# THE MIRACULOUS MEDAL

ITS ORIGIN, HISTORY, CIRCULATION, RESULTS

M. ALADEL, C.M.

SENSUS FIDELIUM PRESS

Gastonia, North Carolina

ISBN: 978-1-962639-26-2

For more information, please visit sensusfideliumpress.com

# DEDICATION

TO: The Most Compassionate Virgin Mary, mother of God, conceived without sin.

Oh Mary, conceived without sin, Virgin incomparable, august Mother of Jesus, thou who hast adopted us for thy children, and who hast given us so many proofs of thy maternal tenderness, deign to accept this little book, feeble token of our gratitude and love!

Oh! may it be instrumental in attracting and attaching inviolably to thee, the hearts of all who read it!

O Mary, conceived without sin, pray for us who have recourse to thee!

AUTHOR'S DECLARATION.

In conformity with the decree of Pope Urban VIII, we declare that the terms miracle, revelation, apparition, and other expressions of a similar nature here employed, have, in our intention, no other than a purely historical value, and that we submit unreservedly the entire contents of this book to the judgment of the Apostolic See.

PREFACE OF THE AMERICAN PUBLISHER.

Since the hour when the Beloved Disciple took the Blessed Virgin to his own, the followers of her Divine Son have always cherished a reverential affection for her above all other creatures. They have regarded her as the ideal of all that is true and pure and sweet and noble in the Christian life, and they have honored her as the most favored of mortals, the greatest of saints, the masterpiece of the Almighty. The peculiar veneration paid to her by the Apostles, was caught up by the first Christians, who regarded her with awe because of her great dignity; and when she died, her memory was held in benediction. But death could not sever her from those who, in the person of St. John, had been given to her for her children. She still lived for the Church. From the time when the faithful took refuge in the Catacombs to the fifth century, when the Council of Ephesus solemnly sanctioned the homage paid to her as the Mother of God, her intercession was often invoked; and from that day, devotion towards her has increased until our own age, when the nations of the earth unite to proclaim her Blessed.

Often has Mary given signal proofs of the pleasure she takes in the devotion of her clients and of the power she possesses to grant their petitions. Graces asked through her mediation have been suddenly obtained; wonders in the way of cures and conversions have been wrought at her shrines; disasters have been averted; plagues have been made to cease; and, to crown all her favors, apparitions have occurred, in which she has shown herself, radiant with the lustre of Heaven, to her loyal servants; and, in some instances, she has left something like the scapular, the Miraculous Medal and the fount in the grotto of Lourdes, as memorials of her visit.

These manifestations of her maternal solicitude have of late been more frequent, more renowned, and more efficacious than ever. As the end draws near and the dangers increase, her anxiety for the sanctification of her own bursts its bonds and urges her to find new ways to the hearts of men. Among the most recent of these demonstrations, the Miraculous Medal is one of the most remarkable. How it originated, how rapidly and widely it has circulated, and how gloriously it has fulfilled its mission, are told in this book. A more interesting and edifying history could not easily have been written. To all children of Mary, in America as elsewhere, it will be welcome, and for them this edition has been prepared by

THE PUBLISHER.

May 4, 1880.

# Contents

# Sister Catherine, Daughter of Charity—Her Birth—Early Life—Vocation—Entrance into the Community—Apparitionof the Blessed Virgin—The Medal—Sister Catherine is sent to d'Enghien Hospital—Her humble, hidden Life—Her Death.

It is an extensively credited assumption, that those who are favored with supernatural communications should have something extraordinary in their person and mode of life. One easily invests them with an ideal of perfection, which, in some measure, sets them apart from most mankind. But if, at any time, an occasion occurs to prove that such an assumption is erroneous, if we discover in these divine confidants' weaknesses or only infirmities, we are astonished and tempted to be scandalized. Among the Christians who knew St. Paul only by reputation, some were disappointed on a closer acquaintance; they said his appearance was too unprepossessing and his language too unrefined for an apostle. Were not the Jews scandalized that Our Lord ate and drank like others, that His parents were poor, that He came from Nazareth, and that He conversed with sinners? So true is it that we are always disposed to judge by appearances.

Not so with God. He sees the depths of our hearts, and often what appears contemptible in the eyes of the world, is great in His. Simplicity and purity He prizes especially. Exterior qualities, gifts of intellect, birth, and education, are of little value to Him, and when He has an important mission to confide, it is ordinarily to people not possessing these qualifications. Thus, does He display His wisdom and power, in using what is weak, to accomplish great results. Sometimes, He chooses for His instruments subjects that are even imperfect, permitting them to commit faults to keep them in all humility, and convince them that the favors they receive are not accorded their own merits, but are the gift of God's pure bounty.

These observations naturally prelude Sister Catherine's biography; they explain in advance the difficulties which might arise in the mind of the reader at the contrast between a life so simple and ordinary and the graces showered upon her.

Sister Catherine (Zoé Labouré) was born May 2, 1806, in a little village of the Côte-d'Or Mountains, called Fain-les-Moutiers, of the parish of Moutiers-Saint-Jean. This last place, particularly dear to St. Vincent, was not far from the cradle of St. Bernard, that great servant of Mary, nor from the spot where St. Chantal passed a part of her life, as if in the soil as well as the blood there was a predisposition to certain qualities or hereditary virtues.

Her parents, sincere Christians, were held in esteem. They cultivated their farm and enjoyed that competency which arises from rural labor joined to simplicity of life. God had blessed their union with a numerous family, seven sons and three daughters.

At an early age, the sons left the paternal roof; little Zoé, with her sisters, remained under the mother's eye, but this mother, God took from Zoé, ere she had completed her eighth year. Already capable of feeling the extent of this sacrifice, it seemed to her as if the Blessed Virgin wished to be her only Mother.

An aunt, living at Rémy, took Zoé and the youngest sister to live with her; but the father, a pious man, who in his youth had even thought of embracing the ecclesiastical state, preferred having the children under his own eye, and at the end of two years they were brought home.

Another motive, also, impelled him to act thus. The eldest sister thought seriously of leaving her family to enter the Community of Daughters of Charity, and the poor father could not bear the idea of confiding his house to mercenary hands. And thus, at an age when other children think only of their sports, Zoé was inured to hard work.

At the age of twelve, with a pure and fervent heart, she made her First Communion in the church of Moutiers-Saint-Jean. Henceforth, her only desire was to be solely His who had just given Himself to her for the first time.

Very soon after, the eldest sister left home to postulate at Langres; and Zoé, now little mistress of the house, did the cooking, with the assistance of a woman for the roughest work. She carried the field hands their meals, and never shrank from any duty however laborious or severe.

Moutiers-Saint-Jean possesses an establishment of the Sisters of St. Vincent de Paul. Zoé went to see them as often as her household duties permitted, and the good Sister-Servant, who loved her much, encouraged the child in her laborious life; yet the latter never spoke to the Sister of her growing vocation, but awaited, with a secret impatience, until her sister (two years her junior) would be able to take charge of the house. It was she to whom Zoé confided her dearest desires, and then commenced for the two that tender intimacy of life, one of pure labor and duty, and whose only relaxations were attending the services of the parish church.

The two young girls, thinking themselves able to dispense with the servant, dismissed her, and now shared between them all the work. Zoé, who was very sedate and trustworthy, watched over everything with the utmost vigilance, and took care of her sister with a mother's tenderness.

One of her favorite occupations was the charge of the pigeon house, which always contained from seven to eight hundred pigeons. So faithfully did she perform this duty that they all knew her, and as soon as she appeared they came flying around her in the shape of a crown. It was, says her sister, a most charming spectacle—innocence attracting the birds, which are its symbol.

In youth, we see her, already modest in deportment, serious in character, pious and recollected in the parochial church which she regularly attended, kneeling upon the cold stones even in winter. And this was not the only mortification she practiced; to bodily fatigue, she added from her tenderest youth that of fasting every Wednesday and Saturday. It was for a long time without her father's knowledge; at length, discovering his daughter's pious ruse, he endeavored to dissuade her; but all his reproaches were not able to overcome her love of penance, she believed it her duty to prefer the interior voice of God to that of her father.

In all this we clearly discern the character of the future Sister, with its virtues and defects. On one side, we see true simplicity, unselfishness, constant application to the most laborious duties under the safeguard of innocence and fervor; on the other, a disposition accustomed to governing, and which could not yield without an internal struggle.

During this life of rural toil, she never lost sight of her vocation. Several times was her hand asked in marriage, but she invariably answered that, long affianced to Jesus her good Savior, she wished no other spouse than Him. But had she yet made a choice of the Community she would enter? It is doubtful, especially when we consider the following event of her life, which deeply impressed her, and always remained grave in the memory of her dear sister who related it.

Being still in her father's house at Fain-les-Moutiers, she had a dream, which we may consider as an inspiration from God and a preparation for her vocation.

It seemed to her that she was in the Purgatorian chapel of the village church. An aged priest of venerable appearance and remarkable countenance appeared in the chapel and began to vest himself for Mass; she assisted at it, deeply impressed with the presence of this unknown priest. At the end of Mass, he made her a sign to approach, but affrighted, she drew back, yet ever keeping her eyes fixed upon him.

Leaving the church, she went to visit a sick person in the village. Here, she again finds herself with the aged priest, who addresses her in these words: "My daughter, it is well to nurse the sick; you fly from me now, but one day you will be happy to come to me. God has His designs upon you, do not forget it." Amazed and filled with fear, the young girl still flies his presence. On leaving the house, it seemed to her that her feet scarcely touched the ground, and just at the moment of entering her home she awoke and recognized that what had passed was only a dream.

She was now eighteen years old, knowing scarcely how to read, much less write; as she was doubtless aware that this would be an obstacle to her admission into a Community, she obtained her father's permission to visit her sister-in-law, who kept a boarding school at Châtillon, and there receive a little instruction. Her father, fearing to lose her, reluctantly consented to her departure.

Incessantly occupied with thoughts of the vision we have already related, she spoke of it to the Curé of Châtillon, who said to her: "I believe, my child, that this old man is St. Vincent, who calls you to be a Daughter of Charity." Her sister-in-law having taken her to see the Sisters at Châtillon, she was astonished on entering their parlor to behold a picture, the perfect portrait of the priest who had said to her in her dream: "My daughter, you fly from me now, but one day you will be happy to come to me. God has His designs upon you, do not forget it." She immediately inquired the name of the original, and when told that it was St. Vincent, the mystery vanished; she understood that it was he who was to be her Father.

This circumstance was not of a nature to quench the ardor of her desires. She remained but a short time with her sister-in-law. The humble country girl was ill at ease amidst the young ladies of the school, and she learned nothing.

It was at this time she became acquainted with Sister Victoire Séjole, who was afterwards placed over the house at Moutiers-Saint-Jean. Though young, already thoroughly devoted to God and His poor, Sister Victoire divined the candor of this soul and its sufferings; she immediately begged her Sister-Servant to admit Zoé as a postulant without delay, offering herself to bestow particular pains upon her, instructing her in whatever was indispensable for her as a Daughter of Charity.

But Zoé could not yet profit by the interest good Sister Victoire had taken in her; this happiness was to be dearly bought.

When she acquainted her father with her intentions, the poor father's heart rebelled; he had already given his eldest daughter to St. Vincent's family, and now, to sacrifice her who for years had so wisely directed his household, seemed indeed beyond his strength. He considered a means of dissuading her from her plans and thought he had found it by sending her to Paris, to one of his sons who kept a restaurant, telling him to seek by various distractions to extinguish in the sister's heart all the idea of her vocation. Time of trial and suffering for the young aspirant, who, far from losing the desire of consecrating herself to God, only sighed more ardently after the happy day when she could quit the world.

She now thought of writing to her sister-in-law at Châtillon, and interested her in the matter. The latter, touched by this mark of confidence, had Zoé come to her, and finally obtained the father's consent. Zoé became a postulant in the house of the Sisters at Châtillon, in the beginning of the year 1830.

Zoé Labouré was very happy to find, at last, the end of those severe trials which had lasted almost two years. The 21st of April 1830, she reached that much desired haven, the Seminary.[1]

Behold her, then, in possession of all that had been the cherished object of her desires and affections from earliest childhood! Her soul could now dilate itself in prayer, and in the joyful consciousness of being entirely devoted to the service of its God.

During the whole of her Seminary term, she had the happiness of having for Director of her conscience M. Jean Marie Aladel, of venerated memory, a priest of eminent piety, excellent judgment and great experience, austere as a hermit, indefatigable in work, a true son of St. Vincent de Paul. He was a prudent guide for her in the extraordinary ways whither God had called her. He knew how to hold her in check against the illusions of imagination, and especially the seductions of pride at the same time, that he encouraged her to walk in the paths of perfection by the practice of the most solid virtues. M. Aladel did not lose sight of her, even after she was sent to the Hospital d'Enghien. He thereby gained much for his own sanctification and the mission confided to him.

Informed by her of God's designs, he devoted himself unreservedly to the propagation of devotion to Mary Immaculate, and during the last years of his life, to extend among the young girls educated by the Sisters of St. Vincent, the association of Children of Mary. He died in 1865, eleven years before his spiritual daughter.[2]

Three days before the magnificent ceremony of the translation of St. Vincent de Paul's relics to the chapel of St. Lazare, a feast which was the signal of renewed life for the Congregation of the Mission, Sister Labouré was favored with a prophetic vision. The same God who had called Vincent from the charge of his father's flocks to make him a vessel of election, was now going to confide to a poor country girl the secrets of His mercy. Let us give the account of this first impression in her own simple language.

"It was Wednesday before the translation of St. Vincent de Paul's relics. Happy and delighted at the idea of taking part in this grand celebration, it seemed to me that I no longer cared for anything on earth.

"I begged St. Vincent to give me whatever graces I needed, also to bestow the same upon his two families and all France. It appeared to me that France was in sore need of them. In fine, I prayed St. Vincent to teach me what I ought to ask, and that I might ask it with a lively faith."

She returned from St. Lazare's filled with the thought of her blessed Father and believed that she found him again at the Community. "I had," said she, "the consolation of seeing his heart above the little shrine where his relics are exposed. It appeared to me three successive days in a different manner: First, of a pale, clear color, and this denoted peace, serenity, innocence and union.

"Afterwards, I saw it the color of fire, symbolic of the charity that should be enkindled in hearts. It seemed to me that charity was to be reanimated and extended even to the extremities of the world.

"Lastly, it appeared a very dark red, a livid hue, which plunged my heart in sadness. It filled me with fears I could scarcely overcome. I know not why, nor how, but this sadness seemed to relate to a change of government."

It was strange, indeed, that Sister Labouré, at that time, should have these political forebodings.

An interior voice said to her: "The heart of St. Vincent is profoundly afflicted at the great misfortunes which will overwhelm France." The last day of the octave, she saw the same heart vermilion color, and the interior voice whispered: "The heart of St. Vincent is a little consoled, because he has obtained from God (through Mary's intercession) protection for his two families in the midst of these disasters; they shall not perish, and God will use them to revive the Faith."

To ease her mind, she related this vision to her confessor, who told her to think no more about it; Sister Labouré never dreamed of aught but obeying, and in no way did she ever reveal it to her companions.

We find this singular favor mentioned in a letter written by Sister Catherine, in the year 1856, at the command of M. Aladel. The year she entered the Seminary, this worthy missionary was almost the only chaplain of the Community. The Congregation of the Mission, scarcely restored at this epoch, counted at its Mother House but nine priests in all, and at least half that number were in the Seminary. M. Étienne, of venerated memory, was Procurator General, and M. Salhorgne, Superior of St. Vincent's two families. If the laborers were few, the deficiency was supplied by the devotedness of these few, who multiplied themselves for the service of the Community. The Divine bounty has prepared for their charity a beautiful recompense.

According to the notes which Sister Catherine wrote later in obedience to M. Aladel, the humble daughter during all her Seminary term enjoyed the undisguised sight of Him whose presence is concealed from our senses in the Sacrament of His love. "Except," said she, "when I doubted, then I saw nothing, because I wished to fathom the mystery, fearing to be deceived."

Our Lord deigned to show Himself to His humble servant, conformably to the mysteries of the day, and, in connection with this, she mentions one circumstance relative to the change of government, which could not have been foreseen by human means.

"On the Feast of the Holy Trinity," says she, "Our Lord during Holy Mass appeared to me in the Most Blessed Sacrament as a king with the cross upon His breast. Just at the Gospel, it seemed to me that the cross and all His regal ornaments fell at His feet, and He remained thus despoiled. It was then the gloomiest and saddest thoughts oppressed me, for I understood from this that the king would be stripped of his royal garb, and great disasters would ensue."

When the humble daughter had these forebodings concerning the king, he was then apparently at the pinnacle of fortune. The siege of Algiers was in progress, and everything predicted the happy success of his arms. During the early part of July, this almost impregnable fortress of the pirates fell into the power of France; the whole kingdom rejoiced at the memorable victory, and the churches resounded with hymns of thanksgiving.

Alas! this triumph was to be quickly followed by a bloody revolution, which would overthrow the throne and menace the altars. That very month, the clergy and religious communities of Paris were seized with terror. M. Aladel was greatly alarmed for the Daughters of Charity and the Missionaries, but Sister Labouré never ceased to reassure him, saying that the two communities had nothing to fear, they would not perish.

One day she told him that a bishop had sought refuge at St. Lazare's, that he could be received without hesitation, and might remain there in safety. M. Aladel paid little attention to these predictions, but returning sadly to his house, he was accosted on entering by M. Salhorgne, who told him that Mgr. Frayssinous, Bishop of Hermopolis, and Minister of Religious Worship under Charles X, had just come, begging an asylum from the persecution that pursued him.

These revelations bore an impression of truth which it was difficult to ignore; so in feigning to mistrust them, M. Aladel listened with the deepest interest. He began to persuade himself that the spirit of God inspired this young Sister; and after seeing the accomplishment of several things she had foretold, he now felt disposed to give credence to other and more marvelous communications she had confided to him.

According to her testimony, the Most Holy Virgin had appeared to her, these apparitions were repeated various times, she had been charged to acquaint her director with what she had seen and heard, an important mission had been confided to her, that of having struck and circulated a medal in honor of the Immaculate Conception.

The third chapter of this volume gives a detailed account of these visions, just as they have been transmitted to us from the hand of the Sister herself.

Notwithstanding the sensible assurances of the Sister's veracity, M. Aladel listened to these communications with mistrust, as he tells us himself, in the canonical investigation prescribed in 1836 by Mgr. de Quélen; he professed to consider them of little value, as if they had been the pious vagaries of a young girl's imagination. He told her to regard them in the same light, and he even went so far as to humble her, and reproach her with a want of submission. The poor Sister, unable to convince him, dared speak no more of the apparitions of the Blessed Virgin; she never mentioned the subject to him except when she felt herself tormented and constrained to do so by an almost irresistible desire.

"Such was the reason," says M. Aladel, "that she spoke to him concerning the matter but three times, although the visions were much oftener repeated." After thus relieving her heart, she became perfectly calm. The investigation also shows us that Sister Catherine sought no other confidant of her secrets than her confessor; she never mentioned them to her Superior or anyone else. It was to M. Aladel Mary had directed her, to him only did she speak, and she even exacted of him the promise that her name would never be mentioned.[3]

After this pledge, M. Aladel related the vision to M. Étienne and others, but without designating the Sister's identity, directly or indirectly. We shall see later how Providence always guarded her secret.

These celestial communications, we may easily imagine, produced in the soul of Sister Labouré profound impressions, which usually remained even after she had finished her devotions, and which rendered her in some degree oblivious of what was passing around her. It is related that after one of these apparitions she rises like the others at the given signal, leaves the chapel, and takes her place in the refectory, but remains so absorbed that she never thinks of touching the meal apportioned to her.

Sister Caillaud, third Directress, going her rounds, says bluntly to her: "Ah! Sister Labouré, are you still in an ecstasy?" This recalls her to herself, and the good Directress, who knows not how truly she has spoken, suspects nothing.

Meanwhile, Sister Catherine approached the end of her Seminary term, and in spite of her affirmations at once so artless and so exact, her director always refused to credit them. She had the affliction of leaving the Mother House without being able to obtain anything, even a hope.

It was because the affair was graver than she thought; the supernatural origin of the favor he was directed to communicate to the public could be contested, and the prudent Director saw that in such a matter he could neither exact too many proofs, nor take too many precautions.

Sister Labouré was clothed with the holy habit in the month of January 1831, and sent under the name of Sister Catherine to the Hospital d'Enghien in the faubourg St. Antoine. Here she could continue her communications with M. Aladel. This good father did not lose sight of her; though apparently giving no credit to his penitent revelations, he was studying her carefully to convince himself whether these visions were the product of a weak, enthusiastic mind and excited imagination. But the more he studied her, the more confident he felt that there was nothing of this in Sister Labouré. The judgment formed of her by the Directresses of the Seminary was, that she had a somewhat reserved but calm, positive character, which M. Aladel qualified as cold and even apathetic.

This last epithet, however, was not applicable to Sister Catherine, in whom her companions, on the contrary, recognized a very impulsive temperament. But his opinion proves, at least, that there was no excessive imagination. Moreover, she proved herself solidly grounded in virtue, whilst no one ever perceived anything extraordinary in her demeanor, and especially in her devotion.

Before going to her new destination, Sister Labouré spent some days in one of the large establishments of Paris. Wishing to examine the young Sister more leisurely, M. Aladel made a pretext of visiting the Sisters at this house. The account of these visions had already been circulated throughout the Community, and it was known that M. Aladel had received the Sisters' confidence; hence, as soon as he appeared, the Sisters surrounded him, and each one eagerly plied him with questions. He had his eye upon Sister Catherine, who, without being disconcerted, quietly mingled her inquiries with the others. The worthy missionary was reassured, understanding that the Sister kept her secret.

The last time the Blessed Virgin appeared to Sister Labouré in the sanctuary of the Mother House, she said to her: "My daughter, henceforth you will see me no more, but you will hear my voice during your meditations." And, indeed, during the whole course of her life, she had frequent communications of this kind. They were no longer sensible apparitions, but mental visions, that she well knew how to distinguish from the illusions of imagination or the impressions of a pious fervor.

Her mission had not been accomplished regarding the medal. Some months elapsed, and the Immaculate Virgin complained to Sister Catherine that her orders had not been executed.

"But, my good Mother," replied Sister Catherine, "you see that he will not believe me." "Be calm," was the answer; "a day will come when he does what I desire; he is my servant, and he would fear to displease me."

These words were soon verified.

When the pious missionary received this communication, he began to reflect seriously. "If Mary is displeased," said he, "it is not with the young Sister, whose position prevents her doing anything; it must be with me." This thought troubled him.[4] A long time previous, he had related these visions to M. Étienne, then Procurator General. One day, at the beginning of the year 1832, when they had gone together on a visit to Mgr. de Quélen, M. Aladel profited by the opportunity to speak to the latter of these apparitions, and especially of his own embarrassment, since the Blessed Virgin had complained to the Sister of the delay in fulfilling her commands.

Mgr. de Quélen replied that, seeing nothing in it at all contrary to faith, he had no objection to the medal being struck at once. He even asked them to send him some of the first.

The ravages of the cholera, which had broken out meanwhile, retarded the execution of this design until June; the 30th of that month, two thousand medals were struck, and M. Aladel hastened to send some of them to the Archbishop of Paris.

Mgr. de Quélen wished to make an immediate trial of its efficacy; he was very much troubled concerning the spiritual condition of the former Archbishop of Mechlin, Mgr. de Pradt, now on the verge of death; he desired his conversion so much the more earnestly, as the death of this prelate might be the occasion of scandal and grave disorders, such as have accompanied the interment of the constitutional bishop Gregory. Providing himself with a medal, he went to visit the sick man. At first, he was refused admittance, but very soon the dying man repents of it, and sends him an apology, with a request to call again. In this interview, he testifies to His Grace a sincere repentance for his past life, retracts all his errors, and after receiving the Last Sacraments, he dies that very night in the arms of the archbishop, who, filled with a holy joy, eagerly imparts this consoling news to M. Aladel.

The worthy missionary sent a medal to Sister Catherine, who received it with great devotion and respect [5] and said: "Now it must be disseminated." This was easy to do among the Daughters of Charity, who had all heard whispers of these apparitions; the eagerness to receive the medals was general, they were distributed freely, and cures and conversions multiplied themselves accordingly in all ranks of society, so that very soon the medal received the appellation of miraculous.

A witness of these wonders, the heart of Father Aladel dilated with joy, and he believed it his duty to publish a notice of the origin of the medal, and thus satisfy all the inquiries addressed him on the subject. For the glory of God and Mary, he added an account of all the consoling facts that had come to his knowledge.

What said Sister Catherine in hearing of these wonderful occurrences? Less than anyone; she was astonished; doubtless her joy was great, but it was confined within the silence of her heart. Occasionally she sent some new message to M. Aladel, begging him to have an altar erected commemorative of the apparition, and telling him that many graces and indulgences would be attached thereto, and fall most abundantly upon himself and the Community.

She urged him also to solicit spiritual favors, assuring him that he might ask freely, for all his requests would be granted.

But this worthy priest, whose position in the Community, as we have already said, was that of simple chaplain, prudently kept silence, holding himself in reserve until the favorable moment should arrive for him to act. Some years after, M. Étienne, his intimate friend, was elected Superior General, and he was made assistant of the Congregation and Director of the Daughters of Charity; in concert, they formed the design of erecting to the Immaculate Mary an altar more in accordance with her maternal bounty and the gratitude of her children. Providence itself seemed to co-operate with the execution of their plan, the Community receiving from the government just then a present of two magnificent blocks of white marble, in recognition of the Sisters' services to the cholera patients and their orphans. One was destined for an altar, the other for a statue of the Immaculate Mary.

Meanwhile, the number of inmates at the Mother House, the Seminary especially, increased daily. The new life infused into the Community had awakened many vocations, and the center of reunion had become inadequate in size to its purposes, the chapel particularly was much too small. In enlarging it, the architect had a difficult problem to resolve he must respect the sanctuary honored by Mary's visit, and yet extend the enclosure. He did so by adding side aisles, on a lower foundation, surrounded with galleries. If the edifice, always too low and small, gained nothing in the way of art, it has, at least, the advantage of preserving intact the exact spot where the Most Holy Virgin appeared.

The former altar was taken into the side chapel dedicated to St. Vincent, and the holy founder was there represented holding that heart, burning with love of God and the poor, as it had appeared to Sister Catherine in the vision. A plaster statue of the Immaculate Conception temporarily occupied the place over the main altar, destined for the marble statue, which for various causes was not solemnly inaugurated till 1856.

It was a day of great rejoicing for the Mother House; the statue was not a cold, mute representation; ... it was an eloquent image of Mary; here had this merciful Mother spoken and promised her graces; daily experience had confirmed these promises, and the statue still awakens in the hearts of those who come to pray at her feet, the deepest and tender emotions. Yes, Mary is indeed here. She speaks to the hearts of her children. She makes them feel that she loves and protects them!

Sister Catherine said also to M. Aladel, in the early period of her vocation: "The Blessed Virgin wishes you to establish a Congregation, of which you will be the Superior. It is a Sodality of Children of Mary; the Blessed Virgin will shower many graces upon it, and indulgences will be granted it."

The reader will see, during the volume, how this work was realized, and how admirably Providence has extended the association.

She also told him that the month of May would be celebrated with much magnificence and become universal in the Church; that the month of St. Joseph would likewise be kept with solemnity; that devotion to this great Saint would greatly increase, as well as devotion to the Sacred Heart of Jesus.

So many miracles wrought everywhere and every day, so many signal testimonies of Mary's protection, made it an obligation on the Community, and especially the Seminary where they had originated, to perpetuate so precious a souvenir.

Two pictures were therefore ordered, one representing the vision of the medal, the other that of St. Vincent's heart. The artist, wishing to depict the Blessed Virgin as accurately as possible, consulted M. Aladel as to the color of the veil. ——

The missionary's embarrassment was great; he had forgotten this item but attaching more importance to the details than Sister Catherine thought, he wrote to her, and under the pretext of warning her against the illusions of the demon, he asked her to describe again the Blessed Virgin's appearance in the vision of the medal. Sister Catherine made this answer: "Just now, my Father, it would be impossible for me to recall all that I saw, one detail alone remains, it is, that the Blessed Virgin's veil was the color of morning light."

This was just what M. Aladel wished to know, and precisely the only thing Sister Catherine could recollect.

These little incidents, regulated by Providence, were not lost; they increased the confidence of the wise Director. When the pictures were placed in the Seminary, M. Aladel discreetly took measures to have Sister Catherine come to see them, just at the very time he would be there as if by chance. Another Sister, accidentally meeting them there, has a suspicion of the truth, and turning suddenly to the worthy Father, she says: "This is certainly the Sister who had the vision!" He is greatly embarrassed and sees no way of extricating himself from the difficulty, except by calling upon Sister Catherine to answer. She laughed, saying: "You have guessed well," but with such simplicity that the other Sister said to the Father: "Oh! I see plainly that it is not she; you would not have asked her to tell me."

During her long life, Sister Catherine was subjected to trials of this sort.

The details Mgr. de Quélen had received from M. Aladel concerning the vision of the medal interested him deeply, and he was anxious to become acquainted with the favored Sister. M. Aladel replied that the Sister insisted upon remaining unknown. "As for that," said His Grace, "she can put on a veil and speak to me without being seen." M. Aladel excused himself anew, saying it was for him a secret of the confessional.

M. Ratisbonne, miraculously converted in 1842 by the apparition of the Miraculous Medal, also ardently desired to speak with the Sister first favored by this celestial vision, and he often but vainly entreated her Director's permission.

Those around her frequently asked embarrassing questions, or expressed their suspicions. When too closely pressed, she found means of making the curious feel their indiscretion, so that it was not repeated. Moreover, her great simplicity ordinarily disconcerted her interrogators.

On several occasions, the Blessed Virgin seemed to aid her; thus, in the investigation of 1836, and in the deposition made to the Promoter, M. Aladel declared that he had vainly endeavored to persuade Sister Catherine to be present, he could not overcome her repugnance; and moreover, they would interrogate her to no purpose, she had forgotten everything concerning the event.

The same thing happened one day, it is said, in the presence of M. Étienne, then Superior General; he could not succeed in making her speak; she remembered nothing. It is this which gave rise to the rumor in the Community, that the vision was completely effaced from the memory of the Sister who had been favored with it.

Thanks to this opinion, Sister Catherine was enabled to remain long years truly concealed in her modest duties; employed first in the kitchen, then in the clothes-room; afterwards, for nearly forty years, she had charge of the old men's ward of the Hospital d'Enghien, combining with this duty the care of the poultry yard.

She loved these humble duties. Everything was kept in perfect order, and for her there was no greater happiness than that of being among her poor. At the end of her life, she spoke of it as her chief consolation. "I have always," said she, "loved to stay at home; whenever there was question of a walk, I yielded my turn to others that I might serve my poor."

And this was true. One walk only was she unwilling to forego, that which led to the Community, and she knew no other road but that to the Mother House. When she could make this visit, she never yielded her turn.

Her attraction for silence and the hidden life always kept her in the rear, as the place most suitable for her, and most favorable to the spirit of recollection. She ceded to none the lowest and most repulsive duties of her ward, duties which she termed the pearls of a Daughter of Charity; she moved calmly and quietly, avoiding precipitation, and when advanced in years, the young Sisters, her assistants, often heard from her lips these words: "Ah! my dear, do not be so agitated, be more gentle."

She regarded as one of the most cherished souvenirs of her community life, that of her first Sister-Servant, "a dear soul," said she, "who every year sent the first fruits of her garden to the indigent families of the faubourg, or to her old men. The Sisters were not allowed to touch them until this had been done."

This aged Superior was Sister Savard, who never supposed that Sister Catherine was favored with especial graces, and particularly with the vision of the Blessed Virgin.

Our humble daughter Catherine respected and loved all the Sisters under whom she served, and never did she utter a word against them; she saw only their virtues and good qualities.

"Child of duty and labor, but especially of humility," says her last Superior, "Sister Catherine was not truly appreciated except by those who studied her sufficiently to perceive the great simplicity, uprightness, and purity pervading her soul, her mind, her heart, her whole person.

"Never arrogating to herself the slightest merit on account of the singular favors with which the Immaculate Virgin had loaded her, she said, one day towards the close of her life, when Providence permitted a slight allusion to this subject: 'I, favored Sister! I have been only an instrument; it was not for myself the Blessed Virgin appeared to me. I knew nothing, not even how to write; it was in the Community I learned all I know; and because of my ignorance the Blessed Virgin chose me, that no one might doubt."

Is not the conclusion inspired by the spirit of St. Vincent, "I have been chosen, because being nothing, no one could doubt that such great things are the work of God."

Sister Catherine cared little for the esteem or contempt of others. Despite her rigid silence, there always hovered over her the suspicion that it was she who had seen the Blessed Virgin; no one dared tell her so; but in consequence of the suspicion, she was more closely observed, and more severely judged than any one else, and if by chance her companions discovered in her some slight weakness of nature, or even the absence of some heroic virtue, the thought was immediately rejected that the Blessed Virgin had chosen so ordinary a person.

The testimony of one of her first companions confirms the impression on this point, an impression repeated a hundred-fold. This companion writes to Sister Dufès: "Having passed six years with Sister Catherine, and worked constantly with her one year, I could cite a great number of details full of interest and edification; but I am forced to confess that her life was so simple, so uniform, that I find nothing in it to remark. Notwithstanding the whispered assurances that she was the Sister so favored by the Blessed Virgin, I scarcely credited it, so much was her life like that of others. Sometimes, I sought to enlighten myself indirectly on the subject by questioning her as to the impression such extraordinary occurrences had produced in the Seminary, hoping that her answers would betray her, and thereby satisfy my curiosity, but she replied with so much simplicity that my hopes were always deceived."

It is true, Sister Catherine had nothing remarkable about her, and yet nothing common or trivial.

Her height was above the medium; her regular features bore the seal of modesty; and her clear blue eye was indicative of candor. She was industrious, simple, and not the least mystical in her spiritual exercises; she affected neither great virtues nor particular devotions, well pleased to cherish them in the depths of her heart and practice them according to the rule with fidelity and exactness.

After her death, some notes were found written by her own hand during one of the annual retreats. Everything in them is simple, solid, practical, and there is not one word of allusion to the extraordinary graces she had received; even when addressing the Blessed Virgin, nothing recalls the familiarity with which Mary had treated her. Here are some extracts, in which no changes have been made except those of fault-spelling.

"I will take Mary for my model at the commencement of all my actions; in everything, I will consider if Mary were engaged thus, how, and wherefore she would do this, with what intention. Oh! how beautiful and consoling is the name of Mary ... Mary!

"Resolution to offer myself to God without reserve, to bear every little contradiction in a spirit of humility and penance, to beg in all my prayers that the will of God may be accomplished in me. O my God! do with me as Thou wilt! O Mary! grant me your love, without which I perish; bestow upon me all the graces I need! O Immaculate Heart of Mary! obtain for me the faith and love which attached you to the foot of the cross of Jesus Christ!

"O sweet objects of my affections, Jesus and Mary, let me suffer for you, let me die for you, let me be all for you and no longer anything for myself!

"Not to complain of the little contradictions I meet with among the poor, and to pray for those who cause me suffering. O Mary, obtain for me this grace, through your virginal purity!

"To employ my time well, and not to spend one moment unprofitably. O Mary, happy are those who serve you and put their confidence in you!

"O Mary, Mary, Mary, pray, pray, pray for us, poor sinners, now and at the hour of our death! Mary, O Mary!

"In my temptations and times of spiritual dryness, I will always have recourse to Mary, who is purity itself. O Mary, conceived without sin!——

"O Mary, make me love you, and it will not be difficult to imitate you!

"Humility, simplicity, and charity are the foundation of our holy vocation. O Mary, make me understand these holy virtues! St. Vincent, pray, pray for us!

"O Mary, conceived without sin, pray, pray for us! Deign, O Queen of Angels and of men, to cast a favorable eye upon the whole world ... especially upon France ... and each person in particular! O Mary, inspire us what to ask of you for our happiness!"

Sister Catherine lived forty-six years in a large establishment, under the direction of five successive Superiors; she was brought in contact with many companions of different dispositions and different degrees of virtue, consequently the esteem in which she was held varied. If they sometimes gave her to understand that her mind was failing, such things troubled her little, and she always quietly went her way, receiving kindness with grateful simplicity, and ungracious words without flinching.

Faithful to the rule with such uniform exactness, that merit seems to disappear before habit, she never uttered a word against charity. Even when age had given her some privileges over her young companions, rarely did she allow herself to blame or advise them; not, at least, unless they consulted her, then she advised submission. "Everything is in that," said she, "without obedience, Community life is not possible." To the very end of her days, her obedience to her Superior was as perfect as when she left the Seminary.

We must not, however, suppose that Sister Catherine was of a yielding, gentle temperament, to which obedience was natural; no, on the contrary, she had a strong will and quick temper. Thoroughly versed in household labors, she performed her part with great care and assiduity, and directed most scrupulously all that was entrusted to her charge. Her impulsive temper sometimes displayed itself in little sallies of impatience, the firm tone of her words revealing at times what virtue ordinarily caused her to repress. When the first heat was over, she immediately repented of it and humbled herself.

It was often observed that this first movement of surprise, just ready to escape, was held captive, not by human respect, but by a superior will; thus, proving that her implicit obedience was due her fidelity to grace.

Understanding her nature, we can now form an idea of what Sister Catherine suffered from the opposition she experienced in realizing her mission; even though these contradictions, especially after the medal had been struck, were more apparent than real on the part of her wise Director, they were none the less painful to her. Might we not say that these trials constituted an interior martyrdom sustained by God and known to him alone?

Sister Catherine, despite her strong constitution, was not exempt from physical suffering, and her companions were sometimes astonished at the simplicity with which she asked for little comforts that a mortified soul would have denied itself. These slight defects formed a veil that obscured the sight of many, and partially concealed the beauties of her soul.

Apparently, the very depths of this simple nature might be read at a glance, and yet she faithfully guarded the secrets of God. In her were seen, by a singular contrast, prudence and discretion allied to perfect simplicity. Thus, whilst some found her a little too thoughtful of her health, others observed that on all great feasts of the Blessed Virgin, particularly that of the Immaculate Conception, she was either sick or suffering acute pain, which trials the humble Sister received as a favor from her celestial Mother.

The Superior of the Hospital d'Enghien relates that, one year, when Sister Catherine had gone with several of her companions to spend the beautiful Feast of December 8th at the Community, on getting into the omnibus that evening she fell and broke her wrist. She said not a word, and no one perceived the accident. Some minutes after, seeing that she held her arm in her handkerchief, Sister Dufès inquired what had happened. "Ah! Sister," she quietly replied, "I am holding my bouquet; every year the Blessed Virgin sends me one of this sort."

Detachment from the esteem and affection of creatures was still another trait characteristic of our dear Sister. God sufficed her; that God who had manifested Himself to her in so wonderful a manner, that Immaculate Virgin whose charms had ravished her heart, were her sole joy and delight. The Blessed Virgin, pointing to the sacred tabernacle where her divine Son reposes, had said to her: "In all your trials, my daughter, it is there you must seek consolation." Faithful to these words of her good Mother, Sister Catherine in moments of trial sought the chapel, whence she soon returned to her occupations with renewed serenity of soul and countenance ever cheerful. Jesus and Mary alone received the confidence of her sufferings and her fervor, so that her virtues in a measure were concealed from creatures.

One of the Sisters of the house says that, having often observed her closely to discover, if possible, some trace of her communications with God, she could find nothing especial except that during prayer she did not cast down her eyes, but always kept them fixed upon the image of Mary. She remarks, also, that Sister Catherine never wept except from great anguish of heart, but many times she saw her shed tears in abundance on listening to some traits of protection or some conversion obtained through the Blessed Virgin's intercession, or, as in 1871, at the evils afflicting the Church and France.

Solidly pious amid companions apparently more so, we see nothing indeed in our humble Sister to distinguish her from others. Only one especial circumstance has been remarked, the importance she attached to the recitation of the chaplet. Let us hear what her Sister-Servant says on this point—

"We were always struck," writes Sister Dufès, "when saying the chaplet in common, with the grave and pious way our dear companion pronounced the words of the Angelical Salutation. And what convinced us of the depth of her respect and devotion was the fact that she, always so humble, so reserved, could not refrain from censuring the indifference, the want of attention, which too often accompanies the recitation of a prayer, so beautiful and efficacious."

Her love for the two families of St. Vincent, far from diminishing with age, only incited her to employ continually in their behalf the sole influence at her disposal, prayer; regularly every week, she offered a Communion to attract the benediction of Heaven upon the Congregation of the Mission; her prayers for her Community were incessant.

Sister Catherine always retained the same duty at the Hospital d'Enghien; with truly admirable solicitude, she nursed the old men entrusted to her, at the same time not neglecting the pigeon house, which recalled the purest and sweetest joys of her childhood. The young girl of former days, whom we have seen with her dear pigeons hovering round her, was now a poor Sister, quite aged, but none the less attentive to her little charge.

Sister Catherine was, then, the soul of the little family in charge of the hospital. During these later years, the number of our Sisters had increased considerably, and consequently the administration of the two houses, d'Enghien and Reuilly, being very difficult for one person, an assistant was sent me for the hospital. If Sister Catherine had not for years been moulded to obedience and abnegation, it would have been hard to her quick, impulsive nature, to recognize the authority of a companion so much younger than herself; but far different were the thoughts of this humble Sister, who always endeavored to abase herself.

"She was the first to tender her perfect submission. 'Sister,' said she, 'be at ease, it suffices that our Superiors have spoken; we will receive Sister Angélique as one sent from God and obey her as we do you.' Her conduct justified her words.

"Although Sister Catherine guarded rigorously the supernatural communications she had received, she occasionally expressed her views to me on actual occurrences, speaking then as if inspired by God.

"Thus, at the time of the Commune, she told me that I would leave the house accompanied by a certain Sister, that I would return the 31st of May, and she assured me I need have no fears, as the Blessed Virgin would take my place and guard the house. At the time, I paid very little attention to the good Sister's words.

"I left, indeed, and realized, contrary to my plans, and without a thought on the subject, all that Sister Catherine had predicted. On my return from the Community, May 31st, I expressed my anxiety concerning the house, which had been in the hands of the Communists, and, it was said, plundered. Sister Catherine endeavored to reassure me, repeating that the Blessed Virgin had taken care of everything, she was confident of it, for the Blessed Virgin had promised her.

"We found on our arrival that this Mother of mercy had, indeed, guarded and saved all, notwithstanding the long occupation of our dear house by a mob of furies, whose Satanic pleasure was to destroy.

"One circumstance struck me most forcibly; these wretches had made useless efforts to overthrow the statue of Mary Immaculate placed in the garden—it had withstood all their sacrilegious attempts.

"Sister Catherine hastened to place upon the head of our august Queen the crown she had taken with her in our exile, telling the Blessed Virgin she restored it in token of gratitude.

"Many times, did Sister Catherine thus reveal her thoughts to me with the simplicity of a child. When her predictions were not realized, she would quietly say: 'Ah! well, Sister, I was mistaken. I believed what I told you. I am very glad the truth is known.'[6]

"Meanwhile, time flew, and our good Sister often spoke of her approaching end. Our venerated Superiors began to feel anxious about losing her, and the Superior General one day sent her to come to the Community that he might receive from her own lips certain communications which he considered very important.

"Sister Catherine, to whom this was wholly unexpected, was almost speechless with amazement. On her return, she expressed to me her emotion, and, for the first time, opened her heart to me concerning that which she had formerly so much feared to reveal.

"This repugnance had vanished; seeing herself on the borders of the tomb, she felt constrained to make known the details which she thought buried with the venerated Father Aladel, and she expressed great grief that devotion to the Immaculate Conception was less lively and general than it had been.

"These communications, moreover, were for myself alone; I did not impart them to the other Sisters. It is true, a greater number were informed of this pious secret, but they never learned it from Sister Catherine herself. All they could observe in connection with it was her ardent love for Mary Immaculate and her zeal for the propagation of the Miraculous Medal, also that, when she heard one of our Sisters express a desire to make the pilgrimage to Lourdes or some other privileged sanctuary of Mary, she could not refrain from saying, somewhat impetuously: 'But why do you wish to go so far? Have you not the Community? Did not the Blessed Virgin appear there as well as at Lourdes?' And a most extraordinary fact is that, without having read any of the publications concerning this miraculous grotto, Sister Catherine was more familiar with what had taken place there than many who had made the pilgrimage. Leaving these incidents aside, never did she utter a word calculated to give the impression that she had any part in the singular favors the Blessed Virgin had lavished upon our humble chapel at the Mother House.

"Since opening her heart to me, this good companion had become very affectionate; it was a rest for her, a consolation to find someone who understood her. Our worthy Father Chevalier, Assistant of the Congregation of the Mission, occasionally visited her to receive her communications concerning the apparition. One day, he spoke to her of the new edition he was preparing of the notice of the medal. 'When M. Aladel's edition of 1842 appeared,' replied Sister Catherine, 'I said to him, truly, that he would never publish another, and that I would never see another edition, because it would not be finished during my lifetime.' 'I shall catch you there,' replied M. Chevalier, who expected it to appear very soon. But unforeseen difficulties having retarded the publication, he subsequently recognized that the good Sister had spoken rightly.

"From the beginning of the year 1876, Sister Catherine alluded very frequently to her death; on all our feast days, she never failed to say: 'It is the last time I shall see this feast.' And when we appeared not to credit her assertion, she added: 'I shall certainly not see the year 1877.' We could not, however, believe her end so near. For some months she had been obliged to keep her bed, and relinquish that active life she had led so many years.

"Her strength was gradually failing; the asthma joined to some affection of the heart undermined her constitution; she felt that she was dying, but it was without a fear, we might say without emotion. One day, when speaking to her of her death: 'You are not afraid, then,' said I, 'dear Sister Catherine.' 'Afraid! Sister!' she exclaimed; 'why should I be afraid? I am going to our Lord, the Blessed Virgin, St. Vincent.'

"And, truly, our dear companion had nothing to fear, for her death was as calm as her life.

"Several days previous, one of our Sisters was talking familiarly with her, when, without any allusion to the subject from the other, our sick Sister said: 'I shall go to Reuilly.' This was the name given the House of Providence, separated from d'Enghien Hospital by a vast garden, and similar to it in the nature of its works. 'What! to Reuilly?' answered her companion; 'you would not have the heart to do so, you who love so well your Enghien, that you have never left.' 'I tell you; I shall go to Reuilly.' 'But when?' 'Ah! that is it!' said Sister Catherine, in a decided, mysterious tone, that disconcerted her companion. After a few moments, she added: 'There will be no need of a hearse at my funeral.' 'Oh! what do you mean?' replied the Sister. 'It will not be needed,' said the sick one, emphatically. 'But why not?' 'They will put me in the chapel at Reuilly.' These words struck her companion, who repeated the conversation to me. 'Keep that to yourself,' said I.

"On the 31st of December, she had several spells of weakness, symptoms of her approaching end. We then proposed to her the last consolations of religion; she gratefully consented and received the Sacraments with indescribable peace and happiness; then, at her request, we recited the litany of the Immaculate Conception.

"Being one day near her bed, speaking to her of Heaven and of the Blessed Virgin, she expressed a desire to have during her agony sixty-three children, each invoking the Blessed Virgin by one of her titles in the litany of the Immaculate Conception, and especially these very consoling words: 'Terror of demons, pray for us.' It was observed that there were not sixty-three invocations in the litany. 'You will find them in the office of the Immaculate Conception,' said she. Measures were taken to comply with her desires, the invocations were written upon slips of paper and kept for the final hour, but, just at the time of her agony, we could not collect the children; she then asked that the litany be recited and had us repeat three times the invocation which makes hell tremble.

"Our Sisters were especially touched to hear her exclaim, with an accent of deep tenderness: 'My dear Community! my dear Mother House!' So true is it, that what we have loved most in life returns to us with renewed vigor at the hour of death!

"Some of her former companions and friends of the House came during the day to see her for a last time; one of them, holding an office in the Seminary, approaching her, said sadly: 'Sister Catherine, are you going to leave us without telling me a word of the Blessed Virgin?' Then the dying Sister leaned towards her and whispered softly in her ear quite a while. 'I ought not to speak,' said she; 'it is M. Chevalier who is commissioned to do that.' ... She continued, without interruption: 'The Blessed Virgin has promised to grant especial graces every time one prays in the chapel, but particularly an increase of purity, that purity of mind, heart, will, which is pure love.'

"This good daughter, animated with the true primitive spirit of the Community, was, in uttering these last words, the unconscious echo of the venerable Mother Legras, whose writings breathe the same thought.

"A Sister-Servant, who came to visit her, approaching the sick Sister, reminded her of the necessities of the Community and of the Seminary, and ended by saying: 'Dear Sister Catherine, when you get to Heaven, do not forget all this, attend to all my commissions.' Sister Catherine answered: 'Sister, my will is good, but I have always been so stupid, so dull, I shall not know how to explain myself, for I am ignorant of the language of Heaven.' Upon which the other, delighted with so much simplicity, was inspired to say: 'Oh! my dear Sister Catherine, in Heaven we do not speak as we do on earth; the soul regards God, the good God regards the soul, and all is understood—that is the language of Heaven.' Our dear Sister's countenance became radiant at this, and she answered: 'Oh! Sister, if it is thus, be tranquil, all your commissions will be fulfilled.'

"M. Chevalier came, also, that day to give her his blessing, and he spoke to her on the same subject. Sister Catherine answered him with faculties undimmed, and said to him, among other things: 'The pilgrimages the Sisters make are not favorable to piety. The Blessed Virgin did not tell me to go so far to pray; it is in the Community chapel she wishes the Sisters to invoke her, that is their true pilgrimage.'

"The poor, to whom she was so devoted, likewise occupied her thoughts.——

"At four in the afternoon, another attack of weakness collected us all around our dear, dying one, but the supreme moment had not yet come. We surrounded her bed until evening. At seven, she seemed to sink into a slumber, and without the least agony or the least sign of suffering, she yielded her last sigh. Scarcely could we perceive that she had ceased to live.... Never have I seen a death so calm and gentle."

"The deepest emotion now filled our hearts; we pondered the celestial interview of our blessed companion with that good God who had so often revealed Himself to her during her Seminary life, and that beautiful Virgin, whose charms can never be depicted on earth.

"It was not sorrow which pervaded our hearts; not a tear was shed in these first moments; we yielded to an indescribable emotion; we felt ourselves near a Saint; the veil of humility under which she had lived so long concealed was now rent, that we might see in her only the soul favored by Heaven.

"Our Sisters disputed the happiness of passing the night beside her venerated remains, a magnetic attraction drawing them to her.

"To perpetuate the fact that she had received these favors whilst still a Seminary Sister, we thought of having her photograph taken, also, in the Seminary habit; it succeeded completely in both costumes.

"We now carried her blessed remains into the chapel. There the Immaculate Virgin watched over her; lilies and roses surrounded her virginal body, and her cherished device—'O Mary! conceived without sin, pray for us who have recourse to thee'—surrounding this little sanctuary, seemed the last echo of her life.

"Then commenced the miracle of glorified humility; this humble Sister, who in life had been scarcely noticed, was suddenly surrounded by persons of every age and condition, who considered it a very great happiness to come, not to pray for her, but to recommend themselves to her blessed intercession.

"As for us who were keeping watch around our dear relic, we could not bear to think of the moment which would take her from us. This house, which had been protected by her presence for forty-six years, would it be deprived of her forever? The thought was heart-breaking; it seemed as if we were about to lose the protection of the Immaculate Virgin, who would henceforth cease to hover over us.

"On the other hand, to keep our dear Sister with us appeared impossible. Our Superiors, being consulted, permitted us to take measures in accordance with our wishes. We had a world of difficulties to surmount.

"'Pray,' said I to our Sisters; and they passed the night supplicating the Immaculate Mary to let our beloved companion remain with us.

"All night long, I vainly tried to think of a suitable resting place for her, when suddenly, at the sound of the four o'clock bell, I thought I heard these words: 'The vault is under the chapel of Reuilly.' 'True enough,' said I, joyfully, like a person who suddenly sees the realization of a long deferred hope. Now I remembered that, during the construction of the chapel, a vault had been made communicating with the children's refectory. Our worthy Mother Mazin had assigned to it no actual purpose, saying we might have use for it hereafter.

"There was no time to lose. We were on the eve of her funeral, and the authorization, so difficult to obtain, had not yet been solicited.

"The vault was hastily prepared, and the petition, sustained by influential persons, succeeded as if by enchantment.

"January 3d, the feast of St. Genevieve, was the day appointed for the interment of her, whom we regarded as the tutelary angel of our house. But the word 'interment' is not appropriate here—'triumph' is the proper expression—for it was a veritable triumph for our humble Sister.

"A deputation was sent from all the houses of our Sisters, that had received timely notice, and the little chapel was much too small to accommodate the numbers that came. Mass over, the funeral cortege which was to accompany the body in procession from d'Enghien Hospital to the vault at Reuilly was organized, as follows: The inmates of our industrial school, Children of Mary, came first, bearing their banner; next to these, all our little orphans; then, our young girls of the Society (both externs and those belonging to the house), wearing the livery of the Immaculate Mary; the parishioners, and lastly, our Sisters preceding the clergy.

"This lengthy procession passed slowly through the long garden walk, and whilst the solemn chants of the Benedictus resounded afar, the modest coffin appeared in sight, covered with lilies and eglantines, emblems of purity and simplicity.

"At the entrance of the vault, the crowd stood aside, and our Children of Mary greeted the arrival of the body by singing the blessed invocation: 'O Mary! conceived without sin, pray for us who have recourse to thee!' It would be impossible to describe the effect of these funeral obsequies, of a nature so entirely new.

"To preserve our treasure, it was necessary to wall up the subterranean entrance, but we had an opening made communicating with the chapel.

"The poor, whom Sister Catherine had nursed, lay a magnificent crown on the tomb of St. Vincent's humble daughter, who, in life, sought only the lowliest paths, and who had supplicated the Blessed Virgin to keep her unknown and unsought. ——"

The life of dear Sister Labouré was the faithful realization of Our Lord's words in the Gospel: "I return Thee thanks, Father, that Thou hast concealed these things from the wise of this world and hast revealed them to little ones." Never were the gifts of God better concealed in a soul, under the double mantle of humility and simplicity.

For forty-six years did she lead a life of obscurity and toil, seeking no other satisfaction than that of pleasing God; she sanctified herself in the lowliest paths by a faithful correspondence to grace, and an exact compliance with the practices of a community life. The favors she received from Heaven never filled her heart with pride; witness of the wonders wrought daily by the medal; she never uttered a word that might lead others to suspect how much more she knew about it than anyone else.

Might we not say, she had chosen for her motto these words of À Kempis: "Love to be unknown and accounted as nothing?" How faithfully these traits portray the true daughter of the humble Vincent de Paul!

What, in Heaven, must be the glory of those whose earthly life was one of self-abasement? Do we not already perceive a faint radiance of this glory? The obsequies of the humble servant of the poor resembled a triumph; by an almost unheard-of exception, her body remains amid her spiritual family; her tomb is visited by persons of every condition, who, with confidence, recommend themselves to her intercession, and many of whom assure us that their petitions have been granted. In fine, this biographical notice discloses what Sister Catherine so carefully concealed, and thus accomplishes Our Lord's promise: "He who humbles himself, shall be exalted."

## Mary's Agency in the Church – THIS AGENCY, EVER MANIFEST, SEEMS TO HAVE DISAPPEARED DURING THE EIGHTEENTH AND IN THE BEGINNING OF THE NINETEENTH CENTURY—MARY APPEARS IN 1830—MOTIVES AND IMPORTANCE OF THIS APPARITION—THE IMMACULATE CONCEPTION

Devotion to the most Blessed Virgin is as ancient as Christianity, and we find traces of it from the very origin of the Church, among all nations who accepted the Gospel. During the first ages, it was concealed in the obscurity of the catacombs, or veiled itself under symbolical forms to escape the profanation of infidels; but when the era of peace succeeded that of bloody persecutions, it reappeared openly and in all the brilliancy of its ravishing beauty. It developed a wonderful growth, especially in the fifth century, after the Council of Ephesus had proclaimed the divine maternity of Mary, thereby sanctioning the exceptional homages rendered her above all the saints.

The image of the Virgin Mother, circulated throughout Christendom, becomes the ornament of churches, the protection of the fireside, and an object of devotion to the faithful. It is at this epoch, especially, we see everywhere gradually disappearing the last vestiges of paganism. The Immaculate Virgin, the Mother of tenderness, the Queen of Angels, the Patroness of regenerated humanity, supplants those vain idols, which for ages had fostered superstition, with its train of vices and errors.

Every Catholic admits that the Church's veneration of Mary rests upon an inviolable foundation—both faith and reason unite in justifying it. Events have proved that God Himself has authorized it, for it has often pleased Him to recompense the confidence and fidelity of her servants, by sensible marks of His power, by extraordinary graces—in a word, by true miracles. By a disposition of His Providence, He has decreed Mary's intervention in the economy of the Church and the sanctification of souls, as He did in the mysteries of the Incarnation and Redemption. Her character of Mediatrix between Heaven and earth obliges her to make this agency felt, to display the power she has received in favor of man. These manifestations of the Blessed Virgin in the Church, these marvelous proofs of her solicitude for us, form an interesting portion of the history of Catholicity. The liturgy is full of such souvenirs, and several feasts have been instituted to commemorate them. Christian countries abound in traditions of this nature; they are one of the sources whence piety derives its nourishment.

The majority of pilgrim shrines owe their origin to some supernatural intervention of the Blessed Virgin. Sometimes she has manifested herself under a visible form, most frequently to a poor shepherd or peasant; again, she has wrought a miracle, as the recovery of a sick person, the conversion of a hardened sinner, or some other prodigy betokening the power of a supernatural agency. Sometimes, a statue, a picture, apparently not fashioned by the hand of man, is accidentally discovered; the neighboring population are touched, their faith is reanimated, and soon a shrine, a chapel, or even a splendid basilica, is erected to protect this gift of Heaven, this pledge of Mary's affection. Innumerable generations repair to the spot, and new favors, new miracles, ineffable consolations, ever attest to the tutelary guardianship of her, who humble, confiding hearts have never invoked in vain. We might cite hundreds of names in support of these assertions.

The history of devotion to Mary in Catholic countries gives rise to an observation worthy of remark, that the faith of a country is in proportion to its devotion to the Blessed Virgin. We can also add that, when God wishes to revive the Faith among any people, He commissions Mary to manifest there her goodness and power.

Every age has furnished the Church with constantly increasing proofs of Mary's mediation; there are epochs in which she seems to be so lavish of her presence, that we might say she lives familiarly among mankind, and that her delights are to converse with them.

Again, on the contrary, she appears to retire, to hold herself aloof from the world, to give no more signs of her intervention. We have a striking example of this in somewhat recent age. More than a century do we find deprived of Mary's sensible mediation; history records in all that period not one of these apparitions, not a new pilgrim shrine founded, not a signal grace obtained through the intercession of the Mother of Mercy. If a few events of this kind took place, they were at least very rare, and have remained in obscurity.

This age, forsaken by the Blessed Virgin, was the eighteenth century, to which we must add the first thirty years of the nineteenth.

At this epoch, when impious rationalism endeavored to efface all idea of the supernatural, when the most firmly established truths were attacked, when among Christians the standard of virtue was lowered and character was of slight esteem in any class or station of society, we might believe that Mary, fatigued with men's ingratitude, had resolved to leave them to their own devices, and let them govern the world according to their ideas of assumed wisdom. She did not renounce her mission of Mediatrix in favor of the Church, she still watched over her great adopted family, she listened to the prayers of her faithful servants, but she remained invisible, she no longer displayed any of those marks of tenderness her maternal heart had lavished upon them in the ages of faith.

We know the consequences of Mary's abandoning the earth, and how these sages who wished to dispense with God governed society. The history of their reign is written in letters of fire, of blood and of filth.

This revolutionary and impious naturalism was prolonged into the nineteenth century; it still exerts a deplorable influence at the present day, but it encounters opposition; the supernatural order is firmly asserted, the truths of Faith are warmly defended, the holy Church is respected and obeyed, its august Head is held in veneration to the very extremities of the earth, God's kingdom is still opposed, but it numbers devoted subjects, who, if needful, would shed their blood in its defense. Indifference, human respect, jeering skepticism, are gradually disappearing, leaving the Church with only sincere friends, or declared enemies. It is a progress no one can ignore.

Whence comes this change? and what the date of so consoling a resurrection? Beyond a doubt, it owes its origin to God's infinite bounty—but the instrument, can it be ignored or contemned? Is it not the Blessed Virgin Mary? Has her mediation not been visible for forty years? Yes, it is Mary who has wrought this astonishing transformation, and through the medal styled miraculous has this series of wonders been inaugurated.

In 1830, Mary for the first time, after an interval of a century and a half, manifest her desire of a reconciliation with earth.

It is the first sign of pardon she accords man, after her long silence.

It is the announcement of a new era which is about to commence.

The apparition of November 27th, in the chapel of the Mother House of the Daughters of Charity, Paris, appears, at first, to be of little importance, yet it was destined to have an immense bearing upon the future and its consequences were to be incalculable.

Like a stream whose source is concealed at the foot of a mountain, but which receives as it advances numberless tributaries, and finally becomes a majestic river, fertilizing the provinces and kingdoms through which it flows; so the vision of the medal has been the initiatory step in a religious movement, which, to-day, extends throughout the world, sitting in justice upon old errors, superannuated prejudices; systems inimical to truth, and fully revealing the true Church and true sanctity, rendering to Mary Immaculate, Mother of God and Mother of men, such tributes of veneration, love and devotion, as she has never received since the preaching of the Gospel.

The reader is already acquainted with Sister Catherine, the humble daughter whom Mary deigned to select for her confidante. The following chapter gives a detailed account of the apparitions.

We have said that this event was the dawn of a new era, the signal of renewed devotion to Mary throughout the world. It seemed as if this tender Mother wished, by lavishing extraordinary graces upon her children, to make them forget the severity with which she had punished their offences.

A rapid glance at the development of devotion to Mary, during half a century, will suffice to show the truth of this affirmation.

The medal, scarcely struck, is circulated by millions; it immediately becomes the instrument of so many cures and conversions, that it is universally styled the Miraculous Medal, a name which clung to it, and which is justified by the constant working of new miracles, as the second part of this book will show. But this medal was destined not only to work miracles, it had an object still higher, it had a dogmatical signification, it was to popularize the belief in the Immaculate Conception of Mary.

As far as is possible for us to penetrate the adorable designs of Providence, everything inclines us to believe that the Immaculate Conception is one of those truths whose proclamation is interwoven with the welfare of modern society, and whose influence upon Catholicity is incalculable. It is the complement of the Blessed Virgin's glory; even with the incomparable prerogative of her divine maternity, her grandeur would still lack something, were she not proclaimed free from original sin. The germ contained in the Holy Scriptures, preserved by tradition, taught by the Fathers and holy Doctors, supported by the Roman pontiffs, solemnized from the earliest ages in many churches, adopted instinctively by the piety of the faithful, and depicted under most graceful forms by brush and chisel of Christian artist, this belief received, through the medal, the seal of a popular devotion. The prayer revealed by the Blessed Virgin herself: "O Mary! conceived without sin, pray for us who have recourse to thee!" this prayer, repeated incessantly by numberless mouths from infancy to old age, by poor and rich, and in every quarter of the globe, entered as a formula into the practices of a Christian life, and hastened, we might safely say, the day when Pius IX was to declare the Immaculate Conception an article of faith.

The wonderful circulation of the medal, and the miracles wrought by means of it, would soon have made the chapel of the rue du Bac a much frequented pilgrim shrine, as many who were indebted to Mary for their cure or conversion wished to testify their gratitude by leaving there ex-voto offerings. But the Superiors of the Community deemed it inadvisable to allow this. However, Divine Providence, wishing to maintain this pious impulse, opened in the very center of Paris a sanctuary, to receive what the chapel of the Daughters of Charity had refused.

The pastor of Notre-Dame-des-Victoires, M. Desgenettes, who had taken a lively interest in the apparition of 1830, was inspired to consecrate his parish to the holy and immaculate Heart of Mary. An Arch confraternity was established for the conversion of sinners; the success was as rapid as it was wonderful, and soon the whole world resounded with accounts of the miracles accorded the associates' prayers. To remind them that Notre-Dame-des-Victoires is allied with the vision of the Sister of St. Vincent de Paul, an article of their rule enjoins them to wear, with respect and devotion, the indulgenced medal of the Immaculate Conception, known as the Miraculous Medal, and they are advised to recite occasionally the prayer engraved upon that medal: "O Mary! conceived without sin, pray for us who have recourse to thee!"

Some years later, in 1846, the Blessed Virgin manifests herself upon the mountain at La Salette to two little shepherd children, charging them to warn mankind of the necessity of doing penance to avert the impending evils.

At Lourdes, in 1858, Mary appears to a poor and ignorant young girl; she tells her name, calling herself by that which is most dear to her: "I am the Immaculate Conception," and she promises abundant benedictions to all who come to pray in that favored place.

In 1871, she appears in the village of Pontmain to some children; she comes to revive their drooping courage and restore hope to their fainting hearts.

It would take too long to enumerate these manifestations of Mary in various parts of Christendom—those images which seem animated; those mysterious voices which warn, which encourage the world; those supernatural revelations to privileged souls—all, we might say, favors of a tender Mother, who pardons her guilty children, and who wishes by multiplied tokens of her love to make them oblivious of her past severity.

To so many marks of the Immaculate Mary's tenderness, the Catholic world has responded by an admirable outburst of filial piety; each year sees hundreds of thousands of pilgrims seeking her privileged sanctuaries; her Feasts are celebrated with admirable splendor; devotion to her is clothed in every form capable of expressing admiration, gratitude, and tenderness. Who could enumerate the churches and monuments everywhere erected in her honor, the associations established under her invocation, the books composed in her praises?

But the homage which eclipses all others, is the definition of the dogma of the Immaculate Conception in 1854. This definition, ardently desired by the devout faithful, enthusiastically welcomed by the whole world, was the grand thought of Pius IX after his elevation to the chair of St. Peter, and it will be recorded in history as the crowning event of his Pontificate, already illustrious for so many other causes.

Mary, by this, has received from her children all the glory it was in their power to procure her; her prerogatives appear in all their luster; she is acknowledged as sovereign mistress of Heaven and earth; she occupies in the economy of religion the true place Divine wisdom has assigned her. Let us hope she will soon display to the world the effects of her powerful protection, that she will crush the infernal serpent's head, that she will calm the storms hell has unchained—in fine, that she will assure the triumph of the Church and the reign of Jesus Christ in justice and truth.

# APPARITIONS OF THE BLESSED VIRGIN TO SISTER CATHERINE: FIRST APPARITION: THE ANGEL CONDUCTS THE SISTER TO THE CHAPEL; MARY CONVERSES WITH HER—SECOND APPARITION: MARY UPON A GLOBE, HER HANDS EMITTING RAYS OF LIGHT, SYMBOLIC OF GRACE; MARY ORDERS A MEDAL TO BE STRUCK—THIRD APPARITION: MARY RENEWS THE COMMAND.

## APPARITIONS OF THE BLESSED VIRGIN TO SISTER CATHERINE

When Sister Catherine was favored with these apparitions of the Blessed Virgin she related by word of mouth to her director, what she had seen and heard, and he, though apparently attaching little importance to her communications, carefully took note of them. The Sister never thought of writing them, she judged herself incapable of doing so, and, moreover, in her opinion, it would have been contrary to humility.

In 1856, when events had confirmed the truth of her predictions, M. Aladel told her to commit to writing all she could recollect of the supernatural visitations of 1830. She obeyed, despite her repugnance, and sketched an account of her vision of St. Vincent's heart, which we have already read, and that of the apparitions of the Blessed Virgin.

In obedience, she again wrote in 1876, an account of these same apparitions.

Finally, another copy, not dated, was found among her papers after death.

These three narrations accord perfectly in the main yet differ sufficiently in detail to prove that one was not copied from the other.

To these manuscripts, in which no change has been made, except a correction of faults in style and orthography, we are indebted for the following account of the apparitions.

It is to be regretted that M. Aladel's notes were almost destroyed; no doubt they contained very interesting details, but what portion of them remains is of little importance.

Before quoting Sister Catherine's own narration, we must remark, that the first vision, having little reference to anything but the Sister herself and St. Vincent's two Communities, M. Aladel did not deem it advisable to have published; also, that although the account of the vision of the medal in the first editions of the notice, seems to differ notably from that related by the Sister, we will see later how these discrepancies can be explained, and that in the main the two versions are identical.

## FIRST APPARITION OF THE BLESSED VIRGIN

### To Sister Catherine Labouré, Daughter of Charity.

Sister Catherine, already favored with celestial visions, ardently desired, with all the simplicity of her nature, to see the Blessed Virgin. To obtain this grace, she invoked her good Angel, St. Vincent, and the Blessed Virgin herself.

On the 18th of July 1830, eve of the Feast of St. Vincent de Paul, the Directress of the Seminary gave an instruction on devotion to the Saints and the Blessed Virgin; this but inflamed our Sister's pious desire. Fully imbued with the thought, she retired for the night, recommending herself to her blessed Father, St. Vincent, and confidently believing that her prayers would be answered.

About half-past eleven o'clock, she hears her name, "Sister Labouré," distinctly called three times; suddenly awaking, she opens her curtain on the side whence the voice proceeds, and what does she perceive? A little child of ravishing beauty, four or five years of age, dressed in white and enveloped in the radiant light beaming from his fair hair and noble person. "Come," said he, in a melodious voice, "come to the chapel, the Blessed Virgin awaits you." But, thought Sister Catherine (she slept in a large dormitory), the others will hear me, I shall be discovered. "Have no fears," said the child, answering her thought, "it is half-past eleven, everybody is asleep, I will accompany you."

At these words, no longer able to resist the invitation of her amiable guide, Sister Catherine dresses hastily and follows the child, who walks always at her left, illuming the places through which he passes; and everywhere along their path, to the Sister's great astonishment, does she find the lamps lighted. Her surprise redoubles, on seeing the door open at the child's touch, and on finding the altar resplendent with lights, "reminding her," she said, "of the midnight Mass."

The child conducts her into the sanctuary; here she kneels, whilst her celestial guide remains standing a little behind at her left.

The moments of waiting seem long to Sister Catherine; at last, about midnight, the child says to her: "Behold the Blessed Virgin, behold her!" At that instant, she distinctly hears on the right-hand side of the chapel, a slight noise, like the rustling of a silk robe; a most beautiful lady enters the sanctuary, and takes her seat in the place ordinarily occupied by the Director of the Community, on the left side of the sanctuary. The seat, the attitude, the costume (a white robe of a golden tinge and a blue veil), strongly resemble the representation of St. Anne in the picture adorning the sanctuary. Yet it is not the same countenance, and Sister Catherine is struggling interiorly against doubt. Can this indeed be the Blessed Virgin? she asks herself. Suddenly, the little child, assuming the voice of a man, speaks aloud, and in severe words asks her if the Queen of Heaven may not appear to a poor mortal under whatever form she pleases.

Her doubts all vanish, and following only the impulses of her heart, the Sister throws herself at the Blessed Virgin's feet, familiarly placing her hands upon the Blessed Virgin's knees, like a child beside its mother.

"At this moment," said she, "I felt the sweetest emotion of my life, it would be impossible for me to express it. The Blessed Virgin told me how I must act in all my trials; and pointing with her left hand to the foot of the altar, she told me it was there I must come and lay open my heart, adding that it was there I would receive all needful consolation. Then she also said to me: 'My child, I am going to charge you with a mission; you will suffer many trials on account of it, but you will surmount them, knowing that you endure them for the glory of the good God. You will be contradicted, but you will be sustained by grace, do not fear; with simplicity and confidence, tell all that passes within you to him who is charged with the care of your soul. You will see certain things, you will be inspired in your prayers, give an account to him.'

"I then asked the Blessed Virgin for an explanation of what she had already shown me. She answered: 'My child, the times are very disastrous, great trials are about to come upon

France, the throne will be overturned, the entire world will be in confusion by reason of miseries of every kind.' (The Blessed Virgin looked very sad in saying this.) 'But come to the foot of this altar, here graces will be shed upon all—upon all who ask for them with confidence and fervor.

"'At a certain time, the danger will be great indeed, it will seem as if all were lost, but do not fear, I shall be with you; you will acknowledge my visit, the protection of God and that of St. Vincent upon the two Communities. Have confidence, do not be discouraged, you are in my especial keeping.

"'There will be victims in other Communities.' (Tears were in the Blessed Virgin's eyes as she said this.) 'Among the clergy of Paris there will be victims, Mgr. the Archbishop will die.' (At these words her tears flowed anew.) 'My child, the cross will be despised, it will be trampled underfoot, our Lord's side will be opened anew, the streets will flow with blood, the entire world will be in tribulation.'" (Here the Blessed Virgin could no longer speak, grief was depicted in her countenance.) At these words Sister Catherine thought, when will this take place? And an interior light distinctly indicated to her in forty years.

Another version, also written by her own hand, says forty years, then ten, after which, peace. In connection with this M. Aladel said to her:

"Will you and I see the accomplishment of all these things?" "If we do not, others will," replied the simple daughter.

The Blessed Virgin also entrusted her with several communications for her Director concerning the Daughters of Charity, and told her that he would one day be clothed with the necessary authority for putting them in execution.[7] After this, she said again: "But great troubles will come, the danger will be imminent, yet do not fear, St. Vincent will watch over you, and the protection of God is always here in a particular manner." (The Blessed Virgin still looked very sad.) "I will be with you myself; I will always keep my eye upon you, and I will enrich you with many graces." The Sister adds: "Graces will be bestowed, particularly upon all who ask for them, but they must pray, they must pray.

——

"I could not tell," continues the Sister, "how long I remained with the Blessed Virgin; all I can say is that, after talking with me a long time, she disappeared like a shadow that vanishes."

On arising from her knees, Sister Catherine perceived the child just where she had left him, to throw herself at the Blessed Virgin's feet. He said: "She has gone," and, all resplendent with light as before, he stationed himself anew at her left hand, and conducted her back to the dormitory by the same paths as they had come.

"I believe," continues the narration, "that this child was my Guardian Angel, because I had fervently implored him to procure me the favor of seeing the Blessed Virgin.... Returned to my bed, I heard the clock strike two, and I went to sleep no more."

What has just been recounted was only a part of Sister Catherine's mission, or rather a preparation for a future mission to be given her as a pledge of the Immaculate Mary's tenderness for humanity.

In the month of November of this same year, 1830, Sister Catherine communicates to M. Aladel a new vision; but it is no longer that of an afflicted Mother weeping over the evils menacing her children, or the martyrdom of her dearest friends. This vision recalls the rainbow appearing in a sky still black with storms, or the star shining through the tempest to inspire the mariner with confidence—it is the Virgin Queen, bearing the promise of benediction, salvation, and peace.

M. Aladel relates this to the Promoter of the diocese, and we find it inserted in the verbal process of the investigation, dated February 16, 1836, as follows:

"At half-past five in the evening, whilst the Sisters were in the chapel taking their meditation, the Blessed Virgin appeared to a young Sister as if in an oval picture; she was standing on a globe, only one-half of which was visible; she was clothed in a white robe and a mantle of shining blue, having her hands covered, as it were, with diamonds, whence emanated luminous rays falling upon the earth, but more abundantly upon one portion of it.

"A voice seemed to say: 'These rays are symbolic of the graces Mary obtains for men, and the point upon which they fall most abundantly is France.' Around the picture, written in golden letters, were these words: 'O Mary! conceived without sin, pray for us who have recourse to thee!' This prayer, traced in a semi-circle, began at the Blessed Virgin's right hand, and, passing over her head, terminated at her left hand. The reverse of the picture bore the letter M surmounted by a cross, having a bar at its base, and beneath the monogram of Mary, were the hearts of Jesus and Mary, the first surrounded with a crown of thorns, the other transpierced with a sword. Then she seemed to hear these words: 'A medal must be struck upon this model; those who wear it indulgenced, and repeat this prayer with devotion, will be, in an especial manner, under the protection of the Mother of God.' At that instant, the vision disappeared."

According to the testimony of Sister Catherine's Director, this apparition appeared several times in the course of a few months, always in the chapel of the Mother House of the Daughters of Charity, either during Mass or some of the religious exercises. M. Aladel adds that he was not certain as to their number, but he knows they were repeated thrice, at least, the Sister having mentioned it three different times.

Here is the account written by the Sister's own hand:

"The 27th of November, 1830, which was a Saturday and eve of the first Sunday in Advent, whilst making my meditation in profound silence, at half-past five in the evening, I seemed to hear on the right hand side of the sanctuary something like the rustling of a silk dress, and, glancing in that direction, I perceived the Blessed Virgin standing near St. Joseph's picture; her height was medium, and her countenance so beautiful that it would be impossible for me to describe it. She was standing, clothed in a robe the color of auroral light, the style that is usually called à la vierge—that is, high neck and plain sleeves. Her head was covered with a white veil, which descended on each side to her feet. Her hair was smooth on the forehead, and above was a coif ornamented with a little lace and fitting close to the head. Her face was only partially covered, and her feet rested upon a globe, or rather a hemisphere (at least, I saw but half a globe). Her hands were raised about as high as her waist, and she held in a graceful attitude another globe (a figure of the universe). Her eyes were lifted up to Heaven, and her countenance was radiant as she offered the globe to Our Lord.

## SECOND APPARITION OF THE BLESSED VIRGIN

"Suddenly, her fingers were filled with rings [8] and most beautiful precious stones; the rays gleaming forth and reflected on all sides, enveloped her in such dazzling light that I could see neither her feet nor her robe. The stones were of different sizes, and the rays emanating from them were more or less brilliant in proportion to the size.

"I could not express what I felt, nor what I learned, in these few moments.

"Whilst occupied contemplating this vision, the Blessed Virgin cast her eyes upon me, and a voice said in the depths of my heart: 'The globe that you see represents the entire world, and particularly France, and each person in particular.'

"I would not know how to express the beauty and brilliancy of these rays. And the Blessed Virgin added: 'Behold the symbol of the graces I shed upon those who ask me for them,' thus making me understand how generous she is to all who implore her intercession.... How many favors she grants to those who ask. At this moment I was not myself, I was in raptures! There now formed around the Blessed Virgin a frame slightly oval, upon which appeared, in golden letters, these words: 'O Mary! conceived without sin, pray for us who have recourse to thee!'

"Then I heard a voice which said: 'Have a medal struck upon this model, persons who wear it indulgenced, will receive great graces, especially if they wear it around the neck; graces will be abundantly bestowed upon those who have confidence.'

"Suddenly," says the Sister, "the picture seemed to turn," and she saw the reverse, such as has already been described in the previous account of the investigation.

Sister Catherine's notes do not mention the twelve stars surrounding the monogram of Mary and the two hearts. Yet they are always represented on the medal. It is morally certain that she communicated this detail, by word of mouth, at the time she related the apparitions.

Other notes in Sister Catherine's own handwriting complete the account. She adds that some of these precious stones did not emit rays, and when she expressed her astonishment at this, she was told that they were a figure of the graces we neglect to ask of Mary. On a hasty perusal, our Sister's account of the vision appears to differ from M. Aladel's. We were struck with this and had to study these interesting and authentic documents attentively, in order to decide whether the visions differed essentially or were really the same.

## THIRD APPARITION OF THE BLESSED VIRGIN

According to M. Aladel's testimony in the investigation, the apparitions relative to the medal were always similar, and Sister Catherine, before her death, confirmed this assertion. As we have just learned from our Sister's own words, the Blessed Virgin always appeared with the terrestrial globe under her feet, and at the same time in her virginal hands, pressing it and warming it, as it were, against her maternal heart, and offering it to her Divine Son in her quality of Advocate and Mother, with an ineffable expression of supplication and love.

This is what the Sister saw. Was it all? No, after the first act of sublime intercession, after this most efficacious prayer of our divine Mediatrix, her hands are suddenly filled with graces, under the figure of rings and precious stones, which emit such brilliant rays that all else is invisible, Mary is enveloped in them, and her hands are bent beneath the weight of these treasures. Her eyes are cast upon the humble Sister whose ravished glances can scarcely support this celestial effulgence. At the same time, an oval frame is formed around the vision, and a voice directs the Sister to have a medal struck according to the medal presented. The medal is a faithful reproduction of this picture, now the symbolical part disappears in the sheaves of light.

Sister Catherine being asked if she still saw the globe in the Blessed Virgin's hands, when the luminous sheaves issued from them, answered no, there remained nothing but the rays of light; and that when the Blessed Virgin spoke of the globe, she meant that under her feet, there being no longer any question of the first. Hence, we may conclude, that Sister Catherine's description of the apparition and M. Aladel's agree perfectly. The small globe which the Blessed Virgin holds in her hands, and the large one on which she stands, are both inundated with the same dazzling rays, or enriched with the same graces. The august Mary seems to indicate by the small globe merely a figure of the world, imperfectly represented beneath her feet, thus reminding us that she is all merciful Queen of the human race.

There is yet another variation in the description of the two apparitions. M. Aladel, in conformity with the popular belief, that white and blue combined constitute the Blessed Virgin's livery, as emblems of purity, celestial purity, gives the mantle an azure tint. Sister Catherine expresses the same idea several times in her notes, saying: "White signifies innocence, and blue is the livery of Mary." However, the blue mantle is not mentioned in the notice of the apparition, Sister Catherine speaks only of the robe and veil of auroral light.

When questioned as to a more definite description of this color, she replied that it was a deep white, tinted with the mild, beautiful radiance of dawn,[9] thus wishing, no doubt, to give some idea of the celestial hue of the robe and veil. It is this hue that tortures the artist, for he feels his pencil powerless to depict the beauties of another sphere.

We can understand from the above, how M. Aladel could have mistaken some details furnished by Sister Catherine or have confounded the apparition of the medal with the visions of July 18th and 19th, in which the Blessed Virgin's apparel was white and blue.

However, the accessories of the mantle and its indescribable hue, in no wise affect the reality of the apparition.

We recollect with what indifference, we might say severity, M. Aladel received his penitent's communications, bidding her give no heed to them, but dismiss them from her mind, as altogether unworthy of attention. But Sister Catherine's obedience, attested by her director himself, could not efface the delightful remembrance of what she had seen and heard; to return to Mary's feet was her greatest happiness; the thought never left her, nor the firm conviction that she would see this dear Mother again. And, indeed, in December, she was favored with another vision, similar to that of November 27th, and occurring at the same time, during evening meditation. But there was a striking difference between this and the previous one, the Blessed Virgin, instead of stopping at St. Joseph's picture, passed on, and rested above the tabernacle, a little behind it, and precisely in the place the statue now occupies. The Blessed Virgin appeared to be about forty years of age, according to the Sister's judgment. The apparition was, as it were, framed from the hands in the invocation: "O Mary! conceived without sin, pray for us who have recourse to thee!" traced in golden letters. The reverse presented the monogram of the Blessed Virgin, surmounted by a cross, and beneath were the divine hearts of Jesus and Mary. Sister Labouré was again directed to have a medal struck upon this model. She terminates her account in these words: "To tell you what I understood at the moment the Blessed Virgin offered the globe to Our Lord, would be impossible, or what my feelings were whilst gazing on her! A voice in the depths of my heart said to me: 'These rays are symbolic of the graces the Blessed Virgin obtains for those who ask for them.'"

These few lines, according to her, should be inscribed at the base of the Blessed Virgin's statue. On this occasion, contrary to her usual custom, she could not refrain from an exclamation of joy at the thought of the homages which would be rendered Mary! "Oh! how delightful to hear it said: 'Mary is Queen of the Universe, and particularly of France!' The children will proclaim it, 'She is Queen of each soul!'"

When Sister Labouré related the third apparition of the medal, M. Aladel asked her if she had seen anything written on the reverse. The Sister answered that she had not. "Ah!" said the Father, "ask the Blessed Virgin what to put there."

The young Sister obeyed; and after having prayed a long time, one day during meditation, she seemed to hear a voice saying: "The M and the two hearts express enough."

None of these narrations mention the serpent, yet it always figures in representations of the apparition, and certainly in conformity with Sister Catherine's earliest revelations of the vision. The following shows why we are so positive of this fact.

Towards the close of her life, after a silence of forty-five years, M. Aladel being no more, this good daughter was interiorly constrained to confide to one of her Superiors the communications she had received from the Blessed Virgin, that they might serve to reanimate devotion and gratitude to Mary. Having done this, her mind was relieved; she felt that now she could die in peace.

The Superior, favored with her confidence, wishing to realize one of her venerable companion's most cherished desires, proposes a statue of Mary Immaculate, holding the globe. On asking Sister Catherine if the serpent must be represented under the Blessed Virgin's feet, she answered: "Yes; there was a serpent of a greenish color, with yellow spots." She also remarked that the globe in the Virgin's hands was surmounted by a little cross, that her countenance was neither very youthful nor very joyous, but indicative of gravity mingled with sorrow, that the sorrowful expression vanished as her face became irradiated with love, especially at the moment of her prayer.

Our attempt at representing the vision was successful, although the tint of the robe and veil, the celestial radiance of the face, the splendor of the rays, must always remain an impossibility for art; as the good Sister, whilst declaring her satisfaction, betrayed by her tone of voice and expression the disappointment she felt at the impotency of human skill to depict the beauty of the celestial original.

Thirty-five years before, M. Aladel had vainly attempted a representation of the same apparition, as we learn from a curious fragment, a small design [10] representing the Immaculate Virgin holding the globe, etc., as described by Sister Catherine. His note directing the details is in exact conformity with the Sister's description, except in one particular, the blue mantle. But little satisfied with this attempt, which gave but a confused idea of the apparition, and his own especial impression of it, he relinquished the undertaking, and held to the known model.

We may say, with truth, that nothing can equal the beauty, the grace, the expression of tenderness depicted in the attitude of this Virgin, whose graciously downcast glances and hands, filled with blessings, proclaim her the Mother, inviting her little child to cast itself into her arms, or earnestly entreating the prodigal son to confide in her merciful mediation.

This image of the Immaculate Mother, universally admired and honored, has a mute eloquence which never fails to touch the heart; and, truly, may it ever be styled the miraculous Virgin. Were we to cite only those which have come to our knowledge, a volume would be insufficient to contain an account of all the wonderful conversions, cures, marks of protection, wrought since the appearance of this vision to the present day.

The production of new models, representing the Immaculate Virgin in a different attitude, should never supplant this, which is, as it were, the type of all others; nor weaken the devotion heretofore accorded it by popular gratitude.

# Propagation of the Medal: ITS WONDERFUL CIRCULATION—CANONICAL INVESTIGATION ORDERED BY MGR. DE QUÉLEN.

We have already seen with what mistrust M. Aladel received Sister Catherine's communications, and how he hesitated to assume the mission proposed to him. At last, after grave reflection, after consultations with enlightened persons, and upon the formal authorization of Mgr. de Quélen, Archbishop of Paris, he decided to have the medal of the Immaculate Conception struck. This was in 1832.

When about to depict the details as related by the Sister, many difficulties presented themselves. In what attitude should the Blessed Virgin be represented, for in the apparition she had several? Should a globe be in her hands? Again, at one instant she was enveloped [68]in waves of light, but this could not be gracefully reproduced in an engraving. After mature consideration, it was decided to adopt the already existing model of the Immaculate Virgin, which represents her with hands extended; to this were added the luminous rays escaping from the rings on her fingers, the terrestrial globe on which she stands, and the serpent she crushes under her feet. Around the oval were inscribed these words: "O Mary! conceived without sin, pray for us who have recourse to thee!" The reverse bears the letter M, surmounted by a cross, and the Sacred Hearts of Jesus and Mary below the M, the first surrounded with a crown of thorns, the second pierced by a sword.

"As soon as the medal was struck," says M. Aladel, "it was freely circulated, especially among the Daughters of Charity, who, knowing something of its origin, wore it with great confidence. Shortly after, they gave it to several sick people, six of whom experienced most beneficial results. Three cures and three conversions were wrought, some of them in Paris and some in the diocese of Meaux, all of a very sudden and unexpected nature. And now there was heard everywhere a great demand for the Miraculous Medal, the medal which heals—virtuous mothers of families giving it as a New-Year's present to their children, who received it so gladly and wore it with such respect that no one could doubt how their innocent hearts prized it. All the pious hastened to procure it as soon as it was known to be within reach; but the event it gives us most pleasure to record here, and which edified us most in these early days of the propagation of the medal, is that, in two cities of the province, nearly all the young people united in wearing the medal as the safeguard of their youth. Four hundred silver medals were sent for, to be indulged for this purpose. Very soon entire parishes in various counties solicited their pastors to get them medals, and in Paris an officer of high rank bought sixty for brother officers at their request.

"Thus, the medals of the Immaculate Conception were circulated in a truly wonderful manner, in all the provinces and among all classes; from every side we heard most consoling things; priests filled with the spirit of God wrote to us that these medals reanimated piety in the cities as well as in the country; grand vicars, enjoying the high esteem due their piety and intellect, prelates, even more distinguished, assured us of their entire confidence in the medals, which they regarded as means sent by Providence to revive the faith so sensibly enfeebled in our age; that in reality they did awaken faith daily in many hearts apparently devoid of it, that they re-established peace and union in families divided by discord, in fine, that not one of all those wearing the medal but had experienced most salutary effects.

"Mgr. de Quélen himself (whose great charity brought him in contact with all classes) told me several times that he had given the medal to numbers of sick persons of every condition in life, and never had he failed to recognize the blessed results. Very soon he publishes these in a circular of December 15th, 1836, on the occasion of consecrating the parish church of Our Lady of Loretto. It is a fact we are jealous of confirming, and the knowledge of which we desire should reach even the most remote parts of the Catholic world; in our diocese this devotion has become more deeply rooted with time; the afflicted still affirm, increase and extend its marvelous progress; signal favors, graces of healing, preservation and salvation seem to multiply among us, in proportion as we implore the tender pity of Mary conceived without sin. 'We exhort the faithful,' adds he in the beginning of the same circular, 'to wear the medal struck a few years ago in honor of the Blessed Virgin,' and to repeat frequently the prayer inscribed around the image: 'O Mary! conceived without sin, pray for us who have recourse to thee!'

"Moreover, in every part of France have we witnessed the increasing eagerness of the faithful of all ages, sexes and conditions, to procure the Miraculous Medal. Careless

Christians, hardened sinners, Protestants, the impious and even Jews, asked for it, received it with pleasure and wore it with religious veneration.

"Not only in France were we forced to admire the propagation of the medal; it spread rapidly and extensively throughout Switzerland, Piedmont, Italy, Spain, Belgium, England, America, in the Levant, and even China. It is also said, that at Naples, as soon as they heard of it, the Metropolitan Chapter sent for some to one of our establishments in that city, that the king had silver medals struck for all the royal family and court, and a million of another medal, which were distributed during the cholera—that the image is there venerated in nearly every house, and the picture in several churches. At Rome, the Superior Generals of religious orders took pains to circulate it, and the Sovereign Pontiff himself, placed it at the foot of his crucifix. We also received a letter informing us that His Holiness gave it to several people as a particular mark of his pontifical affection.

"Moreover, to estimate the propagation of this medal, it suffices to consult the registry of M. Vachette, to whom was entrusted the striking of it.[11] This examen shows that, from June 1832, to the present time, he has sold: 1st, two millions in silver or gold; 2nd, eighteen millions of a cheaper metal. According to him, eleven other manufacturers in Paris have sold the same quantity; at Lyons, four others with whom he was acquainted, at least double the number; and in many other cities, whether of France or foreign countries, the manufacture and sales are incalculable."

Struck with this marvelous propagation, and the universal anxiety to learn the origin of the medal, Sister Catherine's pious Director published, in 1834, a short notice containing a brief narration of the apparition, and of the graces obtained by means of the medal. This book sold rapidly, and new editions had to be printed; when the eighth appeared in 1842, the number of copies sold amounted to a hundred and thirty thousand, and each successive edition was increased by well authenticated accounts of many new miraculous occurrences.

In consequence of all this, the venerable priest found himself engaged in a vast and active correspondence, which, to the end of his days, filled his heart with ineffable consolation, at the thought of his thus assisting in the accomplishment of the Immaculate Mary's promises throughout the universe.

Among the communications he received in the course of the year 1836, there was one which appeared to him the confirmation of Sister Catherine's vision. He published it in the notice of the medal. It was the vision of a Swiss religious, already favored with many extraordinary graces. We reproduce it here for the edification of the reader:

"The 17th of August 1835, the first day of her retreat, this religious, in an ecstasy after Holy Communion, sees Our Lord seated upon a throne of glory, and holding a sword in His hand. 'Where goest thou, and what seekest thou?' He asked. 'O Jesus!' she answered, 'I go to Thee, and it is Thyself alone I seek!' 'Where dost thou seek Me, in what and through whom?' 'Lord, in myself I seek Thee, in Thy holy will and through Mary.' Here Our Lord disappeared, and the religious, awaking from her ecstasy, was reflecting upon His words, when there suddenly appeared to her the Blessed Virgin, all lovely and resplendent. She held in her hand a medal, on which was engraved her image and the inscription: 'O Mary! conceived without sin, pray for us who have recourse to thee!' And sheaves of light gleamed from her hands. 'These rays,' said Mary to her, 'are symbols of the graces I obtain for men.' She then turned the medal, and the religious saw on the reverse the letter M surmounted by a little cross, beneath which were the Sacred Hearts of Jesus and Mary. 'Wear this medal,' said the Queen of Heaven, 'and thou wilt enjoy my very especial protection; take pains, also, that all who are in any pressing necessity wear it, that efforts are made to procure it for them.... Be in readiness, for I will put it upon thee myself, on the Feast of my beloved servant Bernard; today, I leave it in thy hands.' The Blessed Virgin afterwards reproached her for misplacing the medal and taking little pains to find it; the religious acknowledged indeed, that she had received it in July, and that having lost it, she really gave herself no anxiety, considering it merely an ordinary medal, knowing neither its origin nor its effects till this vision. This is attested by the Superior of the Community. The Blessed Virgin kept her promise, and on the 20th of the same month, the Feast of St. Bernard, she placed on the neck of the religious, the medal she had already put in her hands, recommending her to wear it respectfully, to repeat the invocation frequently, and to apply herself to the invitation of the Immaculate Mary's virtues.

"During her retreat in August 1836, she sees the medal every day, suspended, as it were, in the air. At first, it appeared very high, shining a few moments like the sun, then like gold; again, it seemed not so high and was apparently of silver; finally, very near the earth, and of a baser metal. The religious gazed in admiration, though without comprehending the meaning of this vision, until Vespers, when it was explained to her. A sweet but unfamiliar voice asked her which of these medals she preferred. She answered, the most brilliant, and the same voice congratulating her on the choice she had made, told her, that the brilliant medal shining like the sun, was that of faithful Christians, who, in wearing it, honor Mary perfectly, and contribute to her glory; the gold medal, that of pious persons who have a tender and filial devotion to Mary, but who keeping it within their hearts, advance but slightly this divine Mother's cause; the silver medal, that of all who wear it with respect and devotion, but who sometimes lack constancy and generosity in imitating Mary's virtues—finally, that the brass medal, represented that of all, who contenting themselves with invoking Mary, take no pains to walk in her footsteps, and thus remain sadly attached to earth. The same voice added, that there is, however, a very especial and peculiar union among these various persons, marked, we might say, with the precious seal of Mary Immaculate; they all necessarily aid one another in a very particular manner by prayer, so that with this powerful assistance, the third can elevate the last, the second sustain the third, and the first, thus happily attract all the others.

"These details have been communicated to us, from the abbey of Our Lady of Hermits at Einsiedlen, so renowned for the great virtues of its fervent religious, and the immense concourse of pilgrims, who repair hither from all parts of the world."

Up to this time, the medal had received only the verbal approbation of the Archbishop of Paris; a formal authorization was necessary to assure the faithful of its authenticity, and to conform moreover to the laws of the Church, which exact a canonical judgment, before permitting the introduction of new images in the liturgical worship. A juridical examination was consequently requested, in order to confirm the origin of the medal.

Mgr. de Quélen willingly complied, and by his order an investigation was begun February 16th, 1836, under the direction of M. Quentin, Vicar General, Promoter of the diocese; it was prolonged into the month of July and had not less than nineteen sittings.

We still possess the verbal process of this inquiry. Various witnesses appeared, the principal of whom was Sister Catherine's Director, M. Aladel.

In the course of the process, the Promoter asked, why God had chosen the Daughters of Charity for so rare a favor, and not one of those convents noted for the observance of an austere rule, such as rigorous fasts, mortifications, etc. For it was not in a contemplative order, but in the Mother House of this modest institution so useful to humanity, in the chapel which for a long time contained the mortal remains of St. Vincent, the father of the poor, that the apparition, which was the model of the medal, took place.

We believe the reason of this preference is to be found in the two usages observed among the Daughters of Charity, from the beginning of their Society; the first, an act of consecration to the Blessed Virgin on the Feast of the Immaculate Conception; the second, the ending each decade of the chaplet by the following profession of faith: "O Most Holy Virgin! I believe and confess thy Holy and Immaculate Conception, pure and without spot! O Most Pure Virgin! by thy virginal purity, by thy Immaculate Conception and thy glorious quality of Mother of God, obtain for me of thy dear Son, humility, charity, great purity of heart, body and soul, holy perseverance in my dear vocation, the gift of prayer, a good life and a happy death."

The proofs admitted in the inquiry to establish the authenticity of the vision of the medal, are:

1st. The Sister's character—she is a poor young country girl, uneducated and without talent—of solid but simple piety, good judgment, and calm, sedate mind; we perceive at once that everything about her excludes all suspicion of deceit or illusion. The better to preserve her incognito, she will not allow her name to be mentioned, and she even refused to appear before the Promoter of the investigation.

2nd. The wisdom of the Sister's Director, who took all possible precautions to guard against deception, and who yielded to his penitent's reiterated entreaties, only from fear of displeasing the Blessed Virgin, and by the advice of his Superiors.

3rd. The apparition contains nothing, either in its character or object, opposed to the teachings of the Church, but is, on the contrary, conducive to edification. Being several times renewed and always in the same manner, we may conclude that the Sister's imagination had nothing whatever to do with it.

4th. The wonderful circulation of the medal, confirmed by the testimony of the first engraver, M. Vachette, and the extensive sales of copies of the notice, reaching 109,000 in sixteen months, as attested by the publisher, M. Bailly, must be regarded as a confirmation of its supernatural origin.

5th. The extraordinary graces obtained through the instrumentality of the medal, cures and conversions, several of which are legally attested by the deposition of reliable witnesses, who appeared before the Promoter and signed the verbal process, give a last proof to the fact it was sought to establish, namely, that the Miraculous Medal must be of divine origin. Such is the formal conclusion, in the report addressed to the Archbishop by the Promoter, at the end of the inquiry.

Unfortunately, the ecclesiastical authority did not pronounce judgment; we know not why the inquiry did not receive the sanction to which it apparently led. The death of Mgr. de Quélen, at the end of the year 1839, caused all proceedings to be abandoned. Everything still remains in the domain of private devotions, and the model of the Immaculate Virgin, with its symbolical attributes, is not yet authorized as an object of public veneration in the churches.

This deplorable omission is so much the more difficult to understand, as, personally, Mgr. de Quélen took a serious interest in the apparition of 1830, the compass of which he comprehended. It was he who urged M. Aladel to have the medal struck; he expressed a wish to have some of the first; he received them and experienced their efficacy. Before ordering the investigation, he had summoned to him the Mother General of the Daughters of Charity, together with the officers forming her council, and other Sisters well versed in Community affairs, to learn from them what usages of the Community could have drawn down upon it such a favor as the Blessed Virgin had just bestowed. Not content with possessing the Miraculous Medal, the pious prelate had in his own chamber a statue of the Immaculate Conception after the Sister's model. It was cast in bronze, under his own eyes, as he wished to assist at the operation. When, in 1839, the solemn octave of the Immaculate Conception was celebrated in the diocese of Paris, for the first time, this statue, on a throne surrounded with flowers, was exposed to the veneration of the faithful. On the 1st of January of this same year, he consecrated his diocese to Mary Immaculate.

In commemoration of this, he had a picture painted, which represents him standing at the foot of Mary's statue, his eyes fixed upon her with love and confidence. The statue rests upon a globe which bears these words: "Virgo fidelis." And the invocation, "Regina, sine labe concepta, ora pro nobis," is inscribed upon the picture.

On the Feast of the Assumption, he presented this picture to his chapter, that it might, he said, be a monument of his devotion and that of the chapter of Paris to the Immaculate Conception of the Mother of God.[12]

A medal, bearing date of January 1, 1839, reproduces this picture upon one of its faces. On the other is a vessel, tempest-tossed, and a star guiding it to the haven of peace. These words of St. Bernard, "Respice stellam, voca Mariam,[13] explain the allegory. The following lines complete the explanation:

"Vana, Hyacinthe, furit; Stella maris auspice, vincis."[14]

# DEVELOPMENT OF THE DEVOTION TO THE IMMACULATE CONCEPTION

The principal end of the Blessed Virgin's apparition to Sister Catherine was to develop among the faithful, devotion to the Immaculate Conception; and the medal was the instrument used to accomplish this. Its influence was so prompt and perceptible that, in the year 1836, the Promoter charged with directing the canonical inquiry attributed to it, in a great measure, the wonderful development of devotion to the Virgin Immaculate. This pious impulse, once firmly rooted, continued to increase throughout the world; but, according to the ordinary ways of Providence, whilst the effects struck the eyes of all, the cause was forgotten, it was forgotten especially that God had chosen a modest Daughter of Charity to revive in the Church devotion to the Blessed Virgin. The medal was known everywhere, it was worn by everyone, it accomplished numberless prodigies, but whence did it come? This no one thought of asking. It is miraculous; that epithet includes its name, its origin, its value, and the humble Daughter who received it from Mary, to bestow upon mankind, silently admires these astonishing results, and says, like her blessed Father: "I am nothing in all this but a vile instrument, I cannot attribute to myself any of the glory without committing an act of injustice."

The august Virgin had said that the graces obtained for mankind through her intercession would be particularly abundant in France. Events have proved the reality of the promise. It is in France, especially, that the medal has been propagated, miracles multiplied, and devotion to the Immaculate Conception most rapidly developed; it may be said, with truth, that that country has, indeed, merited the title of Mary's kingdom. As, among all the French dioceses, Paris was the one favored with these apparitions of the Blessed Virgin, so was Paris the one to inaugurate the religious movement. Faithful echo of the Church's ancient traditions concerning the Immaculate Conception, a prelate, whose piety equaled his nobility of character, and whose virtue received a new luster from the fire of persecution, Mgr. de Quélen distinguished himself among all the bishops by his zeal in honoring the privilege so dear to Mary. A witness of the influence exerted by the medal upon the sensibly increasing devotion of the faithful to Mary conceived without sin and struck with the already abundant fruits of this devotion in the conversion of sinners, the pious Archbishop was filled with joy. Incited by a just hope of seeing the gifts of Heaven still more abundantly multiplied, if devotion to Mary were produced under new forms, he addressed a petition to the Sovereign Pontiff with the view of obtaining from His Holiness: 1st. To celebrate solemnly, on the second Sunday of Advent, the Immaculate Conception of Mary, that devotion might be maintained and strengthened among the faithful; 2nd. To add to the preface, Et te in Immaculata Conceptione; 3rd. A plenary indulgence, in perpetuity, for this same day.

Our Holy Father, Pope Gregory XVI, approved the Archbishop's petition, and granted it by a rescript of December 7, 1838. The privileges he had just obtained, in honor of Mary, conceived without sin, this venerable prelate joyfully published the first of the following January in a solemn circular, which clearly depicts his eminent piety. We here reproduce it for our readers' edification:

"Circular of the Archbishop of Paris on the subject of the Feast of the Immaculate Conception of the Blessed Virgin Mary, Mother of God.

"Hyacinthe Louis De Quélen, by the divine mercy and grace of the Holy Apostolic See, Archbishop of Paris, etc.

"To the clergy and faithful of our diocese, health, and benediction in our Lord Jesus Christ.

"We do not wish, dearly beloved brethren, to await the end of the year which begins to-day, and which we dare regard as one fruitful in all manner of spiritual blessings, ere announcing to you the new favor we have just received from the Holy Apostolic See, so much have we loved to persuade ourselves that the joy of your hearts will equal our own, so confident are we that this favor is for us, the presage of multiplied graces, and that it becomes henceforth for our diocese an abundant source of sanctification and salvation.

"Let us hasten to proclaim this favor: it treats of devotion to our august Queen, Mother and Mistress, the Most Holy and Immaculate Virgin Mary, honored especially in the mystery of her most pure Conception.

"Mary was conceived without sin: Behold what the Catholic Church, what the infallible Church, what the true and only Church of Jesus Christ authorizes us to teach, without, however, declaring it an article of Faith,[15] what she prevents us denying publicly, what she instils into all the faithful, when in her general council, she declares, she proclaims, that in the decree treating of original sin, her intention is not to include therein the Blessed and Immaculate Virgin Mary, Mother of God.[16] Behold! what the Sovereign Pontiffs permit us to say, that always, and with a view of nourishing the piety of Mary's servants, who invoke her by recalling the first of her privileges, that which approaches nearest the sanctity of God, always do they deign to second these prayers, and zealously open the treasure of indulgences of which they are the supreme dispensers, in favor of a devotion so legitimate.

"Mary was conceived without sin. Behold! what the Church of Paris glories in professing and maintaining; what her Doctors hold it an honor to teach and defend; what her children are jealous of preserving as one of their dearest possessions after the sacred dogmas of faith; what they do not hesitate to regard as an immediate con[83]sequence of their faith, not believing it possible to separate in Mary, the title of Immaculate Virgin from that of Virgin Mother of God, and not considering it possible to refuse the privilege of a Conception without spot, to her who was to receive and who indeed did receive, that of the divine Maternity. Behold! what respect and love for the Word made Flesh, inspire for the chaste bosom the Most High sanctified, because He was to descend there, and there clothe Himself with our nature, there become man by the operation of the Holy Ghost.

"Mary was conceived without sin. Behold! what for years, has been repeated thousands and thousands of times, not in this great city or diocese only, but in every part of France, among strangers and in the most distant countries. Behold! the cry of hope which suffering danger, public or private necessities, have wrung from mouths accustomed to bless God, and celebrate the praises of His Holy Mother. Behold! what has been written, engraved, religiously deposed, wherever there were spiritual or temporal favors to be asked, graces of protection, of healing or conversion; at the entrance of cities, at the doors of dwellings, on the breast of the sick, on the couch of the dying. Behold! what in these later times especially, has taken such deep root in all Christian hearts, what has received an extraordinary impulse, what has been propagated in so remarkable a manner, what seems to justify moreover, (the fact can no longer be disguised) the numberless graces obtained through the invocation of Mary conceived without sin.

"Mary was conceived without sin. Behold! what the chaste generation has taken the pious custom of placing on its heart with the sign of the cross as an impenetrable buckler against the inflamed darts of Satan, and under which its innocence and virtue are shielded.

Behold! what inspires it, fortifies it, renders it invincible in combats with the demon of darkness; what makes it victorious over all the seductions of the world and the attacks of hell; what attracts, what leads it to follow Mary in the path of angelic perfection, and makes it taste that celestial word which is not given to all to understand; finally, behold! what everywhere and in all conditions, fills with holy emulation, souls truly pious; what encourages them to walk with constancy in the ways of justice; what communicates to them a just horror of sin and the highest esteem for sanctifying grace, of which the Immaculate Virgin is for them the faithful mirror and venerable sanctuary.

"And behold, also, our very dear brethren, what has urged, and determined us to regard as a consolation, a duty of our episcopate to second your piety in this regard, at the same time, that we satisfy our devotion to this Immaculate Virgin, to whom we are indebted for many signal benefits. We thought it not a rash zeal, to supplicate our Holy Father, the Pope, to deign confide to us the means of increasing devotion to Mary Immaculate in her Conception, to render it easier and thus more popular. The Feast of the Blessed Virgin's Conception, being now in France only one of devotion, we have feared that even if the memory of it were not gradually effaced, it might become insensibly neglected, and the fruits of sanctification and salvation diminished.

"The Sovereign Pontiff has deigned to accord our humble request. The rescript we have received, our very dear brethren, sufficiently testifies how our petitions have been welcomed, our prayers answered, upon what foundation the regulations we are going to prescribe rest, and the advantages we have had reason to expect from them. We long, yes, we long, from lively gratitude, from tender love to Mary, to give vent to our transports and salute her solemnly by the title of Immaculate in her Conception that day, for distant day it seems to our hearts, when we will be permitted to proclaim it joyfully before the assembled faithful, and during the celebration of the holy mysteries.

"O Mary! thou whom wisdom hast possessed in the beginning of thy ways, cloud divinely fruitful, always in light and never in shade, new Eve, who didst crush the infernal serpent's head; courageous Judith, glory of Jerusalem, joy of Israel, honor of thy people, amiable Esther, exempt from the common law which presses as a yoke of anathema upon all the children of Adam, full of grace, blessed among all women. O Mary! conceived without sin, pray for us who have recourse to thee! By thy most Holy Virginity and thy Immaculate Conception, O most Holy Virgin! obtain for us purity of heart and body, in the name of the Father, and of the Son, and of the Holy Ghost. Amen!"

But this does not satisfy the prelate's piety; he also entreats the Sovereign Pontiff that the belief in the Immaculate Conception be expressed in the litanies of the Blessed Virgin. The Holy Father grants this petition and permits the addition to the litany of the invocation: "Regina sine labe concepta, ora pro nobis." Then Monseigneur, in a new circular of June 24th, orders that the Sunday following its reception, this invocation should be chanted three times at Benediction, and in future chanted or recited every time the litany was chanted or recited, adding that no prayer-book without this invocation inserted in the litany would have his approbation. The prelate also exhorted all the clergy, pastors, and others, to instill into the faithful, devotion to the Immaculate Conception, recommending the use of the formula, "Regina sine labe concepta, ora pro nobis."

At last, seeing the near approach of that epoch so dear and solemn, he could not refrain, despite his extreme weakness and the violent sufferings of a mortal malady, from giving vent to his feelings in a third circular, which displays at the same time his zeal for the Immaculate Virgin's honor and his indefatigable solicitude for the welfare of his flock.

The feast and octave of the Immaculate Conception, announced and prepared with so much zeal by the pious Bishop, were celebrated with extraordinary solemnity in all the churches throughout the diocese of Paris, and especially at Notre Dame. It was one of the last consolations this great prelate enjoyed upon earth. He died the 31st of December, crowning a life rich in virtues and sacrifices, by an act of filial homage to Mary Immaculate, and a final testimony of tender solicitude for the flock he was about to leave. He loved this flock during life, and before dying, he confides it to the inexhaustible charity of the Immaculate Heart of the Mother of Jesus, he conceals it under the mantle of her purity, that he may feel assured of the victory over the enemies of its happiness. He had consecrated his person, his diocese and all France to this Virgin, conceived without sin. Was it not to her maternal protection the venerable prelate owed that generous submission, that admirable tranquility, that tender love and sweet serenity of the just, when he was hovering on the brink of eternity? He had placed all his confidence in thee, O Mary! at that last moment, he invoked thee as the Star of the Sea that was to guide him to Heaven, and it was under thy auspices his beautiful soul winged its flight to the bosom of its God.

In emulation of the example of the illustrious Archbishop of the capital, the other Archbishops and Bishops of France petition the Holy See for the same privileges, publishing them in their respective dioceses by solemn circulars, and proclaiming them a new source of benediction for the people. Thus, in the same year, 1839, the Archbishops of Toulouse and Bourges, the Bishops of Montauban, Pamiers, Carcassonne, Fréjus, Châlons, Saint-Flour and Limoges; in 1840, the Cardinal Archbishop of Rouen, the Archbishop of Lyons and Besançon, the Bishops of Bayeux, Évreux, Séez, Coutance, Saint-Dié, La Rochelle, Tulle, Ajaccio, Nantes and Amiens; in 1841, the Archbishop of Bordeaux, the Bishops of Versailles, of Nîmes and Luçon, Mende and Périgueux. We are fully persuaded, and even assured, of the fact that a great number of the dioceses in France requested and obtained the same privileges; but we cite only those of which we ourselves have kept note.

"What should be our transports of joy, confidence, admiration, and gratitude, at this universal tribute of honor and homage to the Virgin conceived without spot! All earth unites with Heaven in a concert of praise and thanksgiving, proclaiming that Mary has been conceived without sin; all hearts vie with one another in celebrating the signal favors, the miraculous cures and conversions God has deigned to accord those who invoke the Blessed Virgin under the title of Immaculate in her Conception." (Circular of the Archbishop of Bourges.)

"This new luster bestowed upon the devotion to Mary conceived without sin, should console religion and raise our hopes.... Oh! in this desolated region, how should we rejoice to see appear in Heaven, if not an omen of the end of all combats, at least the pledge of new triumphs and new conquests!" (Circular of the Archbishop of Digne.)

May this beautiful devotion, be powerful in attracting the benedictions of Heaven upon earth, ever increase. Let us fervently implore the Immaculate Mother of God to enkindle it in all hearts, to bless that France whose protectress she has so often proved herself, to preserve and augment therein faith and piety, and to make all the children of France but one family, united by the bonds of religion and charity. Let us also implore the same grace for all countries, all peoples. Let each one of us wear the precious sign of her maternal tenderness, this Miraculous Medal, which, recalling to our minds the first and most glorious of her privileges, she gives us as the pledge of all her favors.

Oh! if we knew the gift of our Mother! oh! if we understood the excess of her bounty! Does she not seem longing to give us knowledge, when she displays to us the abundance of her riches and the prodigies of her liberality, in those rays of grace she showers upon us like a deluge of love and mercy? Does she not likewise unveil to us the mystery of her charity, in the image of her heart united to that of the divine Jesus? ... The same fire consumes them, the same zeal devours them, thirst for our salvation. This union of love and sacrifice is very clearly represented by the august Mary's initial joined to the sacred sign of the cross above the two hearts, as an authentic testimony, of the co-operation of the Mother of the Savior in the salvation of the human race.

Wear then, little children, this cherished medal, this precious souvenir of the best of mothers; learn and love to say: "O Mary! conceived without sin, pray for us who have recourse to thee!"

Morning Star, she will be delighted to guide your first steps and to keep you in the paths of innocence. Wear it, Christian youth, and amidst the numberless dangers lurking in your paths repeat frequently: "O Mary! conceived without sin, pray for us who have recourse to thee!" Virgin most faithful, she will preserve you from all peril. Wear it, fathers, and mothers; say often: "O Mary! conceived without sin, pray for us who have recourse to thee!" And the Mother of Jesus will shed upon you and your families the most abundant benedictions. Wear it, ye old and infirm; say also: "O Mary! conceived without sin, pray for us who have recourse to thee!" Help of Christians, she will aid you in sanctifying your sufferings and the closing years of life. Wear it, souls consecrated to God, and never cease repeating: "O Mary! conceived without sin, pray for us who have recourse to thee!" Queen of Virgins, she will implant in the garden of your heart those fruits and flowers which constitute the delight of the Spouse, and which will form your crown at the nuptials of the Lamb. Amidst the trials and tribulations of life, let us invoke Mary, conceived without sin, and our tears will be dried, our sufferings assuaged, our sorrows sweetened, for she dispenses the dew of all graces. In our combats against the demon, the world and the flesh, let us appeal to Mary, conceived without sin; Strength of combatants and Crown of victors, she will shield us against their most violent assaults and assure us of the victory; but oh! when standing on the brink of that moment which summons us before the Sovereign Judge, then especially must we invoke Mary, conceived without sin, and she whom the Church calls Gate of Heaven will herself receive our last sigh and introduce our soul into the abode of glory and perfect happiness.

And you also, poor sinners, though covered with the wounds of sin, buried in the deepest abysses of passion, the arm of an avenging God lifted to descend upon your guilty head, despair seizing your soul, raise your eyes to the Star of the Sea; you are not bereft of Mary's compassion; take the medal, cry from the depths of your hearts, "O Mary! conceived without sin, pray for us who have recourse to thee!" Unfailing Refuge of sinners, her charitable hand will apply to your cruel wounds a healing ointment; she will rescue you from the depths whence you have fallen, she will turn aside the formidable blows of Divine justice, she will pour over your soul the balm of sweet hope, she will guide you anew in the paths of righteousness and conduct you even to the haven of a blessed eternity.

Would that all might taste this means of salvation! the dismal shades of voluntary death would soon cease to terrify our cities and rural districts. Yes, the short prayer, "O Mary! conceived without sin, pray for us who have recourse to thee!" made with faith, would, even amidst the violent agitation of a homicidal thought, banish the tempter; a simple glance at the medal of the Immaculate Mary would dissipate despair. "No one commits suicide under the eyes of a mother," said very truly, His Eminence, the Cardinal Archbishop of Rouen. And the same might be said of many other crimes of daily occurrence.

Oh! you whose souls are cruelly afflicted night and day, virtuous wives, who shed burning tears over the irreligion of a tenderly-loved husband; sorrowful mothers, bitterly deploring the wanderings of a child reared in the bosom of an eminently Christian family, but drawn into the vortex of bad example; pious sisters, praying fervently and incessantly for the conversion of a brother, who once, like yourselves, enjoyed the sweet consolations of religion; Christian children, secretly bewailing the indifference of a father who seems to have lost, long since, the precious gift of Faith, console yourselves; a new hope is offered you, and it comes to you through the beneficent hands of Mary; offer, give the image of this tender Mother to the dear objects of your solicitude; the thought of this precious medal or a glance at it, will banish many a temptation, for we may say with truth of the soul as well as of the body, "no one commits suicide under the eyes of a mother." If they refuse your offer do not despair; Mary will find her way to these hardened hearts, and in spite of themselves, she will take them under her protection; imitate the pious ruse of many others, who in a like extremity, have stealthily slipped the precious medal under the pillow of the impenitent sick on the verge of death; imitate those mothers, those wives, those Christian daughters, who carefully concealed in the clothing of that child, that spouse, that father, the medal they had refused to wear, do this, and one day they will appreciate the pledge of your piety and tenderness. No, no, never does anyone wear in vain, the medal of her to whom the Church applies these words of Scripture. "He who finds me, will find life, and will obtain salvation from the Lord." [17]

But it is not enough to wear the medal as a mere pledge of the Immaculate Mary's love; we must regard it also, as an assistant in reaching perfection. This Mother, all amiable, proposes herself to our imitation, she places herself, in a measure, before our eyes, that seeing her so pure and perfect, we may be attracted by her charms. It is the image of her beauty and goodness she brings us from Heaven. It is a mirror in which we learn to know the Sun of Justice, by the perfections with which he has enriched His divine Mother.... It is on one side, the picture of what we should be, and on the other, an eloquent lesson of what we should practice. The shining purity of the Immaculate Mary, reveals to us the beauty of our soul, created in the image of the thrice holy God, and exciting in us, the love of that amiable virtue which makes us resemble the angels, it necessarily inspires us with the most vivid horror of evil, and causes us to shun the slightest imperfections, since they tarnish this divine resemblance.

And, as though it were not enough to excite our fervor by the sight of her ravishing beauty, this faithful Virgin discovers to us the means of preserving innocence or recovering it, should we have been so unfortunate as to lose it. This is the lesson of the symbolic figures engraved on the reverse of the medal: "Nothing shall be written on the reverse of the medal; ... what is already there says enough to the Christian soul." The Sacred Heart of Jesus and Mary placed beneath the cross tell us that purity is preserved or restored by love and union with our Lord.... Love covers a multitude of sins; love is the bond of perfection, the consummation of all virtues.... Love assures fidelity. It must be stronger than death to make us die to the world, to sin and ourselves, that we may be attached inseparably to Jesus crucified. There is also another lesson to be learned—that taught by Mary's holy name, united to the sign of the cross. It is placed above the two hearts because true love leads to sacrifice; it immolates, it fastens, it nails to the cross of Jesus Christ, and this union of sufferings on earth is the pledge of a glorious and eternal union hereafter.

Children of Mary, respond to her loving tenderness; be docile to the salutary lessons of our divine Mother, gratefully acknowledge this inappreciable testimony of her ingenious liberality. Go to Mary with the simplicity of a child, who lovingly clings to her bountiful hand until he obtains the object of his desires. Amidst all the storms of life, let your eyes be fixed upon this Star of the Sea. Invoke Mary; ever seek her amiable protection; she will never refuse to hear our petitions. May her remembrance and love reign always in our minds and hearts! May we repeat incessantly this sweet invocation: "O Mary! conceived without sin, pray for us who have recourse to thee!" and when strength and speech have failed us may the Miraculous Medal be pressed to our dying lips, and the last throb of our heart protest that we wish to die murmuring: "O Mary! conceived without sin, pray for us who have recourse to thee!"

# EXTRAORDINARY GRACES OBTAINED THROUGH THE INSTRUMENTALITY OF THE MIRACULOUS MEDAL

## I.

### Graces Obtained from 1832 to 1835.

"Bless the God of heaven," said the angel to Tobias and his son; "chant His praises among all mankind for the blessings with which He has loaded you, for it is good to conceal the secret of the king, but it is glorious to reveal and publish the works of God. Elenim sacramentum regis abscondere bonum est; opera autem Dei revelare et confiteri honorificum est."[18] Blessed, then, always and everywhere, be the God of heaven and earth, for the numberless benefits He has been pleased to confer upon us through Mary! Let us adore the mysterious destiny of the Mother of the King of Kings, "who, by reason of this title, truly merits the name of Queen," says St. Athanasius; and let us rob neither God nor Mary of the honor and glory due them. Let us publish the Lord's works of power and goodness to man through the mediation of the Immaculate Virgin, whom He has established Depositary and Dispensatrix of the treasures of His mercy, that mercy which embraces our corporal infirmities as well as spiritual needs.

An account of the extraordinary graces obtained by means of the Immaculate Conception Medal will be for all Christian souls a source of precious benedictions. At the view of these prodigies of mercy, these marvelous cures and conversions, the reader will be led to thank God and glorify His Holy Mother; those who have already loved Mary will be incited to still greater love; careless Christians, those who are tried by suffering, those who have the misfortune to be in a state of sin, will feel their confidence awakened, and they will tenderly invoke her whom the Church so justly styles Health of the weak, Refuge of sinners, Comforter of the afflicted.

Experience proves this. Everyone knows, moreover, that an example of virtue or an event which clearly reveals God's agency, acts much more powerfully on the soul than a simple consideration of the subject or a series of arguments. "Verba movent, exempla trahunt—words can move, example attract."

We also hope for something more from the publication of these accounts—we hope by them to convince the faithful that Mary's dearest title is that of Immaculate, and that she knows not how to refuse the petitions of those who, with lively faith, invoke her by this dearest title. It is, moreover, the Church of Rome which thus reveals, as it were, all the merciful tenderness of Mary's Heart, and presents us the devotion to her spotless Conception as the sure means of enriching ourselves from the exhaustless treasures of that Heart and according to all our necessities. "Sacra Virgo Maria ... sentiant omnes tuam juvamen quicumque celebrant tuam sanctam Conceptionem;"[19] and surely this prayer of the Mother of all churches—prayer which we might readily style prophetic—has long since been answered. We have recently seen a compilation, made in 1663 by a Jesuit father, with the approbation of the Ordinary, containing an account of sixty-two conversions or cures effected in different places by the invocation of Mary conceived without sin, and apparently nothing less than miraculous. It is also a well-known fact, mentioned in the life of B. Peter Fourrier, founder of the Congregation of Notre Dame, that these simple words, "Mary was conceived without sin," worn with faith, brought relief to a multitude of sick persons during an epidemic. The same means obtained not less visible protection at Nemours, when that city was in imminent danger of being sacked, and at Paris in 1830. But we confine ourselves to the graces obtained through the Miraculous Medal. Our choice of examples will show that, in bestowing especial favors upon France, the Immaculate Mary gives no less striking proofs of her protection in other countries where the medal is known and piously worn.

Among the traits of protection obtained through the medal in the diocese of Paris, nine (three conversions and six cures) underwent a detailed examination and were pronounced veritable by the Promoter in the investigation of 1836. We mention them in this edition, adding to each one's title the word—Attested.

Quite a few incidents printed in the edition of 1842 we have omitted here, to insert (without greatly increasing the size of the volume) more recent accounts equally reliable, thus proving that the medal is not less miraculous in our day than at the time of the apparition.

The extraordinary graces of which it has been the instrument, would have formed an uninterrupted series from the year 1832 till the present, if unfortunately, neglecting to keep note of them, an interval of several years had not crept into the documents in our possession.

For the future, please God, no such omission will occur, and all the authenticated accounts which come to our knowledge will be carefully registered for the glory of Mary conceived without sin, and the edification of her servants.

## CONVERSION OF A SOLDIER AT ALENÇON—1833.

On the 14th of April 1833, there was brought to the hospital of Alençon (Orne) a sick soldier, who came from the hospital of Vitré (Ile-et-Vilaine). His impiety there had greatly distressed the hospitable ladies of St. Augustin, in charge of that establishment, a circumstance communicated to us by persons who witnessed the insulting manner in which he rewarded the kind attentions of their unfailing charity. Arrived at the hospital Alençon, we soon saw what he was, irreligious, impious, and brutally rude. The chaplain hastened to visit him and condole with him on his sufferings; and as the opening of the Jubilee very naturally paved the way for a few words on that extraordinary grace, he gently exhorted the sick man to imitate the example of other soldiers who were preparing to profit by it, but his words were answered by insults. The chaplain did not insist and contented himself for several days with merely visiting him, and kindly sympathizing with his sufferings; the sick man scarcely replied, and seemed much annoyed, even at the visits.

The Daughters of Charity in charge of this hospital met with no better treatment, notwithstanding the kind attention they lavished on him. His malady increased; seeing that it was becoming very necessary for him to receive the consolations of religion, the chaplain urged him again to make his peace with the good God, but he was answered by blasphemies. "Ah! yes, the good God, little He cares for me." In answer to this the abbé made a few observations full of charity, and the patient continued: "Your good God does not like the French; you say He is good, and He loves me; if He loved me, would he afflict me like this, have I deserved it?" These outbursts of impiety only inflamed the charitable zeal of the minister of a God who died for sinners, and inspired him with forcible language, to depict the justice and merciful goodness of the Lord. The sick man soon interrupted him by invectives: "You worry me; let me alone; go away from here; I need neither you nor your sermons," and he turned over to avoid seeing the priest.

His treatment to the Sisters was no better; and he continued to utter the most horrible blasphemies against religion, and those who reminded him of it; he carried this to such a degree, that the other soldiers were indignant, especially at his outrageous behavior, after any one has spoken to him about his soul, or there had been prayers or a little spiritual reading in the room—he appeared dissatisfied, until he had vomited forth his stock of blasphemies and imprecations. Some days passed and nothing was said to him on the subject of religion, but every care for his bodily comfort was redoubled; no one now scarcely dared hope for his return to God, for his malady increased, and likewise his impiety; all contented themselves with praying for him and recommending him to the prayers of others. The Sister in charge of that ward, having great confidence in the Blessed Virgin's promises to all under the protection of the medal, felt urged interiorly to hang one at the foot of his bed; she yielded to the apparent inspiration, and, unknown to him, the medal was there. He still showed no signs of relenting, and even became indignant when some of the other soldiers prepared themselves, by confession, to gain the Jubilee. The medal had now been six days hanging at the foot of his bed, and many and fervent were the prayers offered up to God for this miserable creature's conversion, although nearly everyone despaired of it. One day, when all the convalescents of the ward were assisting at Benediction of the Blessed Sacrament, the Sister approached his bed, detached the medal and held it up before him. "Look," said she, "at this medal, it is miraculous; I hung it to your bed several days ago, and thereby put you under the Blessed Virgin's especial protection. With her powerful assistance, I confidently hope for your conversion. Look at this good Mother, she is praying for you now." He never raised his eyes, but already grace was working in his heart, for he showed no signs of irritation which had heretofore been the inevitable consequence of mentioning religion. Profiting by this, the Sister spoke to him of God's mercy, and begged him again to cast a glance at the medal she had just hung at the foot of his bed on the inner side. After being repeatedly urged, he opened his eyes and looked towards it. "I do not see your medal," said he to the Sister, "but I see the candle which, doubtless, you have just lit; yes, it is certainly a light." It was five o'clock in the afternoon, June 13th; his bed was so placed that it could not receive any reflection of the sun's rays, and the chaplain, after examining the spot felt assured that at no time could a reflection strike it in that direction. "You are mistaken," said she, "look at it carefully." He repeated in the most positive manner, "I see it distinctly, it is certainly a light." Astonished beyond expression, but fearing her patient's sight was affected, the Sister showed him other and more distant objects; these he distinguished perfectly, and continued to see this light for a quarter of an hour. During this interval, the Sister spoke to him of God; suddenly, fear and love filled his heart. "I do not wish to die as I am!" he exclaimed, "tell the chaplain to come immediately and hear my confession." Hearing one of the other patients utter an oath, "oh! make that miserable man hush!" said he, to the Sister; "oh! I beg you to make him stop swearing."

"I was still ignorant," says the chaplain, "of the origin and effects of this medal. It was a very familiar object, and I regarded it as nothing more than an ordinary medal. When told that the sick man wanted me, I went joyfully, and saw for myself what a complete change had taken place in him. Congratulating and encouraging him, without knowing the cause of this change, I hastened to ask him if he wished me to hear his confession. He replied in the affirmative and made it without delay; I had every opportunity of admiring his goodwill and the pleasure he manifested at each repetition of my visit. I endeavored to make him explain himself and asked if he had not acted from mere civility or a desire to rid himself of the importunities by which he had been beset so long. "No," he answered, "I sent for you, because I wished seriously to make my confession and arise from my state of sin." Henceforth he was no longer the same man; he was now as docile, patient, gentle and edifying in all his words and ways, as he had formerly been unmanageable, brutal, and scandalous. He eagerly desired the Last Sacraments, which, after proper preparation, he received with lively faith. His happiness seemed beyond expression, and though suffering intensely, no one ever heard the least sign of impatience escape his lips. He continued to give the most unequivocal signs of a true conversion; peace and resignation were depicted in his countenance, and to his last sigh, which he breathed June 27th, 1833, did he persevere most faithfully.

NOTE. —These details are attested by M. Yver Bordeaux, chaplain of the Hotel Dieu; by the Sisters of Charity; by a woman patient named Bidon; Julien Prével, an infirmarian; by Jean François Royer, of the Seventh Cuirassiers; Marie Favry, infirmarian, all eye witnesses, besides a large number of other soldiers who left the city whilst we were investigating the matter.

## CURE OF MADEMOISELLE AURELIE B. (PARIS)—1833.

### Attested.

The account of this cure was sent to us by the person herself in the month of May, 1834.

On the 3rd of November 1833, I was attacked by typhoid fever, for which I was treated by a skillful physician and the Sisters of Charity, who spared no pains for my recovery. At the end of a month, I was able to get a little nourishment, and I had the happiness of assisting at the Holy Mass and receiving Holy Communion on the Feast of the Immaculate Conception. I was still very weak, and utterly incapable of any exertion. In this state of exhaustion, I took a little chocolate. The fever soon returned and continued with daily increasing violence until Christmas. Then the physician said there was no longer any hope of my recovery. Another physician was called in, who, after an examination, declared me consumptive to the last degree, but said they might try the effect of a few blisters. Those proved of no benefit. The 27th of December, the physicians finding me extremely ill, informed the Sisters that my death was imminent. Moreover, I had been cold for two days. About half-past six that day, I received the last Sacraments, and at nine everyone thought I would soon breathe my last. Suddenly, one of the good Sisters around my couch thought of putting the medal on me. I kissed it continually with great confidence and began to feel better. My condition the next morning was a matter of astonishment to the physician, and I continued to improve so rapidly that, at the end of two days, the fever had entirely disappeared. My appetite was ravenous, I soon resumed my occupations, and ever since have been in perfect health. I doubt not, Monsieur, that I owe my recovery to Mary, my good Mother, my love for whom seems to have increased; my greatest happiness being to decorate her altars, and my most earnest desire that of consecrating myself to God in a Community whose works have so touching a connection with the sublime destiny of the Mother of Jesus; it is under her protection I expect the accomplishment of my designs.

Yours very respectfully,

Aurelie B.

Note. —The nine Sisters of the establishment have attested the truth of these details, and one of the two physicians does not hesitate to declare her recovery supernatural.

Moreover, this young person has ever since remained in perfect health. Her prayers are granted, the Immaculate Mary has also obtained for her the grace of being received into the Community she wished to enter, which is the reason we do not give her name.

### CURE OF A RELIGIOUS (PARIS)—1834. —Attested.

This fact is known to many; however, to prevent too great a number of visitors, the Superior requests us not to publish the name of the Community.

A young religious, twenty-seven and a-half years old and eight years professed, in an Order especially consecrated to the Blessed Virgin (Paris), had been kept in the infirmary by various maladies, for the space of five months. At the very time she appeared convalescent, an accident of the gravest nature happened; her left thigh bone became disjointed and shrunken, the limb was attacked by paralysis, and the sick religious lay upon her bed one month, without experiencing the slightest alleviation from human remedies. Two physicians and a surgeon being consulted at various times, pronounced the displacing of the bone due an irritating humor; but they could not check it, even by means of cauterizing and issues, so that after a long and painful treatment, she remained a cripple. She now had recourse to the Blessed Virgin as a child to its good mother; a religious of the house having brought her one of those medals called miraculous, which had been given her, she received it gratefully, applied it to the afflicted member and commenced, Saturday, March 1st, 1834, a novena to the Blessed Virgin. All human remedies seemed unavailing; she lost her appetite and was unable to sleep. She was also racked with high fever; however, having snatched a little repose during the Wednesday night after beginning the novena, she was suddenly awakened by a very painful commotion, which re-established the bones in their place; the leg which had been shortened about six inches, became lengthened almost even with the other, and recovered its usual strength. On visiting her next morning, the physicians were greatly astonished, but gave orders that she should not leave her bed yet. On Sunday, the last day of the novena, the fact of the cure was established beyond a doubt. The religious arose quite naturally, and without any assistance, ran to kiss the feet of Mary's statue, placed over the infirmary fire-place; then, dressed in her habit, and accompanied by the Mother Infirmarian, she descended about a dozen steps to the chapel to adore the Blessed Sacrament, after which she repaired to the community room, where the Superior with her Mothers and Sisters were assembled, to give her the kiss of congratulation. This touching scene was terminated by the recitation of the Te Deum, and Sub Tuum. No trace of disease remained, except a slight weakness for a few days, and as this was felt only in the sound limb, it was evidently the result of her having been six months in bed.

Two of the physicians acknowledged, with all the Community, that it was a supernatural favor. One of them has even declared in a certificate of May 4th, 1834, that without wishing to characterize a fact as extraordinary, he observes that in this circumstance there are: 1st, spontaneous disjointing; 2nd, spontaneous diminution, three days convalescence, and these last two are, to the extent of his knowledge, without parallel in the records of surgery.

The religious has never had another attack of this infirmity.

### CURE OF A SICK PERSON (CHÂLONS SUR MARNE)—1834.

The Abbé Bégin, an eyewitness of this cure, which took place at the hospital St. Maur, where he is chaplain, has prepared a verbal process which attests: 1st, that the patient was really afflicted; 2d, that she was cured March 14th, 1834; 3d, that she declares no other means were employed than the medal and prayer. This verbal process is signed by a hundred people of the above-mentioned hospital.

"Madame C.H., a widow, aged seventy, a charity patient at the hospital St. Maur, was, in consequence of a fall the 7th of August, 1833, crippled to such a degree that it was with great difficulty she could walk, even with the aid of a crutch, and sometimes the additional assistance of another person's arm; she could scarcely seat herself, and to rise was still more of an effort. To ascend the stairs was almost impossible, she could accomplish it only by grasping as she went along whatever lay within reach. She could not stoop or kneel; the left limb, which was the principal seat of her malady, she dragged helplessly after her, not being able to bend it.

"Such was her sad condition at the beginning of March 1834. However, she heard something that enkindled a ray of hope in her heart. Someone had spoken to her the January previous of a medal said to be miraculous; it bore on one side the image of Mary crushing the infernal serpent's head, her hands full of graces figured by rays of light proceeding from them, and the invocation: 'O Mary! conceived without sin, pray for us who have recourse to thee!' on the other, the Sacred Hearts of Jesus and Mary, with the letter M surmounted by a cross. She was also informed of the wonders it had wrought, and her heart awoke to the consoling hope of realizing some benefit from the medal which had been promised her. How she sighed for the happy moment when it would be in her possession! How long the time of waiting appeared! At last, her desires were gratified; the 6th of March she received, as if it were a present from Heaven, the long wished-for medal, and hastened, by the reception of the Sacrament of Penance, to prepare herself for the desired favor. Next day, the first Wednesday in the month, she commenced by Holy Communion a novena to the Sacred Hearts of Jesus and Mary. Twenty times, day and night, did she press to her lips the precious medal hung around her neck. For several days of the novena, our Lord severely tried her faith anew. Her sufferings increased greatly, likewise her fervor and confidence, and soon the most blessed results were the recompense of this poor woman's prayers.

"Seven days of the novena had not elapsed ere she was relieved of the sufferings that had so cruelly afflicted her for seven months. I could not depict the astonishment and admiration of everyone who saw on the morning of March 14th this person so helpless the very evening before, walking with all ease imaginable, bend, kneel, go up and down high steps. One spoke of it to another for mutual edification, and, in turn, came to congratulate her on her recovery, and give thanks to God and Mary. The Superior, who had bestowed constant care upon the sick woman during her crippled state and had thus been a daily witness of her sufferings, returned solemn thanks for this extraordinary grace, the whole Community chanting a Te Deum in their chapel.

"P.S.—I forgot to say that the widow has the free use of all her limbs and has never since had a return of her former infirmity."

The following is what Monseigneur thought proper to append to the verbal process, an extract from which we have just read: "We certify that credence can, and ought to, be placed in the testimony of the Abbé Bégin, that of the Sisters and so many other eye-witnesses who have spoken conscientiously and from no motive save that of zeal for the truth.

"† M.S.F.V., Bishop of Châlons.

"Châlons, May 30, 1834. "

## CONVERSIONS OF M. DE CASTILLON, CAPTAIN IN THE 21ST LIGHT GUARDS; AND OF A WOMAN—1834.

Extract from a letter of Sister C. (Herault) to M.E.:

"November 13, 1834.

"It should be the duty of children to glorify their mother, and a very sweet one it is for me to acquaint you with two incidents manifesting the boundless charity of Mary conceived without sin.

"The first relates to a sick soldier in our house. Though we had already witnessed the efficacy of the medal, in effecting the conversion of several soldiers most obstinate in resisting grace, no conversion was so striking as this. M. Frederick de Castillon, aged thirty-five, Captain in the 21st Light Guards, entered the hospital, April 29th, in the last stage of consumption, and attacked by paralysis of the left side. We nursed him for a long time, his condition grew alarmingly worse, but how could we mention religion to a young soldier who boasted of having none? I kept myself always informed of his state and contented myself (apparently) with watching the progress of the disease. Several times I attempted to make him realize his danger, but in vain. One day, when he was much worse, and I had an opportunity of seeing him alone, I ventured to inquire if he were a Catholic. 'Yes, Sister,' he replied, looking steadily at me. I then asked him to accept a medal, to wear it, and frequently invoke the Immaculate Mary, telling him at the same time that, if he did so with faith, this good Mother would obtain for him all the graces he needed, for bearing his sufferings patiently and meritoriously. He received it gratefully but did not put it on.

"But our confidence in the Blessed Virgin's influence over him was not diminished, especially when we saw him place the medal on the side of his bed. The Sister in charge of that hall had already slipped one in his pillowcase. Several days passed, his strength was gradually ebbing away, and after many ineffectual efforts to obtain his consent to see a priest, I asked a clergyman to visit him notwithstanding, and I introduced him into the sick man's presence just as someone came to tell me he could not live through that night (October 15th). We found him extremely ill, but still inflexible. After a few moments, I withdrew, and left him alone with the charitable priest, who could get nothing from him but these despairing words: 'Leave me in peace, to-morrow I shall be dead, and all will be over!' Of course, there was nothing else to be done but comply with his request, and you can imagine how painful it was. We redoubled our petitions to the Immaculate Virgin, and this good Mother soon wrought a change in the unfortunate man's heart.

"Next day, he asked the physician to tell him candidly if his case were hopeless, because he wished to arrange his affairs. That same evening, as soon as the Sister in charge of the hall entered, he said to her very gently and penitently: 'Oh! how sorry I am to have treated the Superior so badly, and the good priest she brought me! Present my apologies to them, I beg you, and ask them to come again.' You know we delayed not a moment in going to see him. Next morning, he began his new life, and during the nine days M. Castillon still lived the chaplain visited him several times every day, remaining two hours at a time. One of his brother officers, coming to see him just after his first confession: 'If you had been here a few minutes sooner,' said M. de Castillon, with an utter disregard of human respect, 'you would have found me in good company. I was with the curé, and I could not have been in better.' He had the happiness of receiving the Last Sacraments with the most admirable disposition. Here are his dying words, which he asked this gentleman to commit to writing: 'I die in the religion of my fathers, I love and revere it, I humbly beg God's pardon for not always having practiced it publicly.' And he expired in the peace of the Lord, October 23rd.

"I now relate the second conversion, that of a woman who, for eighteen years, had been a public scandal, living with a wretch who had abandoned wife and children for her. To such wicked conduct, she added a more than ordinary degree of impiety, boasting that she believed neither in God nor hell, and mocking at everything religion held sacred. Although dangerously ill, she declared that she would never make a confession. Sister N., seeing the rapid progress of the disease and near approach of death, had recourse to the Blessed Virgin; she put a medal around the woman's neck, and began a novena for her conversion, relying upon the assistance of her who, every day, gives us continually increasing proofs that she is our Mother and a most merciful one. Before the novena was finished, this poor creature, yielding to grace, made her confession, and renounced forever the wretch who had been her curse, manifesting as much sorrow for her past life, and proving herself as pious as she had heretofore been shamelessly impious.

"The above facts, Monsieur, I have thought it my duty to make known to you, for the edification of the faithful and the glory of Mary. May these examples of her power and bounty, lead all sinners to cast themselves into her arms!"

NOTE. —These two events are truly a confirmation of what St. Bernard says, "that no one ever invokes Mary in vain;" but what a misfortune for those who refuse her succor! A very reliable individual once told us, that a sick person to whom a medal had been given, and who began to feel the effects of grace, suddenly insisted upon having the medal taken off, saying: "It hurts me; I can wear it no longer." To quiet him it was taken off, and he soon expired without the slightest sign of conversion. The person relating to this, was an eyewitness; it happened in the month of October, 1834.

## CONVERSION AND CURE OF MME. PÉRON AND CURE OF HER DAUGHTER. —Attested.

Note. —It is Mme. Péron herself who gives us all the details. She lives in Paris, rue des Petites-Écuries, No. 24. We quote her own account, written February 26th, 1835, from her dictation, and in presence of the Sister who visited her in her sickness.

"I was sick eight years and afflicted with very considerable hemorrhages. I suffered much and almost continually. I was without strength; I took but little nourishment, and that little increased my malady, which was gradually exhausting me. I do not remember having had during these eight years, more than eight entire days of relief from pain; the rest of the time I passed on the bed, unable to perform the work necessary to aid my poor husband in supporting the family. I have even been confined to my bed for as long as eighteen months without intermission. I consulted several physicians, who prescribed the remedies usual in such cases, but all to no purpose. My husband, not being able to afford such expense, and seeing no hope of my recovery, lost courage and was almost in despair. Some kind persons sought to cheer him: 'You must not be so low-spirited, my poor Bourbonnais, you must bear up under these trials and show your strength of character; your wife is very sick, but she will recover, and your friends will not abandon you.' As for myself, seeing that medicines had no effect and cost us a great deal of money,

I dispensed with doctors, and was a long time without seeing one, having resigned myself to a slow death.

"A neighbor who understood my position, came one day to see me, and urged me not to give up thus, but to have the physician again. I opposed it because we had not the wherewith to remunerate him. She then proposed to call in a Sister of Charity. I observed that not being in want, perhaps the Sisters would refuse to come, as it might thus deprive them of their services, others more unfortunate than myself. This good lady insisted, and I yielded.

"Next morning, I received a visit from Sister Marie (of St. Vincent de Paul's parish), who brought me some assistance, encouraged me to support my sufferings, and did her best to console me. I can truly say that happiness entered my house with this good Sister. She soon sent a physician, who, after examining me and understanding my case, told her, as I have since learned, that it was a hopeless one, I had a very little while to live, and ought to be sent to the hospital to spare my family the sad spectacle of my death. Hearing this, Sister Marie believed it her duty to give my soul especial attention. I was not an enemy to religion, but I was not very practical; I went sometimes to the parish functions, when my sufferings and occupations permitted, but (and I say it to my shame) I had not approached the Sacraments for years. When the Sister, after several other questions, asked me if I went to confession, blushing, I said 'no.' She begged me to do so, and I replied: 'When I am cured, I will.' The good Sister, little satisfied with my evasive answer, urged me again to see a priest. 'Sister,' said I, 'I don't like to be persecuted with things of this sort, when I am cured, I will go to confession.' I saw that this answer grieved her, but she never remitted her visits and kind attention. My malady increased. One Saturday or Sunday night, at the commencement of October 1834, my whole body was cold, and vainly did my friends endeavor to restore a natural warmth, the chill of death seemed on me. They spoke of reciting the prayers for the dying; I understood a part of what was said, but myself was speechless. Whilst I was so ill, my husband told our eldest daughter to go to bed, and he, thinking me easier because I was feebly breathing, threw himself, without undressing, upon the bed to snatch a little repose; but, getting up a few minutes later, he came to me, put his hand on my face, and was horrified to find it covered with a cold sweat. He thought me dead, and called aloud: 'Euphemie,' (this is our eldest daughter's name), 'Euphemie, alas! thy mother is dead!' Euphemie arose and mingled her lamentations with those of her father. Their cries awakened Madame Pellevé, our neighbor, who came to console them. 'Ah! madame,' said my husband, on seeing her, 'my wife is dead!' Having begged him to be resigned to God's will, this lady approached me, and, placing her hand upon my heart: 'No,' she exclaimed, 'she is not dead, her heart still beats.' They kindled a fire and succeeded in restoring a little warmth to my body.

"Madame Pellevé went betimes to inform Sister Marie of all this, and the latter hastened to tell the physician. 'I am not at all surprised,' he answered, 'this lady has two incurable diseases. Besides these hemorrhages, she is in the last stage of consumption, as I have already told you, and if not dead before this, she will not live through the day.' My chest had, indeed, been very weak for some time, and the physicians in consultation had all said I could never be cured.

"At two o'clock in the afternoon I received a visit from Sister Marie, who found me not quite so ill; I could speak. 'Do you love the Blessed Virgin very much?' said she. 'Yes, Sister,' I had indeed always practiced some devotion in honor of this good Mother. 'If you love her very much, I can give you something to cure you.' 'Oh! yes, I shall soon be well.' I spoke of death, for I felt that it was near. Then she showed me a medal and said: 'Take this medal of the Blessed Virgin, who will cure you, if you have great confidence in her.' The sight of the medal filled me with joy; I took it and kissed it fervently, for I truly longed to be cured. The Sister now recited aloud the little prayer which I could not read and urged me to repeat it daily; I promised to add five Paters and five Aves. She then put the medal around my neck. At that instant, there passed through me a new, strange feeling, a general revolution in my whole body, a thrill through all my members. It was not a painful sensation, on the contrary, I began to shed tears of joy. I was not cured, but I felt that I was going to be cured, and I experienced a confidence that came not from myself.

"Sister Marie left me in this state; after her departure, my husband who had remained motionless at the foot of my bed said: 'Put all your confidence in the Blessed Virgin; we are going to make a novena for you.' Towards evening I could raise myself up in bed, which was very astonishing, considering my extreme exhaustion, but a few hours previous. On Tuesday I requested some broth, which was given to me at last, and a little while after I took some soup. My strength returned; I felt that I was cured. Finally, on Thursday, I wished to go to church to thank the Blessed Virgin. This suggestion was opposed, but I insisted and at length went. Whilst on the way and alone (for I preferred going by myself), I met Sister Marie, who did not recognize me; I took her hand: 'Oh!' said she, 'it is really yourself!' 'Yes, Sister, it is I; indeed, I am going to Mass: I am cured!' 'And what has cured you so quickly?' 'The Blessed Virgin, and I am going to thank her.' The Sister was lost in astonishment. I recounted to her how it had all come about in less than three days, and I kept on to church and heard Mass. Since then, I have had no return of my malady; I enjoy good health; I go about my duties, performing a regular day's work, and to the Miraculous Medal am I indebted for it all."

Not only Madame Péron's body but her soul, did the Blessed Virgin restore to health; she soon chose a director and went to confession, and she has continued to do so ever since; her life is really very edifying. As she deeply regrets having lived so long estranged from God, her greatest happiness now is in frequently approaching the Sacraments; two things awaken her tears, the recollection of her past life, and gratitude for her twofold recovery.

Nor is this all; the Blessed Virgin seems to have chosen this family for the purpose of displaying in it the wonders of her power. Madam Péron had a daughter aged sixteen, who, after her mother's recovery, gave herself to God in an especial manner, employing in exercises of piety, all her leisure moments, and edifying her companions in the parish confraternity, whenever she could take part in their devotions for, she lived in another quarter.

The father also was deeply touched at the favors accorded his wife; he wears the medal, and he has experienced its blessed effects.

Madame Péron still has another daughter, a little girl six years and a-half old, who had great difficulty in speaking, or rather, who did not speak at all, although she was not mute. Her utterance was so impeded that she scarcely ever finished a word, thus disconcerting the most patient. It was so much the more deplorable, as she was quite a bright child. 'What a pity she does not talk!' said everyone who witnessed her infirmity. When Sister Marie saw this little girl, 'Why do you not send her to school,' said she to the mother, 'instead of keeping her home all day?' 'You hear how she talks,' answered the mother, who did not like to have her child's infirmity exposed. However, she yielded to the Sister's wishes, and little Hortense was sent to the Sister's parish school. Her imperfect speech did not improve, it would sometimes take her five minutes to pronounce half a word. Some days after, Sister Marie, who deeply pitied the child, spoke to her mother of a novena for curing this defect. "Cure Hortense, Sister! it is impossible, it is a natural defect!" The Sister, with increasing anxiety insisted. The novena was commenced on Saturday; it consisted in hearing Mass every day and reciting a few prayers in honor of the Blessed Virgin. The medal was hung around the little girl's neck, and she was to take part in all the exercises of the novena. For several days there was no change, but Thursday after the Mass of the Blessed Sacrament, Hortense, on leaving church, could speak as distinctly and with as much ease as anyone. Those who first heard her were struck with admiration, the news soon spread, and from all sides came persons to see her; they questioned her, and the child answered, they scanned her to see if it were really the same, and recognizing her, they returned, saying: "This is certainly a great miracle, a sudden cure of a natural defect!"

Little Hortense, showing her medal with delight, would say to all who knew and congratulated her: "The Blessed Virgin has cured me."

In thanksgiving for so great a benefit, the child was consecrated to Mary on the 21st of November, Feast of the Presentation, in the same chapel where the apparition of the medal took place, and, in commemoration of this great event of her life, she was to wear only blue and white until her First Communion. Before this ceremony, she made her confession, with every evidence of understanding thoroughly the importance of the act. When asked if she loves the Blessed Virgin, "Oh! yes," she answers, "I love her with more than all my heart!" an expression invented, it seems, solely by the fulness of her gratitude. She prizes her brass medal so highly that she would not exchange it for one of silver or gold, and she wishes it to be put in the tomb with her when she dies. "We hope, Hortense," said her father not long ago, (he always finds a new pleasure in hearing her talk), "we hope, when you die, that you will leave us this medal as a souvenir of yourself and a relic of the Blessed Virgin." "Certainly, papa, if it gives you so much pleasure, but I promised the Blessed Virgin, the day of my consecration, that the medal should never leave me, but should even descend with me into the tomb when I died."

We publish these details, with the cordial approbation of this family, fully imbued with ever increasing gratitude to Mary Immaculate.

These two accounts have been confirmed by nine other people.

## CONVERSION OF SEVERAL SOLDIERS (HOTEL DES INVALIDES)—1834.
### —Attested.

Note. —All these edifying details, which have already produced a most beneficial effect upon many young men, were given us and attested by Sisters Radier and Pourrat, who, having charge of that ward, were witnesses of the facts, and also instruments of divine mercy in operating these prodigies.

"We had in St. Vincent's ward, number 20, royal hotel des Invalides, Paris, a soldier who had been spitting blood about six months, and who, it was thought, would soon die of consumption. He was naturally polite and grateful for the attentions bestowed upon him, but he showed no signs of religion; his morals were bad, and it was a well-known fact that, for twenty years, his life had been one of scandal.

"It appeared, however, that faith was not entirely extinguished in his heart, for another patient, his neighbor, being on the point of death and refusing to see a priest, this one entreated him to yield, and was instrumental in bringing about his conversion. Alas, his own turn soon came, we saw him growing worse day by day, he was wasting visibly, and had not once mentioned receiving the Sacraments. As he had urged his neighbor to prepare for death, we hoped he would make his own preparation, without being reminded of it, or, at least, that he would willingly comply with the first suggestion. On the contrary, he absolutely resisted all our entreaties, saying: 'I am an honest man, Sister, I have neither killed nor robbed.' 'Even so,' we would answer, 'we all stand in need of God's mercy, we are all sinners.' 'Oh! Sister, just leave me in peace, I beg you.'

"However, he began to realize that he had been sinking for several days, and he said aloud: 'There is no hope for me!' This thought appeared to distress him. One day (it was Wednesday, the 26th of November), the disease took such a sudden turn for the worse, we feared he would not live through the day, and being unable to make any religious impression on him, we warned the chaplain of his condition and his resistance to all our entreaties. The latter went to see him. Our patient received him with great respect, but wishing to get rid of him adroitly, said: 'I am acquainted with the curé.' A little while after, the curé visited him, and conversed with him for some time. On leaving his bedside, the venerable, zealous pastor came to us and said: 'Your patient is very low, and I have not succeeded in getting him to do anything for his soul; indeed, I did not urge him too much, for fear he might say no, and then would not revoke it, like so many others, after once giving a decided negative.'

"The same day a lady of his acquaintance also came to see him, and earnestly but vainly urged him to make his peace with God. To get rid of her importunity he said: 'I know the curé; he has already been to see me and will return this evening.' The curé returned indeed, according to promise; the sick man, on seeing him, jumped out of bed to show that he was not so ill as to make confession a very pressing matter. The curé, a true Samaritan, rendered him all the little services imaginable, helping him back to bed, and even offering to dress his blister; he then spoke to him about his soul, but without avail, for after an hour's conversation he came to us and said: 'I am deeply grieved, for I have done my utmost, but it has had no effect upon him.' We asked the curé if we must call him during the night, in case the sick man grew worse. 'I think,' said he, 'you had better not, unless he asks for me.' A little later one of us reminded him again of the chaplain, who was passing, but he got enraged and began to swear, so that we had to drop the subject, despite our distress at the thought of his appearing so unprepared before his God. Our grief was so much the greater in proportion to his extreme danger, for the death rattle was already in his throat, and it did not seem possible that he could survive the night. It was then my young companion said to me: 'Oh! Sister, perhaps our sins, as our holy St. Vincent says, have been the cause of this man's impenitence.' Expecting nothing more from the patient, Sister Radier now turned all her hopes towards the Blessed Virgin. During night prayers thoughts of the medal came into her mind, and she said to herself: 'If we put the medal on him perhaps the Blessed Virgin will obtain his conversion,' and she determined to make a novena. After prayers she said to her companion: 'Let us go see the sick man and put a medal on him; perhaps the Blessed Virgin will grant our petitions.' She went immediately and found him up and in a state of great agitation, and about to leave the room; all the other patients saw it clearly and said that it was with the intention of committing suicide. The Sister cautiously took away his knife and whatever else might be used in this way, slipped unperceived the medal between his two mattresses, and returned to us very sadly, saying: 'Let us fervently invoke the Blessed Virgin, for I very much fear this poor man will kill himself during the night.'

"Next day, immediately after rising, and even before seeing the Sister who had kept watch, one of us hastened to visit our patient, and not without most dire forebodings, but, to our astonishment, his mind was calm and he seemed better. On inquiring how he felt, 'Very well, Sister,' he answered, 'I passed a good night, I slept well (which I have not done for a long time), and I am better in consequence.' As the Sister retired, he called to her, saying: 'Sister, I wish to make my confession, oh! send the curé to me!' 'You wish to confess?' replied the Sister, 'take care; are you going to do as you did all day yesterday, do you really want him?' 'Yes, Sister, upon my honor.' 'Well, since you wish him, I will go for him, it will certainly be well for you to confess your sins, for it is said that your life has not always been edifying.' Then, without the slightest human respect, he began to mention his sins aloud, and with great sentiments of compunction; we could scarcely induce him to stop. The curé came, and he made his confession, which lasted an hour. Afterwards, one of us having come to see him, he exclaimed joyfully at our reproach: 'Oh! Sister, how happy I am, I have been to confession, I have received absolution, and the curé is to return this evening. Since my First Communion, this is the happiest day of my life!' He appeared deeply affected and expressed a most ardent desire to receive the good God. 'Do you know what we did?' 'What was it, Sister?' 'We put between your mattresses a Miraculous Medal of the Blessed Virgin.' 'Ah! then, that is why I passed such a comfortable night; moreover,

I felt as if there was something about me that wrought a wonderful change, and I do not know why I did not search my bed; I thought of doing so.' The Sister then produced the medal, which he kissed with respect and affection. 'It is this,' he exclaimed, 'that gave me strength to brave human respect. I must place it on my breast; I will give you a ribbon to attach it to my decoration,' (he wore the cross of honor.) The first ribbon offered being a little faded, 'No, Sister,' said he, 'not that, but this; the Blessed Virgin must have a new ribbon.' The Sister, regarding his weak state, placed the medal in such a manner that it was somewhat concealed. 'Oh! do not hide it, Sister,' said he; 'put it beside my cross, I shall not blush to show it.'

"In the afternoon the curé asked us how our patient was, and he was not less edified than ourselves at the account we gave of his admirable dispositions. Preparations were made to give him the last Sacraments. At the sight of the Holy Viaticum, he was so penetrated with emotion that he begged pardon aloud of God for all the sins of his life in detail, and it was with the utmost difficulty he could be persuaded to lower his voice, his heart being too full to contain itself. He passed the following night and the next day in the same dispositions of faith, regret and piety, until Monday morning, December 1st, when he peacefully rendered his soul to God, and we have every confidence that it was received into the arms of His mercy.

"We relate what we saw and heard; it took place in our ward, which numbers sixty patients, the majority of whom witnessed a part of these details."

Note. —Before burial, the Sister took the medal off his corpse, and the patient in the next bed begged to have it, so persuaded was he that it had been the instrument of this touching conversion.

This consoling return to God was followed by several others not less striking or less sincere, and in that very institution, by the same means—the medal. Quite lately two have taken place, but the details are so very much like the above that for this reason alone we refrain from giving them.

All this has been confirmed by M. Ancelin, curé of the Invalides.

### CURE OF M. FERMIN, A PRIEST—1834.

This account was sent us by the Superior General of St. Sulpice, who was anxious that we should have it. The venerable priest of this very estimable Community, who was favored with this grace, wrote the details himself, and they were attested by the Superior and the Director of the grand Seminary of Rheims, both of whom were witnesses.

"To the glory of Mary conceived without sin, I, Jean Baptiste Fermin, unworthy servant of the Blessed Virgin, and subject of M. Olier, have, together with my Superior and confrères, thought it my duty to transmit to our very honored Father, an account of the special favor accorded me.

"Many persons knew what I suffered for six whole years, how I was worn out with a nervous, worrying cough, whose attacks were so frequent and so prolonged that one can scarcely imagine how I ever survived them. My physician himself told me that, for the first three years, my life was in imminent danger, and if in the last three I was less exposed to death at every step, as it were, the giving way of my stomach, the weakness of my chest, were such that all my days were filled with bitterness, and new crosses were laid upon me. In this condition, what ecclesiastical fasts could I keep? Four or five years ago, the desire to comply, to some degree, with the precepts of the Church led me to fast the Ember week before Christmas, and the prejudice to my health was such that I was not permitted to fast again even for a day. Abstinence from meat became impossible, and for having attempted this slight mortification, how much I suffered in consequence, even in the very month of July 1834! Whilst my health was so impaired, and I saw only a lingering end to my afflictions, it pleased my Superiors to give me a year's rest. I received with gratitude this additional evidence of their consideration for me and endeavored to co-operate with them in re-establishing my health, of which they had been so thoughtful; but, in my condition, the recuperative powers of nature were of slight avail. Even amidst perfect quiet and rest for four whole months, I experienced but little alleviation of my sufferings, for though my chest became, at least, apparently stronger, my stomach grew weaker and more disordered, so that I was obliged to diet, which, added to the dieting I had already practiced, reduced me to such a state of exhaustion that I could not foresee the consequences.

"O, Mary, how deplorable was my condition when you cast upon me a look of mercy! On the 15th of November 1834, I was sent a medal, struck in honor of the Immaculate Conception, and already celebrated as the instrument of many miracles. In receiving it, I was penetrated, for the first time, with a strong feeling of confidence, that this was the Heaven-sent means by which I would reach the end of my afflictions; I had not foreseen this hope, still less had I excited it, for I believe I can say, conscientiously, that I felt naturally disinclined to ask a favor of which I deemed myself unworthy. However, the feeling became so strong that I thought it my duty to consider it prayerfully the next morning; and not to oppose so good an impulse, I determined to make a novena, and I commenced it on the 16th. From that moment my confidence was boundless, and like a child who reasons no longer, but sees only what he feels sure of obtaining, it sustained me amidst the new trials to which I was subjected; for on the 19th, and several days after, my sufferings were redoubled, affecting at once both stomach and chest. On the 22d I felt considerably better, on the 23d I believed myself strong enough to abandon a diet on which I had subsisted a long time, and on the 24th I wished to eat just what was served the Community; that very morning I commenced, like the hearty seminarians, to take a little dry bread and wine, and it agreed with me. Thus, my desires were accomplished. I had implored the Blessed Virgin to give me health to live according to the rule, and she had done so; but a good Mother like Mary would not leave her work imperfect, and she chose the very day of her Conception to bestow upon me her crowning favors. I was still troubled with a slight indisposition of the stomach accompanying digestion after dinner, but it was not positive suffering, and even this remnant of my old infirmity disappeared entirely. On the eve of that Feast my devotion to Mary, which had lost a little of its first fervor, was, when I least expected it, excited anew, and I felt urged to implore the consummation of a good work so happily begun. I did so that evening, and next morning at prayers, at Mass, at my thanksgiving, and it was in finishing this last exercise before a statue of the Blessed Virgin, after a most fervent prayer, that I realized the recompense of my confidence—I felt assured that my petitions had been granted. Since then, I have experienced no indisposition worthy of attention. I was able to fast the Ember week before Christmas and the eve of that great solemnity; I sang the ten o'clock High Mass the fourth Sunday in Advent; I followed all the offices of the choir on those days the Church consecrates to the celebration of our Divine Master's birth, and, instead of regretting these efforts, I find in each one of them a new motive for blessing the Lord and testifying my gratitude to our good Mother.

J.B. FERMIN."

"Though surpassing our hopes, we have witnessed the speedy and perfect recovery of M.J. Fermin, which appears to be something supernatural, since he employed no other remedies than great devotion to the Blessed Virgin and a novena in her honor.

"AUBRY, RAIGECOURT GOURNAY."

## II.

## Graces Obtained during the Year 1835, in France, Switzerland, Savoy and Turkey.

### CURE OF MADEMOISELLE JOUBERT.

Note. —The account of this very striking cure was sent us by M. Poinsel, Vicar General of Limoges, whom I took the liberty of asking for it.

"Bishopric of Limoges.

"Glory to God! honor to Mary!

"The 10th of February 1834, Mlle. Joubert, aged twenty-nine years, a person of solid piety, was suddenly cured of a painful and very serious infirmity. For more than a year, she had carried her left arm in a sling, by reason of an unaccountable disease which extended from the shoulder to the hand, and was of such a nature that the afflicted member seemed dead; when necessary to be handled, it had to be done with extreme precaution, and even then the pain was so excessive that often the patient fell sick in consequence. The disease was successively styled rheumatic gout, inflammatory and gangrenous rheumatism; science employed in combating it, baths, shower baths, poultices, liniments of all sorts, vain remedies which only aggravated the evil and varied the suffering. Sometimes amputation was spoken of: 'Would to God, Mademoiselle, you had but one arm!' said the physician, not concealing his anxiety and fears of her death, as spring approached, for the diseased arm was pale, livid, and frightful to behold.

The young lady, a true Christian, was resigned to all; by meditations upon the cross, she encouraged herself to suffer, and, perceiving the progress of the disease, she thought only of dying the precious death of the just. A friend, one day, proposed to her that she should wear the medal with confidence, and make a novena to Mary. She acted upon the suggestion; at the end of the novena, on the usual day of her confession (she was accustomed to confessing weekly), she approached the sacred tribunal, and lo! at the very instant when recollected, contrite and humbled, she received the moral effect of the priest's benediction and holy words, an extraordinary physical change took place in the arm heretofore judged incurable, it suddenly became unloosed and free, all suffering vanished! 'I scarcely knew where I was,' said she, 'but it seemed to me as if a cord that had been tightly drawn around my arm was unwound, ring after ring, and I was cured! My surprise, my joy, were extreme and beyond all power of expression!'

"On reaching home, she exclaimed: 'A miracle! light a taper, light two, come, come, see the miracle! I can move my arm, animation is restored to it, I am cured!' Oh! how great the joy of that family! They surrounded the favored one, they looked at, they touched the resuscitated member, they tested its powers in various ways, making her lift divers objects and execute a variety of movements; then, all the members of this truly Christian family, moved even to tears, fell on their knees, and recited that hymn of thanksgiving, the Te Deum.

"Since then, (that is, for more than a year), her arm has been perfectly well. The physician himself was struck with this event, which it would be difficult to attribute to concealed resources, or the sudden agency of nature. What is nature without the intervention and action of God? He is sole Master of nature, life and death are at His will. It is not necessary, then, to reason so much on the subject; a little faith will easily make us recognize here a special grace of God, through the intercession of Mary, our kind, sweet Mother, to whom we must ever repair, invoking her with love and confidence.

"Such is the simple and conscientious account of the event given me, the undersigned, by the person herself, in answer to my questions, in the presence of an intelligent, reliable individual who saw all, having several times dressed the arm, and who, by reason of her skill and long experience, was well calculated to judge of the danger.

"In attestation of which, etc.

"POINSEL, Vicar General.

"February 14, 1835. "

These details are confirmed by two letters of Madame and Mademoiselle Joubert, by the testimony of the Superior of the Daughters of Charity of Limoges, and that of M. Dumonteil, a lawyer and friend of the family.

### CONVERSIONS AND CURES WROUGHT IN SWITZERLAND.

Letter from Sister Boubat, Superioress of the Daughters of Charity in Chesne:

"February 12, 1835.

"I have not great miracles to recount to-day, but the facts I give are certainly very striking traits of protection. However, I shall tell them just as they are, and let you judge them for yourself. Those of which I was not an eyewitness have been told me by very reliable parties who were.

"1st. A woman who had been sick a long time, and given up by the doctors, received, one evening, the Miraculous Medal, and was restored to her usual health that night; feeling perfectly well, she said to her husband next morning that she would get up and prepare breakfast. He treated this as nonsense, and when she really did arise, his astonishment was great, and beyond all bounds when he found that her health was fully restored.

"2nd. In the same village, a young mother had two children, one six the other eight years old. The latter was attacked by a violent malady, described to me as a convulsion, and died in a few days. The younger had a similar attack and seemed on the verge of death. The poor mother was in the depths of grief, when someone thought of offering her a medal. She received it as a treasure. It was evening; she put it on the dying child, who soon fell asleep, and slept soundly the whole night. In the morning he awoke perfectly cured! This good woman afterwards came to me to get medals for herself and some others. Oh! I wish you could have seen her as she wept for joy whilst expressing to me, with all simplicity, the transport of her soul! Never will I forget it, so deep was the impression it made upon me.

"3rd. A child five years old had been racked for several months by a fever, which resisted all efforts to check it. One day, he was in his grandmother's arms when the paroxysm began. This woman, full of faith, applied the medal; the child soon grew better, and the fever never troubled him again.

"The attending physician was a relation; on seeing him after this, the child ran towards him, exclaiming with all the animation and artlessness of his age: 'I am cured, but it was not you who cured me, it was the medal.' He repeats these words nearly every time he sees the doctor.

"4th. A young man, on his deathbed, filled all his friends with serious apprehensions for his salvation. After several vain efforts of the most charitable zeal, the curé induced him to accept a medal, and very soon the dying man expressed a wish to confess. He expired in the most edifying dispositions.

"5th. Three sinners obstinately refused to assist at the exercises of a mission given in their parish, and even sought to oppose it. One of the missionaries persuaded them to accept a medal, and as soon as they had received it, a great change was visible. They not only made the mission, most devoutly, but became its zealous advocates.

"I get these details from a very venerable curé, who gave them to me himself.

"6th. There came to me recently a woman from the neighboring mountainous district, who said without any previous explanation: 'You cured one of my daughters whom all the physicians had given up; I now wish you to give me the same thing.' I tried at once to recollect what medicines I had prescribed, and asked question after question concerning the nature of the malady, to know what remedy I had dispensed. After puzzling my brain to discover, she told me it was a piece, thus suddenly reminding me that I had given a medal to a young woman from that place, who came to consult me about her failing health. To verify the fact, I sent word for the young woman to come to see me.

"I pass over in silence a multitude of other events which, without being termed miracles, are none the less real graces; and in my eyes one most precious and great grace for us is, that the Blessed Virgin deigns to make use of our poor little house to propagate devotion to her. Oh! if you could see these good mountaineers of every age and sex come with the greatest confidence and most touching simplicity, asking for na médaillot—a medal. It has affected me deeply, and I cannot sufficiently express my gratitude to our tender and Immaculate Mother.

"Even Protestants have asked us for these medals, and I am assured it was with perfect sincerity. The pastors in Savoy are also very zealous in propagating this devotion to Mary. Since reading the notice, they have mentioned it from the pulpit to their parishioners, many of whom have, in consequence, procured the medal. Likewise, do we see young men about to enter the army fortify themselves with it, and persons undertaking a voyage wearing it as their safeguard; indeed, everyone has recourse to it as the universal remedy for soul and body."

### CURE OF SISTER HYACINTHE, A RELIGIOUS OF CALVARY.

It is the Mother General of the Community who has given us these details. Her letter is dated February 7th, 1835.

"I am overwhelmed with joy; our poor patient is perfectly cured by virtue of the Miraculous Medal. I could say our patients, for our prayers were offered both for the paralytic and that young person whom I told you had been sick eleven months; she was able to remain out of bed only a few hours each day; whenever she could go to Mass, and that was rarely, she had to be assisted, and the support of an arm was necessary when she approached the Holy Table. Since Thursday she walks alone and eats without experiencing the slightest symptom of her former infirmity, except a little weakness. I hope the Lord will finish His work and restore her to perfect health; but let us speak of our dear Sister.

"The following is a copy of the account I wrote of this marvel to our holy Bishop the day before yesterday, after Mass:

"'I acquaint Your Grace with an incident of God's great mercy, displayed to our community in the sudden cure of one of our choir religious, named Hyacinthe, aged forty-seven years. This good Mother, on the 14th of last January, had a stroke of paralysis. It did not affect her head, but immediately fixed itself in the left side, which became motionless and devoid of feeling. We hastened to summon the physician, who bled her freely in the arm; next day we tried leeches, medicines, a blister on the neck, and three days after one upon the paralyzed limb, but to no avail. The poor patient, as well as ourselves, must submit to the decrees of Him who strikes and heals at will. At the end of fifteen days, I was inspired with the thought of making a novena in honor of the Immaculate Conception, the medal of which, called the miraculous, we all wear. On the fourth day of the novena, as we were about to recite the prayers around her bed, the good Mother desired Holy Communion. She was taken to the choir by three people; after receiving, the limb felt a little better, and she could return with the aid of two persons only. Her confidence in the Mother of God increased daily; yesterday she asked permission to come down on the last day of the novena, and this morning, with the assistance of a cane and someone to support her, she came down and had the happiness of receiving Holy Communion. Immediately after, we finished the novena prayers, just at the end of which she was seized with a pain in the paralyzed arm, followed by an icy chill and then a sensation of extreme heat. She came to me with both arms lifted, exclaiming, "I am cured!" And perfectly cured she was, being able to walk and use her limbs as freely as if she had never felt a symptom of paralysis.

"'To give you an idea of our joy and gratitude, Monseigneur, would be impossible. The patient fainted, and I came very near doing the same; it was with difficulty I could continue our prayers of thanksgiving, so marvelous did it seem that the Lord should have granted this favor to our community, under the government of one of His most unworthy servants.'

"I send you this copy, which we had kept, of the letter.

"In the same letter I asked Monseigneur's permission to have a Te Deum chanted at the end of Benediction. His Grace hastened to send word that he not only permitted but ordered it, which order was joyfully complied with. The Vicar General, our Superior, wrote, asking me to defer our Vespers half an hour, as he wished to assist at the Te Deum. Several other ecclesiastics also came and saw our healed ones blessing God. Since that day our good Mother Hyacinthe follows the rules, complies with all her duties, and has never felt the least return of her malady.

"This miracle created great excitement in our city; the laborers who were working at the house having learned it on the spot, immediately spread the news; the evening previous, they had seen our poor Sister dragging her limb, a cane in hand, and almost carried by two persons, and next morning they beheld her perfectly cured! These men, who have seldom much religion, sang the praises of God's power, and asked me to give them medals. I gave a medal to each with great pleasure. Clergymen have come to learn the particulars of this event, and I let the miraculously cured herself recount the wonders of the Lord.

"I must not omit informing you that the physician having vainly exhausted all remedies, had been nine days without seeing the patient; and the very eve of her recovery he told one of our boarders that the disease having settled itself he believed our afflicted one might be able to walk, but she could never use her arm again. On coming next day to visit his other patients, he was surprised beyond expression when she appeared before him perfectly cured. Wishing to get his candid opinion on the subject, I remarked that probably it was not real paralysis, but only numbness. 'It was a strongly marked case of paralysis,' he answered, 'and there is certainly something supernatural in her recovery.'

"In thanksgiving we continue the novena prayers but preface them with the Laudate.

"Make such use of this letter as you may deem advisable. If you insert it in the notice, you are at liberty to name our city and house. Oh! how we long to spread abroad the knowledge and love of God's power, signally displayed in answer to our invocation of the Immaculate Mother of His Divine Son.

"SISTER ST. MARIE,

"Superioress of Calvary of Orleans."

### CURE OF MADAME LEBON (DIJON).

Note. —"The venerable lady upon whom this cure was wrought belongs to a highly honorable family of Dijon, and her personal character is very well calculated to inspire the utmost confidence," says L'Ami de la Religion, in its issue of April 17th, 1835. Moreover, the letter she wrote, March 12th, to one of her friends, and which she was anxious should be transmitted to us, is accompanied by the certificates of the pastors of St. Michael of Dijon, of Dampierre and Beaumont-sur-Vingeanne, also of five members of the municipal council, and several other very reliable persons, some of them members of her family; more than this, it is followed by a detailed account given by the medical attendant, who had charge of her case for sixteen years.

"Dijon, March 12, 1835.

"Madame and Dear Friend:

"You ask me the details of the miraculous way it has pleased God to restore me to health. Well! it might be summed up in these few words: I implored Mary to obtain my recovery, and she did obtain it instantly; having said this, you know all, but you desire me to recall the circumstances of my sickness and my experience subsequent to the cure. I give them as follows:

"You doubtless remember that, for more than twenty years, I could not walk, in consequence of an abscess on the intestines, which left me in such a state of sensibility that ever after a walk of more than a hundred steps I was exposing myself to the most serious accidents. Neither are you ignorant of the fact that, nearly fifteen months ago, by reason of influenza, a second abscess formed, and so increased the irritability that I hovered between life and death, and even when at my best I was scarcely able to drag myself from one room to another. But you have probably never heard that, since the 1st of last December, my condition was so critical that, with great difficulty, could I remain out of bed three or four hours at a time, which made me, as well as those around me, think my end was near and I would not survive the spring.

"This was my condition, dear friend, when someone mentioned to me the medal of the Immaculate Virgin and urged me to get it. I spent a long time deciding to do so, for I considered it presumptuous to solicit the cure of an infirmity the physicians had pronounced incurable. At last, having thought, on the one side, that the more desperate the malady, the greater God's glory should He deign to cure it; and, on the other, that He had wrought the most wonderful miracles for those who were least worthy, I decided to mention it to my confessor. I did so, and he encouraged me to make the novena.

"The 2nd of February, Feast of the Purification, the first day of the novena and one ever memorable for me, I was taken to church in a carriage; my daughter, sole confidante of my intentions, assisted me to the Blessed Virgin's altar, where, after hearing Mass as well as my infirmity would permit, I received Holy Communion. Scarcely had I knelt to make an act of adoration when I was obliged to take my seat. A Sister of Charity, whom I did not know was there, for I had not hoped to receive the medal just yet, put it on my neck. Immediately, I got on my knees to beg the Mother of the afflicted to intercede with her divine Son for the restoration of my health, should He foresee that it would be conducive to God's glory and her honor, to my salvation and the happiness of my husband and children. Scarcely had I pronounced a few words, petitioning our Lord to graciously hear His holy Mother's prayer, ere Mary had interceded, and God in His great mercy had hearkened; I was cured, Madame, entirely cured.... I finished all the prayers of thanksgiving after Communion and those of the novena on my knees, and, without experiencing the slightest inconvenience, my malady had disappeared, and I have never felt the slightest symptom of it since. I walked, unassisted, to the church door, sent away the carriage and returned home on foot.

"I have given you a detail of the facts, but to express the feelings that filled my heart on re-entering my house would be impossible; my joy, my astonishment, were boundless; I could hardly realize it myself. Cured in an instant! The thought was overpowering! It seemed as if I must be in a dream, but my husband's astonishment, my mother's, and that of the servants, who, seeing the great change wrought in me, although they were ignorant of the means, could not forbear exclaiming: 'But a miracle must have been worked upon you!' convinced me that I was not asleep.

"Since that time I walk as well as any one; scarcely was my novena finished ere I could go from one end of the city to the other. It has not been six weeks since my cure, and I have already walked more than three miles at a time and could have accomplished twice as much. You see, Madame and dear friend, that the miracle is a most striking one.

"I now beg of you, as well as all other pious souls, to unite heartily with me in thanking God and His august Mother.

"Your ever devoted,

"ÉLIS. M. DARBEAUMONT LEBON."

The physician's certificate ends thus: "Whatever may have been the cause of a cure, heretofore regarded as impossible by all the doctors who attended Mme. Lebon, it should be considered none the less certain and positive, for the evidence of the fact is indubitable.

"Wherefore, I sign the present attestation, which I declare sincere and true.

"FOURNIER, Doctor.

"Dampierre, March 19, 1835. "

**CURES WROUGHT AT SMYRNA AND CONSTANTINOPLE.**

Extract of a letter from M. Le Leu, Lazarist missionary:

"Constantinople, March 16, 1835.

"It has been a long time since I proposed writing you something about the medal. In my eyes, one of the greatest miracles it has ever worked is the rapidity of its propagation and the confidence it inspires. By our demands upon you for medals, you may judge their effect in this country. We could dispose of thousands and yet not satisfy the innumerable calls we have for them. At Smyrna, it is the same. We had occasion to send a few into the interior of Asia, and the Blessed Virgin showed herself no less powerful or beneficent there than in Europe. At Angora, an old man was deprived of the use of all his limbs and had neither walked nor worked for years; he lived in frightful poverty, and sighed for death, for he was especially grieved at being so long a burden upon a family in indigent circumstances. (In this country there are numbers of Armenian families very devoted to the Blessed Virgin, and this was one of them.) He had no sooner heard of the Miraculous Medal, than he solicited the happiness of obtaining and wearing it. In these countries the Faith has retained its primitive simplicity; this recipient of a medal does not content himself with praying before it, or hanging it around his neck, but he kisses it with profound respect and applies it to the affected part; the Blessed Virgin cannot resist such confidence, and the good old man instantly recovers the use of his limbs—he now works and supports himself.

"Here is another incident: A young woman belonging to a respectable and very pious family had, for a long time, been a prey to a disease, the nature of which neither the French, Greek nor Turkish physicians could understand. Its symptoms were most violent pains in the side, which prevented her walking, eating, or sleeping, and which sometimes disappeared, only to return with renewed violence. Having heard of our medal, this lady felt interiorly urged to employ it for her recovery, but believing herself unworthy of obtaining a direct miracle, she besought the Blessed Virgin to enlighten the physician and make known to him the proper remedy. Thereupon, she went to the country. At the end of several days, she was astonished to see her physician, who exclaimed as soon as he saw her: 'Madame, good news! I have found the remedy for your disease. I am sure of it; in a few days you will be perfectly well. I do not know why it is, but your case has constantly occupied my mind since your departure, and by a careful study of it I have at last discovered the cause of the disease and the manner of treating it.' The lady recognized at once that this knowledge came from above, and she had not implored Mary in vain. Today she is in excellent health. It was from the mouth of her mother I received these details. 'O Monsieur,' exclaimed this good mother, 'how happy I am at my poor daughter's recovery! It is the Blessed Virgin who has restored her to me. If you could only get me a few more of these medals; I am overwhelmed with requests for them.' The physician himself published the details I have just given. So persuaded is he of the efficacy of the medal that he calls it his final remedy and advises his patients to wear it whenever he is at a loss concerning their malady. And the Blessed Virgin has rewarded his faith; for one of his own daughters, a most pious person, but in miserable health, has just experienced its beneficial effects.

"I could mention numberless other incidents, as many conversions as cures, but one more will suffice for today. Not long ago the mother of a family had every symptom of an attack of apoplexy; she had already lost consciousness, when her son, a very pious young man, who wore one of these medals, took it off his neck and put it around hers. He then ran for a doctor and a priest. On reaching the house they were all three astonished to find that she had quite recovered. That evening the son asked his mother for the medal, and she returned it, but a moment after was stricken with another attack. The protection of the Blessed Virgin seemed to have been withdrawn with this sign of her power. He immediately put the medal on her neck again, this time to remain, and she has been well ever since.

"Oh! do not delay, I beg you, in sending us the medals we have asked of you."

## CONVERSION AND CURE OF AN OLD MAN AT CASTERA-LES-BAINS.

Note. —These details are sent to us and attested by M. Bellos, clerk of registration at Auch, and by other very reliable persons.

"In the early part of March 1835, an old man in the parish of Castera-les-Bains (Gers), fell dangerously ill. The venerable parish priest, M. Barère, hastened to visit him, hoping he might persuade the poor creature to cast himself into those arms that were extended on the cross for all sinners. Our patient, who had not been to confession for long years, received him like an infidel as he was, refused all religious assistance, and ended by saying: 'M. curé, I would rather lose my speech than comply with your wishes!' The charitable pastor retiring, though very reluctantly, now thought of the Miraculous Medal he wore, and, taking it off, gave it to one of the households with instructions to put it in the patient's bed; advising, however, in case the ruse were discovered, no allusion to the subject, so as to spare the unhappy one all occasion of invective against religion. But, oh! marvelous to relate! a little while after, the dying man awakens as if from a profound slumber, and earnestly begs that the curé be sent for to hear his confession. At this news, the good pastor flies to his lost sheep, who receives him with every expression of joy, begs his pardon, and asks to receive the Sacrament of Penance. It would be superfluous for us to dwell at length upon the sentiments and language of the charitable minister of religion. He was so touched by his penitent's dispositions, that he did not hesitate to take him the Holy Viaticum next morning. Many of the faithful accompanied the Blessed Sacrament to the sick man's chamber; confessing again, he abjured his errors before all the assistants, and earnestly entreated them to pardon the scandal his past conduct had given them. Everyone was affected to tears, and it was amid this universal emotion that he received the good God, with the deepest sentiments of humility and compunction, and recommending himself to the prayers of all present. In the course of the following night, fearing he might be carried off by a spell of weakness, he requested Extreme Unction, and received it with the same evidence of faith and piety. This conversion was followed by his perfect recovery, and the good old man now blesses Divine Providence, which, through Mary's protection, rescued him from the borders of a frightful abyss into which his infidelity would have plunged him forever.

"The undersigned, who got these details from the mouth of the curé of Castera, vouches for their authenticity. He has neither added to nor taken from them in the slightest, knowing full well that the Blessed Virgin has no need of falsehoods to prove her power and goodness. It is, then, on his word of conscience he gives this fact, which none of the inhabitants of Castera and the neighboring country would deny, even were he incredulous."

## CURE OF ROSALIE MORVILLIERS, ACKNOWLEDGED AS MIRACULOUS BY ALL THE PARISH.

"Hangest (Somme).

"I have mentioned to you the cure wrought by the Miraculous Medal upon a person aged fifty years; the fact is incontestable. Rosalie Morvilliers, the recipient of this favor, had never been free from suffering since her seventh year; an affection of the nerves caused almost constant palpitations of the heart and severe headaches, which, however, did not hinder her performing some slight work without aggravating the malady. But about five years ago, she was afflicted by an unmistakable attack of epilepsy, which threw her family into the greatest consternation. Henceforth, she was obliged to keep her bed, and saw only her most intimate friends; the very sight of a face that was not familiar was sufficient to throw her into dreadful convulsions for several hours. Independent of any external cause, these paroxysms usually came on three times a day, and so violent were they, that it was with great difficulty she could be kept in her room; she uttered most frightful cries, her features were horribly distorted, her mouth covered with foam, and, indeed, according to the testimony of those who usually witnessed the attacks, it was some time before she regained consciousness.

"Such was her condition when someone gave her a Miraculous Medal. She received it with the greatest confidence, and immediately applied it to that part of her head where the pain was most acute; the pain disappeared immediately. From that moment she felt urged to make a novena in honor of the Immaculate Conception for the cure of her epilepsy. But diffidence in mentioning the matter to her director made her defer the execution of this pious design for six weeks. At length, she yielded to her desires, saying she felt fully persuaded that this novena would ensure her recovery through the Blessed Virgin's intercession, and her confidence was not misplaced. The curé immediately began the novena, engaging in it the sodality of the Holy Family. Whilst at Mass on the morning of the last day, the 17th of Mary's month, the patient was seized with the most violent attack possible, the worst she had ever had, although during the novena, the paroxysms had increased in intensity. Suddenly it ceases. A number of persons begin to pray and recite the chaplet; the patient, regarding them with a smile, gently falls asleep. A few minutes after, she opens her eyes and exclaims: 'I am cured! I am cured! The Blessed Virgin has just cured me of epilepsy! Oh! how good she is, how powerful! It seems to me as if there had just been a general revolution throughout my body. I feel confident, my friends, that this disease has been banished from my system forever.'

"It was very easy for the assistants to believe that some extraordinary change had really been wrought in her, for her countenance presented not the slightest vestige of the attack. She now desired to communicate, and oh! with what transports of faith, gratitude and love she received the good God!

"The noise of this cure soon reached the neighboring villages. How beautiful yet, Monsieur, is the simplicity of the faith in these rural districts! Henceforth, everyone wished to wear the medal.

"This event took place on the 17th of May, at nine o'clock in the morning. Since that time the patient has not felt the slightest symptom of epilepsy. She leaves her room, walks about the garden, and receives visitors indiscriminately, without experiencing any ill effects. However, the Blessed Virgin did not cure all her infirmities; she still has the nervous affection that existed before the epileptic attacks, but I should observe that as the novena was made solely for the cure of epilepsy, the Blessed Virgin has obtained all that was asked of her.

"This, Monsieur, is the exact statement. Some, no doubt, would attribute the cure to natural causes; as for ourselves, we, like the patient, feel convinced that it was owing to Mary's powerful intercession. The curé agrees with us, and so do all who glory in the truths of religion. Honored, then, be the power and goodness of Mary conceived without sin!"

## CURE OF A DAUGHTER OF CHARITY AND ANOTHER PERSON (DIOCESE OF MOULINS).

The following letter was sent by a gentleman of unquestionable veracity to the Journal du Bourbonnais, and published in its issue of June 6, 1835:

"Monsieur:

"We are all Mary's children; at the foot of her Divine Son's cross did her maternal heart adopt us as her own. All ages have felt the salutary effects of her powerful protection; our fathers have admired them, we ourselves admire them, and our days are filled with marvels. Even recently has she appeared, shedding torrents of grace upon a privileged kingdom, and this kingdom is France. The vision is verified, for the age which saw it has also witnessed the multiplication of countless miraculous cures and conversions.

"And shall Bourbonnais, our dear country, be accepted in the distribution of Mary's favors? Oh! no; it also shall have a share in this harvest of glory. The truly astonishing rapidity with which the thousand Miraculous Medals brought to our city have been disposed of is to me a sufficient guaranty of our hopes, and it would keep one's pen in daily use to note the wonderful traits of Mary's protection.

"1st. Sister Chapin, of St. Joseph's Hospital, was for more than two years racked by pains and a fever that defied all medical skill.

"This angel of earth lamented her inability to fulfil the duties of her noble vocation; far from abating, her charity, zeal, and resignation seemed to increase with her gradually declining health, which now excited our serious fears. Having vainly exhausted all the resources of medicine, she turned her back upon art and nature that she might address herself to faith alone. Full of confidence in the Miraculous Medal, she began a novena to Mary for the recovery of her health. Before the novena was ended, both pains and fever had disappeared, and henceforth, she began a new existence, her strength returned, and she is happy to prove herself by deeds (fulfilling with ease the most painful duties) what her virtues have ever proclaimed her, a true daughter of St. Vincent de Paul.

"2nd. Yesterday, again, was witnessed in our Bourbonnais, another wonderful trait of Mary's protection. Here are the facts: On Monday, June 1st, at eight o'clock in the evening, in the parish of Montilly, near the borders of Allier and the castle of Beau-Regard, a woman was stricken with a violent rush of blood to the head; the lamentations and piercing cries of the family attracted their neighbors. Two alarming crises succeeded; they were followed by a third, which was thought to be mortal. The patient, after violently struggling against the combined efforts of four men to restrain her, fell motionless and apparently lifeless; her limbs were stiff and chill, her face a livid blue, her features distorted, her eyes fixed, her respiration insensible, death seemed imminent. This frightful attack had lasted about half an hour, when someone present thought of the Miraculous Medal; she approaches the dying woman and lays the medal upon her lips. At that instant the latter arouses from her slumber, she breathes, she clasps her hands as if thanking the person who had restored her to life, she recognizes all around her, speaks to them and thanks them for their kind attentions.

"The next morning, Tuesday, it was not at the gates of death she was to be found, but in the streets of Moulins, where I saw her myself and spoke to her.

"Pardon me, O divine Mary, if among a thousand striking traits of your power and goodness, I dwell upon some which are comparatively slight, it is only because of their recent occurrence in our very midst. Happy shall I esteem myself to awaken among my brethren a passing tribute to Faith, that living, salutary Faith, whose efficacy I have experienced, and whose truths I long to see planted and nourished in all hearts!

"Deign to accord, etc."

We have learned that Sister Chapin's recovery is permanent.

### CURE OF MARIE LACROIX (DIOCESE OF LANGRES).

Note. —It is M. Barillot, Vicar General, who sends us this account:

"Bishopric of Langres, June 20, 1835.

"Monsieur:

"M. Regnault, curé of Ormoy, canton of Chateau-Villain, in our diocese, an excellent pastor and judicious priest, writes me the subjoined letter of the 19th inst.:

"'A very extraordinary thing has just taken place in my parish. A young woman aged twenty went blind in consequence of a fall; her hip was displaced, and she lost all use of her limbs, except the arms. For three months she was at a hospital of Bar-sur-Aube, under treatment for these severe afflictions, but in vain. At last, judging her case hopeless, the physicians sent her back to her parents at Ormoy. Here, as at Bar-sur-Aube, she endured for three months incredible sufferings, not even being able to turn herself in bed or change her position in the slightest. Her recovery was now despaired of by all, and lately the minister received a petition (with the accompanying certificates of the two physicians who had attended her at Bar-sur-Aube) asking her admission into the hospital of Quinze-Vingts. Meanwhile, this young woman, who had always appeared to me very pious and submissive to God's will, having received a Miraculous Medal, immediately begins a novena. Seven days elapse, and her sufferings, far from diminishing, are intensified; on the eighth she is bathed in a profuse perspiration, after which she suddenly rises, dresses herself, and walks through the streets to church, to the great astonishment of all the people, who, seeing her, cannot restrain their tears.

"'I questioned her closely, but did not express my opinion on the subject. I went to Bar-sur-Aube to get additional information; the physician declares it astonishing, especially when we consider her former hopeless condition. The hospital Sisters, the curés of Bar-sur-Aube, the patients, all say it is truly a miracle. The people of Ormoy and even of the vicinity, who come to see her, wonder that I do not mention it from the pulpit. I beg of you to let me know how to act in the affair, and also that you will speak to the Bishop about it.'

"The Bishop has since sent word through me to the curé of Ormoy, to publish this miraculous occurrence to his parishioners; he has also charged me with forwarding you a copy of the good curé's letter, leaving to your discretion the use you may make of it.

"I am, etc.,

"BARILLOT, Canon, Vicar General."

Before printing this, we wished to ascertain if the cure were permanent, and the Vicar General sent us the following response from the curé of Ormoy:

"The cure is permanent; for several months past the young woman has been with the Ursulines of La Chapelle, who consider her physically able to share in the labors of the house; her condition having been attested by three doctors. Her sudden recovery, as mentioned above, leads us to believe that it was surely supernatural. I was far from meriting this favor which had been granted my poor parish. I hope the Blessed Virgin will finish her work.

"November 3, 1835."

### CURES WROUGHT IN THE CHABLAIS DISTRICT (SAVOY).

"Monsieur:

"The country purged of Calvin's heresy by the labors of Geneva's holy bishop, is not a stranger to the blessings figured by the medal's mysterious rays. This wonderful instrument of Mary's liberality has been propagated with astonishing rapidity, though only a few months since we heard of it in our midst. I consider it a pious obligation to offer you a few small stones towards the construction of that temple of glory now in the process of erection, to the honor of her, who has lately proved herself more powerful and merciful on earth than ever before. I am a young villager living amidst my family; I do not announce miracles to you, but merely recount facts just as I have seen or heard them. I could have subjoined a list of signatures, but I did not judge it necessary, the docile, religious heart deeming them superfluous, and the skeptic, fraudulent, like the facts. On a perusal of the first few phrases in each incident, people living in the vicinity will recognize the individuals concerned, and thereby be more deeply impressed.

"1st. In the month of July 1824, Mlle. C., aged twenty-nine years, bade, as she thought, a last adieu to her family; she and some other generous companions were going to one of the large cities in southern Italy to consecrate themselves there to the service of the sick and poor. After a few months' novitiate in a religious house devoted to works of this nature, she was attacked by one of those debilitating, wasting maladies that physicians are at a loss to define. Attributing it to the climate, the Superiors, after twenty-two months' ineffectual treatment at the novitiate, sent her to breathe her natal air. But change of air proved vain also, and the doctors at last ceased their visits, judging the re-establishment of her health an impossibility. About six years ago, she had improved sufficiently to walk a few steps beyond her chamber, and even remain in the open air some minutes, but amelioration was illusory, and since 1830 she had not been able to leave her couch of suffering except for a few instants. Many times, during these last five years was she apparently on the verge of death, and that for several consecutive days, always, however, retaining her hearing and intellectual faculties, since she could respond by signs to the priest who visited her. It was he who gave me these particulars. Her condition had become such that it was judged advisable to administer the Last Sacraments. This house was now a school of edification, where Christians might study the price of sufferings and the heroism of patience. Finally, about the end of last April, this poor creature, so tortured for the past eleven years, conceived a hope of relief through the Miraculous Medal, but, mistrusting the somewhat extraordinary impressions the thought made upon her imagination, it was only from obedience she could be induced to commence a novena. The sole exercises consisted of repeating, three times a day, the invocation: 'O Mary! conceived without sin, pray for us who have recourse to thee!' On Wednesday, April 24th, the second or third day of the novena, she felt an irresistible desire to arise. It was yet very early in the morning; a little child assisted her to dress. Finding that her limbs support her, she begins to think it must be something miraculous, and, filled with joy, she wishes to announce the news to her mother, who is in an adjoining room. Arrived at the door, she is seized with fright, and precipitately turns back; but, being reassured of her newly restored strength by the facility with which she reaches her own chamber, she overcomes herself, and, retracing her steps, seeks the embraces of her mother, her sister and brother. Her unexpected appearance fills them with great emotion, and abundant tears attest to the depths of their joy and gratitude. A clergyman, who often visited this lady, soon heard rumors of her recovery, but gave no credit to them. Meeting her mother on the street not long after, she burst into tears at the sight of him, and was unable to express the cause of her emotion. Suspecting it, he went immediately to the house, and saw for himself what a miracle had been wrought. With Mlle. C., he unites in blessing her powerful protectress, the Immaculate Mary.

"Since that time, April 24, to the present date, June 18th, Mlle. C. rises about seven o'clock, hears Mass on her knees, employs herself in various duties during the day, makes visits and walks of half an hour's or even an hour's duration, and continues well, even her complexion begins to assume a healthy tinge. Her legs are still a little swollen, and she cannot yet take much nourishment.

"The sudden appearance of this person, whom everyone had known to be seriously afflicted for eleven years, created an extraordinary sensation. All eyes were fixed upon her, and many people even followed her. This took place in the capital of the province.

"2nd. In the month of August 1833, my sister, at the sight of a child who barely missed falling through an open trap door, was suddenly attacked by frightful nervous convulsions, which henceforth returned daily, and even as often as fifteen times a day. It was only at the end of two months that remedies, and a four weeks' strict hospital treatment, succeeded in checking them. Last year, they manifested themselves again in the month of February, but disappeared, leaving her a prey to great weakness, and a fever that kept her in bed four weeks.

"In February of this year, the nervous convulsions returned, and with a frequency and force that were truly alarming. The patient wasted visibly, the paroxysms were renewed seven and ten times a day and were of a most frightful character; the circulation of her blood seemed checked, her feet and hands were deathly chilled, she jerked her head with violence and precipitation, an agitated cry escaped her breast; the attack lasted from three to six minutes and left her completely exhausted. The witnesses of this painful spectacle were affected to tears. She was taken to a skillful physician, who after seeing her in one of these convulsions, pronounced the case hopeless, saying, 'it baffled him, he could not understand it.' However, he prescribed remedies. Meanwhile, the first medals arrived in our midst. On Shrove Tuesday, my sister had five attacks, which she assured me were the worst she had ever had. Next day, wearing the medal, she began a novena, and the two convulsions she had that day were the last; never since has she felt the slightest symptom (and that without employing the prescribed remedies), neither has she had a sign of the fever, which last year replaced the less violent convulsions. This cure was wrought in an insensible, but very efficacious manner, the first day of a novena made through the medal. My sister immediately resumed the manifold duties of a laborious household. She attributes, and we also, her recovery to Mary alone. Thousands of times be love and glory to this good Mother!

"3rd. In the Chablais district, on the frontiers of the canton of Geneva, lived a poor widow, the mother of quite a large family. This good woman, about sixty years old, had a natural predisposition to paralysis. At the age of forty-eight, an attack of this disease deprived her of the use of her left arm. At intervals since then, she has had spells of illness so serious and so protracted, that at least a hundred times she seemed on the verge of the tomb. She never consulted a physician, but animated with a lively, persevering faith, she employed only supernatural means. 'God and the Saints are the only good doctors,' she would say, and 'God and the Saints' rewarded her confidence. She has recovered from these hopeless maladies in an extraordinary manner. On the first of last March, her left foot lost the power of supporting her body in walking, doubtless owing to her natural predisposition to paralysis. Persons informed on the subject have given the following description of the convulsive movements of this poor woman's foot: suspended, it preserved its natural position, but on putting it to the ground, it immediately lost its balance; her body was bent, her knee turned out, the sole of her foot exposed, and the left side of her foot was the foundation of support for the left limb in walking. She went thus to church, distant about four minutes' walk; but even in that short space of time, the convulsive movements of the foot were sometimes such that she was not able to keep her balance but fell to the ground. Everyone pitied her, she was always calm and perfectly resigned. Her children had made for her an iron brace which reached to the knee, but after a trial, she was obliged to discard it, the remedy causing more suffering than the disease. During the Lenten season, some charitable persons advised her to seek Mary's assistance through the Miraculous Medal. The good widow did so and wore her medal with the utmost confidence. On Holy Saturday, she perceived that her foot had become steady; the next day, Easter, without any remedies having been used, it resumed its natural position, and since that time, though a little weaker than the right, not once has it given way or turned. She attributes her recovery to the Blessed Virgin, whom she invoked by wearing the medal, so justly styled miraculous.

"I could cite many other less striking cases; one time it is a hardy peasant who attributes to Mary's intercession relief from violent pains; another time, a little child, who in a few days, is completely cured of a large tumor under its arm, accompanied by fever; a mother who tells me how her daughter's ill health is sensibly improved by the application of the medal; or a Protestant girl, who, after wearing it, abjures heresy, etc. Nearly all the children of our village wear the Miraculous Medal around their neck, they recite the invocation, they kiss the precious image and give it to their little sisters and brothers in the cradle to kiss.

# III.

## Graces obtained from 1836 to 1838 in France, Italy, Holland, etc.

### CONVERSION AND CURE OF M. GAETAN (BOULOGNE).

This account was sent me by the curé of Boulogne, February 8, 1836.

"In my parish, a young man named Gaetan U——, aged twenty-seven years, was leading a life of criminal intimacy with a woman. Several years after abandoning his mother and brother, that he might be under no restraint in his shameless course, he was prostrated by a serious pulmonary attack. M. Jean Pulioli, an excellent physician, undertook the case; but the violence or the disease overcame his skill, and the patient (still in the house of the bad character with whom he lived,) was reduced to such a deplorable state of exhaustion, that he could not move himself. From the beginning of his sickness, he had insisted that he would not be worried by a priest. But the disease making very rapid progress, the doctor believed it his duty to warn a priest of his condition. My chaplain went immediately to see him, and earnestly entreated him to put an end to this scandalous situation by marrying the woman, but all in vain. I then paid him a visit, and besides remarking in him neither any intention of marrying her nor of separating from her, I perceived from the excuses he gave, that his soul was enshrouded in impenetrable indifference. Having uselessly exhausted all efforts to effect a change, I concluded it would be better to leave him awhile to quiet and serious reflection and return later to know his decision. I urged him to seek the mediation of that refuge of sinners, the Blessed Virgin, and slipping the Miraculous Medal under his pillow, I left. There was no necessity for my returning to learn his decision, he sent his mother for me, with whom he had become reconciled in the meantime; after informing me of the very just reasons he had for not marrying the woman, he asked me if I would not request her to leave, a commission I willingly accepted. She consented, and immediately abandoned the house. The sick man's peace and joy at this were indescribable; when I showed him the medal, he kissed it most fervently and impulsively, notwithstanding his state of exhaustion. Then, with every mark of sincere repentance, he confessed, received the Holy Viaticum and Extreme Unction, for we expected each moment he would breathe his last. This occurred January 19, 1836. Interiorly, he enjoyed unspeakable peace, a favor he always attributed to the Blessed Virgin. From this time, he began to improve, and in a few days his health was completely re-established. He continues to persevere in his good resolutions, and full of the tenderest affection for his celestial Benefactress, he still reverently wears the medal I gave him, often kissing it with truly filial love.

"Monsieur, I was a witness of the above-mentioned fact; I send it to you, not only with the permission of the newly converted and cured, but at his request, and I hope that the knowledge will redound to the honor and glory of the Omnipotent God, who, through the intercession of the Blessed Virgin, has wrought this double miracle.

"I subjoin the certificate of the physician who attests the disease and its cure."

### CURE OF A JUDGE AT NAPLES.

The judge of the civil tribunal of Naples, M. Joseph Cocchia, seriously debilitated by a chronic disease of the bowels, was afflicted with most violent pains, accompanied by a spasmodic sensation that, continually increasing, banished sleep and appetite, and perceptibly diminished his frame. This was followed by a bilious gastric fever, long and obstinate, of fifty days duration. When freed from the fever, the sick man found himself in a frightful state of emaciation and exhaustion; signs of inflammation in the bowels, and such extreme irritation that the least jolt induced fever, made skillful physicians fear lest these were the symptoms of an incurable malady still more deplorable. Whilst in this pitiable condition, there reached the sick man's ears accounts of the prodigies Divine mercy had wrought in favor of those who wore the medal; he eagerly asked for one, and received it with faith; henceforth, he had no longer any need of medical assistance, for he recovered the strength and perfect health he now enjoys.

### CURE OF F.P. DE MAGISTRIS.

M.F. Paul de Magistris, aged seven years, was attacked about the middle of November 1835, by a bilious gastric fever, which, by reason of accompanying circumstances, threatened to shorten his life. After three weeks' illness, his nervous system was also attacked, and he became a prey to a state of profound drowsiness that resulted in the loss of reason and speech. His afflicted parents, seeing the obstinacy of the disease, notwithstanding all efforts of medical skill to the contrary, considered the case hopeless, and their child lost to them. On the evening of January 9th, the curé administered Extreme Unction, believing, as did all the assistants, that the little sufferer had but a few hours to live. A young person, who came to the house, having mentioned the Miraculous Medal brought from France by the priests of the Congregation of the Mission, it was immediately procured, and, with confidence in its healing powers, applied to the child, whilst all present knelt around his bed and recited the Ave Maris Stella. Scarcely had they finished, ere he was considered out of danger. With renewed confidence in the medal, it was resolved to begin a novena in honor of the Blessed Virgin. During its progress, the disease diminished perceptibly, and the child has now entirely recovered. Its parents, as well as other persons of credit and veracity, among them the attendant physician, attest that, having witnessed his deplorable condition, they feel convinced his recovery was a miracle, resulting from the application of the medal.

February 22, 1836.

### CURE OF A DROPSICAL MAN (SWITZERLAND).

"Soleure, January 19th, 1836.

"Baptiste, a wood sawyer, whom you knew during your sojourn in this city, was confined to his bed for two whole months by an attack of the severest form of dropsy on the chest. One of our best physicians, who attended to him at the beginning of his sickness, having told Baptiste's wife that the case was a hopeless one, the family decided to consult another, M. Gougelmann, at Attyswill, a league from Soleure. After seeing the patient, he also gave the same opinion, and the poor wife's distress was beyond expression. A pious lady, witnessing her grief, gave her a Miraculous Medal. The sick man's arms, legs, and whole body were greatly swollen. His breath was short, and he had scarcely any power of motion; his back, and his elbows upon which he was obliged to lean, were a mass of sores. In this pitiable state, death might be expected any moment. His confessor, having come to visit him, brought the Notice of the miracles wrought through the Miraculous Medal. The sick man on receiving it began to read it aloud, greatly to the astonishment of his wife and the priest, who were both witnesses that he had been almost past the power of speech but a few minutes before. And he continued reading thus until he had finished the little book (it was one of the first editions). This was the evening of January 19. His wife, overcome with fatigue, fell asleep for a few moments, his children were in an adjoining room expecting at any instant to hear the sad news of their father's death. He slept a little towards three o'clock in the morning, and on awaking found himself so well that it was impossible to resist the desire of rising from his bed and throwing himself on his knees before a crucifix, in thanksgiving to Our Lord and His divine Mother. His wife awoke, and not seeing him in bed, called to find out where he was. 'I am well; the Blessed Virgin has cured me,' was the answer of Baptiste, whom she perceived kneeling before the crucifix. The children, hearing the noise, hastened to their father's presence, believing him about to breathe his last, but judge of their surprise at finding him restored to health, and his sores perfectly healed! Imagine, if you can, the joy of this poor family, and the happy effects the news of this wondrous cure produced upon the many who heard it. Baptiste has had excellent health ever since."

### CURE OF FRANÇOIS WENMAKERS, OF BOIS-LE-DUC (HOLLAND).

The Noord Brabander, a Holland journal, printed at Bois-le-Duc, contains in number 68 the following account of an extraordinary cure, which is attributed to the Blessed Virgin:

"Bois-le Duc, June 6th, 1836.

"The 25th of last April, François Wenmakers, a young apprentice, aged fourteen years, fell from a height of about sixteen feet. An affection of the brain and an almost complete paralysis of the lungs, larynx and oesophagus were the result; he was not in a condition to take any medicine into his stomach, or even to swallow the least liquid, and he was deprived of consciousness. One of the physicians, feeling worried at his fixed stare, advised the administration of Extreme Unction; and yet another, the eve of his recovery, declared him on the verge of death. The sick man, moreover, had become nearly blind the last few days. On the 1st of May, advantage was taken of a lucid interval, to give him the Holy Viaticum; and on the 4th of the same month, he received Extreme Unction from one of the chaplains of St. Jean. His parents, who immediately after his fall, had hung a medal of the Immaculate Conception around his neck, seeing there was now no hope of his recovery, except in the divine goodness and the intercession of the Blessed Virgin, began, on the 16th of May, a novena in honor of the Mother of God. Three days after, at about six o'clock in the morning, the patient suddenly asked his mother if the medal around his neck was blessed. She answered yes, regarding the question as the effect of delirium. He immediately kissed it and sat up for the first time since the fall, for heretofore he had been stretched out helpless on the bed, and, for some days past, had been deprived of the use of his limbs. 'Something tells me,' he exclaimed, 'that I must get up, that I am cured!' The astonishment of those present may easily be imagined. The mother called his sisters, who repaired the room with an elder girl, and they, seeing that he stoutly persisted in declaring himself cured, persuaded his mother to let him rise. He did indeed get up, and pointing to a picture in the room, representing the medal, he said: 'It is this good Mother who has cured me.' From that moment the boy's health was perfectly re-established, and his intellectual faculties were brighter than ever.

"Reflections here are superfluous. Glory to God and her who thus rewards the confidence of her servants! The parents and their child will ever remember the blessing they have received, and never cease to publish it!"

### CURE OF ROSALIE DUCAS, OF JAUCHELETTE (BELGIUM).

Rosalie Ducas, of Jauchelette, near Jodoigne, aged four years and a-half, was, on the 9th of November 835, suddenly struck with total blindness without the slightest premonitory symptoms; there was no disease, no weakness, she was in apparently perfect health. Not only was the least light, but the least breath of air so painful, that her face had to be kept constantly covered with a cloth four doubled. This poor child's sufferings night and day were heart-rending! At last, the mother herself was taken sick. Some pious individual procured her a blessed medal of the Immaculate Conception. She took it and commenced a novena. Another medal was put on the child's neck, the 11th of June 1836, about six o'clock in the evening; at midnight, the little one ceased its moans, on the fourth or fifth day of the novena, it opened its eyes. The mother and father redoubled their prayers to the Blessed Virgin, and on the ninth day, towards evening, the child recovered its sight entirely, to the great astonishment of the neighbors and all who were witnesses of the occurrence.

"The curé of Jodoigne-la-Souveraine, who had given the medal, has himself seen the child who lives not more than half a league distant; he positively asserts that it has perfectly recovered its sight, and that not the slightest vestige of the attack remains, which fact is well known, and contributes not a little in exciting devotion to the Immaculate Mary."

### CONVERSION OF THE FATHER OF A FAMILY (BELGIUM).

"There are still in existence here some families who, persistently recognizing in the present clergy only a purely civil power, hold themselves utterly aloof, live in a state of schism, and comply with none of the duties of religion.

"One of these miserable creatures was afflicted with a virulent cancer on the side of his face, which for a long time had been eating away the flesh. The malady increasing, I believed it my duty to visit him and offer the consolations of my ministry. I saw him several times, he was suffering greatly; the oesophagus was exposed, the right side of his emaciated face presented only a deep sore, the eye, starting from its socket, hung suspended over a terrible disfigured mouth; his tongue caused him acute pain; his condition was pitiable indeed, especially as he seemed determined to die impenitent. He was a rough, blunt man, who wanted to hear nothing about priests or Sacraments. In vain was he reminded of our Lord's bountiful kindness and the rigors of His justice, nothing touched him; to all expostulations his invariable reply was: 'God's mercy is great, I will confess to God, the Blessed Virgin, to St. Barbara and the good Saints.' He was the counterpart of those men to whom Jesus Christ said: 'In peccato vestro moriemini—you shall die in your sin.'

"His relations and numerous friends endeavored both by prayers and entreaties to snatch him from perdition, but on the other side visited daily and sustained by his old associates in impiety, he persisted in dying as he had lived, in schism.

"In the meantime, I was obliged to be absent several days. This period was for him one of Divine mercy. A lady of the parish made a last attempt to recall him to God, by bringing him one of those medals of the Immaculate Conception called miraculous. She sent it to him with the request to wear it and put all his confidence in the Blessed Virgin. The sick man took the medal, kissed it respectfully, and put it under his pillow. In giving it to him, his daughter had taken care to acquaint him with its origin and advantages, at the same time urging him, as usual, to make his confession. 'Leave me in peace,' was the wretched father's reply, and she could say no more. Next day, a neighboring curé was sent to administer Extreme Unction to another person in the parish. He came, and forgetting, as it were, the one for whom he had been sent, he thought only of the cancerous patient. 'I felt,' he afterwards told me, 'an inexplicable and irresistible desire to visit him, I could not have returned without seeing him.' He asks someone to announce his arrival to the sick man; this person speaks to the latter and urges him to confess. 'The curé of P. is here,' she adds, 'and would like to see you, if you have no objection.' 'Well, yes, let him come.' The curé went to him immediately; at first there was a slight air of resistance about the patient, but it vanished, the hour of grace had come, he confessed with every indication of true repentance, and received Extreme Unction with an indescribable peace and joy, that never faltered during the four remaining days of his life. The Holy Viaticum could not be administered because he was not able to swallow.

"At noon, on the 18th of last May, the month consecrated to Mary, he died, aged seventy-eight.

"Except his former companions in irreligion, this conversion was a subject of rejoicing to the parish, and doubtless it will rejoice all the servants of Mary who hear of it. May this example, among thousands, inspire sinners with great confidence in the Blessed Virgin, propagate devotion to her, and multiply the medal styled miraculous!

"I have thought it a duty to give these few details, for the purpose of making known the truly visible effects of the protection of the Mother of God, and the ever impenetrable springs of grace in regard to man.

"I have the honor to be, Monsieur, with great esteem, &c."

### CURE OF MLLE. ANTOINETTE VAN ERTRYCK
(BOIS-LE-DUC).

"The protection of the Blessed Virgin, which for the last few months has shown itself so powerful in a neighboring kingdom, has also wrought wonders in Bois-le-Duc. Mary has here likewise given equal proofs of her maternal bounty when we have implored her intercession.

"Mlle. Antoinette Van Ertryck, aged twenty-five years, was for more than twenty months deprived of the use of her limbs; they were stiff and paralyzed, almost without feeling, and stretched motionless on a sort of bench made for the express purpose. Medicine afforded no relief. In this sad condition, wearing a blessed medal of the Immaculate Conception, she thought of making a novena in honor of the Feast, to recover her health. On the last day of the novena, she made a fervent communion. Even after the departure of the priest, who came to administer the Blessed Sacrament, there seemed no change for the better, but she felt a shiver through all her body, like the impression often experienced from sudden cold. Just whilst finishing the last prayers, however, she seemed to hear an interior voice saying to her: 'You are cured.' On attempting to move, she found that her limbs had become flexible, and she was able to walk. The miracle was wrought on Saturday, May 16th. The next day, Sunday, she went to church to return thanks for this blessing to the common Mother of all the faithful. The people of our city, always distinguished for their veneration for the Blessed Virgin, and their confidence in her intercession are not wanting in gratitude, and this new favor will but increase their devotion to Mary Immaculate.

"The duration of the malady, the inutility of medical skill, and her astonishing sudden cure are attested by the doctor.

"A. BOLSIUS, M.D."

### CURE OF A YOUNG GIRL AT CRACOW, POLAND.

Extract from a letter of the Countess Lubinska:

"March 12th, 1837.

"I took into my service, the 20th of last December, a young girl whose excellent qualities elicited my deepest interest.

"After being with me some months, she began to suffer most acute pains in the head; the remedies we employed affording no relief, the attending physician advised her to keep her bed, and did not conceal from her his opinion that these pains proceeded from the humor flowing constantly from her ears, and which seeming to be upon the brain, threatened her life, or at all events, her reason.

"What confirmed this opinion was the fact that whenever she walked rapidly or stooped, she was forced by the pain to throw her head back, as she assured me various times during her sickness. The continued suffering induced her, at last, to follow the physician's advice, and consent, if necessary, to the operation of trepanning. I shuddered at the very idea and made her promise to ascertain if a delay of ten days would be attended with any serious consequences. Upon a negative answer from the physician, I stopped all medicines and determined to try the efficacy of the Miraculous Medal. This was on a Saturday, and the very day observed by her as a strict fast, in thanksgiving to the Blessed Virgin for having miraculously cured her of a mortal typhus, after her mother had dedicated her to Mary. Her confidence in Mary was great; and as I did not give her the medal for some hours after promising it, she told one of her friends, as I have since learned, that her impatience to receive it was almost beyond bounds, and assured her that she would not have hesitated between it and two thousand francs had she been allowed a choice, and we must remember that this girl was very poor. To display more clearly the miraculous nature of the cure, God permitted her sufferings to increase to such a degree that very day, that notwithstanding her patience and resignation, it seemed as if she really could not endure them much longer. Knowing her lively faith and confidence, I deemed it unnecessary to enter into a detailed account of the salutary effects of the medal; I gave it to her; she immediately made with it the sign of the cross upon her poor head, repeated the invocation and fell asleep amidst excessive sufferings. On waking she was perfectly cured and has never since experienced the slightest symptom of the disease.

"Filled with sentiments of the deepest humility and the liveliest gratitude, the miraculously cured now wishes to consecrate herself to God in the religious life.

"Blessed a thousand times be God and the Immaculate Mary, and may we ever appreciate such boundless mercy!"

### CONVERSION OF M. REGNAULT, MAYOR OF POITIERS. —1837

The following account was sent to us by the abbé of Chazelle:

"Poitiers, June 12th, 1837.

"M. Regnault, mayor of Poitiers, had exercised his functions since the year 1830. In some difficulties, occurring during his administration, with the bishop and several of the clergy, he had shown himself just and equitable. His charity to the poor was well known. But far different are these moral virtues, which generally receive their recompense here below, from the Christian virtues so seldom rewarded, except in a better world! M. Regnault never appeared at church, except when his presence as mayor was necessary. A prey for some time to a grave malady, he continued to exercise his functions as long as possible, imposing upon himself for that purpose many sacrifices, and displaying an admirable zeal; but, vanquished by the disease, he was at length forced to suspend his duties, and, since the 1st of last January, to resign altogether. The curé of St. Hilaire, having learned the alarming state of his parishioner's health, hastened to visit him, and offer the consolations of his ministry, but in vain. He repeated his visits. He was received into the house, but not taken to see the patient. He now sent word to the latter that he was at his command and would come immediately when sent for. Meanwhile, the disease made such rapid progress that there was no longer any hope of recovery. Several of his friends, interested in his salvation, were grieved to see him so near death without the slightest preparation for it. One of them brought him a Miraculous Medal, and not being able to see him herself, she asked a woman about the house to give it to him for her. The woman did so, and, fearing he might reject it with contempt, she begged him to receive it for the donor's sake. He took it, saying: 'It is a medal of the Blessed Virgin; I accept it respectfully, God is not to be trifled with.' And, putting it under his pillow, he sent a kind message of thanks to the lady who had given it. Some moments after, he takes it out, contemplates it, and kisses it respectfully.

"Having placed his temporal affairs in order, he now expresses a wish to do the same with his conscience and requests his attendants to send for the parish curé. The latter hastens to the sick man's bedside. 'I have made you come in a hurry,' says the patient, 'I want to have a conversation with you.' After this conversation, he asks the curé to return the next day, as he wishes time to prepare himself for the grand action he contemplates. 'The step I am about to take,' he adds, 'I do with full knowledge and entire conviction.' The curé of St. Hilaire, with whom, as mayor, he had just had a lawsuit, suggested that he make his confession to some other priest; he answered that he wished no one but his pastor. Next day, the curé returned, and as he addressed his penitent by the title of M. the Mayor: 'Do not call me that,' said M. Regnault; 'you are now my father, I am your son, I beg you to address me thus.' The curé paid him frequent visits, and as the disease continued to progress, he suggested administering the Holy Viaticum and Extreme Unction. 'I have not been confirmed,' replied the pious patient, 'I ardently desire to receive Confirmation.' The bishop was soon informed, and, readily forgetting all subject of complaint, and thanking God for this unexpected change, the venerable prelate went at once to the sick man. The happy dispositions of the latter touched him deeply, and he administered to him the Sacrament of Confirmation the very day of his receiving Extreme Unction and the Holy Viaticum.

"It is impossible to give an idea of M. Regnault's faith and truly angelic fervor during this ceremony, or the deep impression made upon him at seeing Monseigneur enter his chamber. It was Saturday, January 21st, the eve of Septuagesima Sunday. Monseigneur addressed him in a few words full of unction and charity, and to inspire him with hope, reminded him of the very touching parable of the next day's Gospel, the laborers in the Father's vineyard, who coming at the last hour received the same recompense as those who had borne the heat and burden of the day. All the assistants were deeply affected at this edifying spectacle, and many were moved to tears. The bishop, on leaving, charged the curé to testify again to M. Regnault how great consolation he had experienced at this happy change, and how much he had been edified at his piety during this touching but long ceremony. 'As first magistrate of the city,' he answered, with a peaceful smile, 'I ought to set good example to those under my administration.' The curé sought by repeated visits to sustain this new-born piety, already tried most severely by the excruciating sufferings of the malady, sufferings which the patient bore with calmness and resignation, offering them to God in expiation of his past offences. To recompense his services to the city during his administration, the government bestowed upon him the cross of honor. The curé could not refrain from congratulating him. 'I do not know,' was the modest answer, 'I do not know what I have done to merit it,' and when reminded of his services to the city, 'Oh! do not speak of them,' said he, 'such things might awaken self-love!' What immense progress virtue makes in the soul in a very little while! It was in these happy dispositions he died, the 2d of the following February, Feast of the Purification. The whole city of Poitiers, we might say, attended the funeral. The bishop, the authorities, and a host of other distinguished personages came to pay their tribute of gratitude and admiration to his memory, and the prefect congratulated the curé of St. Hilaire on so wonderful a conversion."

### MARY'S PROTECTION OF A LITTLE CHILD (PARIS).

Madame Rémond, living number 70, rue Mouffetard, held at her chamber window, on the second story, one of her children, aged twenty-two months. Fainting suddenly, she fell back into the room, and the child was precipitated upon the pavement below. Immediate death might naturally have been expected as the inevitable consequence of such a fall; but no, wonderful to relate, the child was not injured. After reading the Archbishop's circular (upon the occasion of the consecration of the church of Notre Dame de Lorette), in which he recommends all the faithful to wear the Miraculous Medal, the pious parents had hastened to procure one and put it on their child. The Immaculate Mary did not fail to reward their piety. On picking the poor little creature up, and examining it, not even the slightest bruise was discovered. As the mother was a long time recovering from her swoon, it caused great anxiety, and several physicians were called in to see her. They also saw the child and declared its escape wonderful indeed. But by way of precaution, they applied a few leeches to it, and a poultice to one knee which seemed to be the seat of some slight pain. The child had been eating an instant before this terrible fall, which, strange to say, occasioned no vomiting, and immediately after being picked up it took all the little delicacies offered it. Everyone declared this occurrence a miracle, and the innocent little creature itself seemed to proclaim it, by kissing the medal and pressing it to its lips, especially when the subject was mentioned, as we ourselves witnessed when the father showed him to us the 25th of June, 1837.

"The mother recovered perfectly, and she never ceases to thank the Immaculate Mary for the double protection she considers due the medal."

### THE ARCHCONFRATERNITY OF NOTRE DAME DES VICTOIRES.

Scarcely six years since the apparition of 1830, and already the designs of Providence were realized; the Miraculous Medal had awakened devotion to the Blessed Virgin, belief in the Immaculate Conception had penetrated all classes of society, and the innumerable favors accorded those who fervently recited the prayers revealed by Mary, had clearly proved how she prizes this first of all her privileges. But so far, her servants remained isolated, having no bond of union, no central point where they could meet; the majority of those who wore the medal as the livery of the spotless Virgin, knew neither the place, the mode, nor date of its origin.

God was now about to complete the work, by giving to this devotion, an organization and fixed exercises which favored its development, and increased the efficacy of prayer, by the power of association.

Towards the end of the year 1836, a man was raised up to execute the divine plans; this man was M. Dufriche Desgenettes, curé of Notre Dame des Victoires, Paris. From 1820 to 1832, in charge of St. Francis Xavier's Church, he numbered among the religious establishments of his parish, the Mother House of the Daughters of Charity, where the Blessed Virgin had appeared. He was one of the most earnest in thanking God for this grace, and most eager to propagate the medal. It was his desire that the privileged chapel should become a pilgrim shrine, but this desire not being realized, he was chosen by Providence to supply the substitute.

Let us quote his own words, relating how he was led to found the Archconfraternity of the Holy and Immaculate Heart of Mary. "There was in Paris, a parish scarcely known even to many of the Parisians. It is situated in the center of the city, between the Palais Royal and the Bourse, surrounded by theatres and places of dissipation, a quarter swallowed up in the vortex of cupidity and industry, and the most abandoned to every species of criminal indulgence. Its church, dedicated to Notre Dame des Victoires, remained deserted even on the most solemn festivities.... No Sacraments were administered in this parish, not even to the dying.... If, by dint of novel persuasion, the curé obtained permission to visit a person dangerously ill, it was not only on condition of waiting until the patient's faculties were dimmed, but also on another almost insuperable condition, that of presenting himself in a secular habit. What benefit were such visits? They were merely a useless torment to the dying." [20]

Such was the parish confided to M. Desgenettes. With the hope of recalling to God, even a few strayed souls, the poor curé, for four years, employed every means that the most active zeal could suggest, but in vain. Sad and grieved beyond measure, he thought of quitting this ungrateful post, when supernatural communication revived his drooping courage.

On the 3rd of December, Feast of St. Francis Xavier, thoroughly penetrated with the inutility of his ministry in this parish, he was saying Mass at the Blessed Virgin's altar, now the altar of the Archconfraternity.... After the Sanctus, he distinctly heard these words pronounced in a very solemn manner: "Consecrate thy parish to the most Holy and Immaculate Heart of Mary." They did not strike his ears, but seemed to proceed from an interior voice. He immediately recovered peace and liberty of spirit. After finishing his thanksgiving, fearing to be the dupe of an illusion, he endeavored to banish the thought of what was apparently supernatural communication, but the same interior voice resounded again in the depths of his soul. Returned to his house, he begins to compose the statutes of the association, with a view of delivering himself from an importunate idea, and scarcely does he take his pen in hand, ere he is fully enlightened on the subject, and the organization of the work costs him nothing but the manual labor of the writing.[21]

The statutes prepared are submitted to Mgr. de Quélen who approves them, and the 16th of the same month, an archiepiscopal ordinance erects canonically the Association of the Holy and Immaculate Heart of Mary for the conversion of sinners. The first meeting took place on Sunday, the 11th of December. In announcing it at High Mass, the pious pastor expected to see in the evening not more than fifty or sixty persons at most. Judge of his astonishment on finding assembled at the appointed hour, a congregation of about five hundred, a large proportion of whom are men! What had brought them? The majority were ignorant of the object of the meeting. An instruction explaining the motive and end of the exercises made a deep impression; the Benediction was chanted most fervently, and there was a notable increase of fervor during the Litany of the Blessed Virgin, especially at the thrice repeated invocation: "Refugium peccatorum, ora pro nobis." The cause was gained, Mary took possession of the parish of Notre Dame des Victoires.

The good curé still doubted; to assure himself that the association was truly the work of God, he demanded a sign, the conversion of a great sinner, an old man on the borders of the tomb, who had several times refused to see him. His prayer was granted, the old man received him gladly, and became sincerely converted. It was not long before new graces showered upon his parish increased M. Desgenette's confidence, numberless sinners changed their lives, indifferent Christians became practical and fervent, the offices of the Church were attended, the Sacraments frequented, the apparently extinguished Faith was relighted, and this parish, lately so scandalous, soon became one of the most edifying in Paris.

The Confraternity of the most Holy and Immaculate Heart of Mary was not to embrace one parish only. God willed that it should extend throughout France, and even the entire world. M. Desgenettes, who understood this design, addressed himself to the Sovereign Pontiff, and obtained, April 24th, 1838, a brief, erecting the association into an Archconfraternity, with the power of affiliating to itself other associations of the same kind throughout the Church, and granting them a participation in the spiritual favors accorded it. From this day, the Archconfraternity developed wonderfully, and became an inexhaustible source of grace. The church of Notre Dame des Victoires was henceforth numbered among the most celebrated sanctuaries in the world. At all hours may the faithful be seen around its altars in the attitude of prayer and recollection. The re-unions which take place every Sunday present a touching spectacle, a dense crowd composed of persons of every condition, who, after fervently chanting Mary's praises, listen attentively to a long series of petitions received in the course of the week from all quarters of the globe.

These present a picture of all the miseries, all the sufferings, all the corporal and spiritual necessities possible; to which are added numberless acts of thanksgiving for benefits obtained through the associates' prayers. These petitions are so multitudinous that they cannot be announced except in a general manner and by categories; they amount, each week, to the number of twenty-five or thirty thousand, and, for the entire year, form a total of a million and a half. At the time of its founder's death, the Archconfraternity numbered fifteen thousand affiliated confraternities in all quarters of the globe, and more than twenty million associates. At the beginning of this year, 1878, the affiliated confraternities amounted to 17,472.

A bulletin, issued monthly, gives an account of the progress of the Archconfraternity, the exercises which take place at Notre Dame des Victoires, the graces obtained, etc. The first nine numbers were published by M. Desgenettes himself, but at irregular intervals; they are full of interest and edification.

Amidst the wonderful success of his work, the venerable pastor, far from seeking any of the glory, thought only of humbling himself; regarding his share in it as naught but that of a simple instrument, he confesses even his resistance to the inspirations of grace, his doubts, his incredulity;[22] he will not admit that he may be called the founder of this work of mercy; it is God who has done all, it is the Immaculate Heart of Mary, that has opened to poor sinners a new source of graces, as for himself, he was not even the originator of the idea.

These sentiments reveal the soul of a saint; the true servants of God are always humble of heart, and the good they accomplish is in proportion to their self-abasement.

In his deep gratitude to God, the pious curé never forgot the bond attaching Notre Dame des Victoires to the chapel of the Daughters of Charity; he always loved this blessed sanctuary; it was there Mary had concealed the source of those vivifying waters which flowed through his parish; it was there this Mother of divine grace had promised those benedictions which the Archconfraternity reaped so abundantly. To preserve the remembrance of this mysterious relation, he desired that the medal of the association should be the Miraculous Medal. Henceforth, the influence of this medal became confounded with that of the Archconfraternity, the extraordinary graces attributed to the former were often due the associates' prayers, and reciprocally, for example, the conversion of M. Ratisbonne. In this case, as in many others, two equally supernatural means united to obtain the same result.

It is related that M. Desgenettes, seeing the Daughters of Charity frequently around the altar of the most Holy Heart of Mary at Notre Dame des Victoires, would sometimes say to them: "My good Sisters, I am much pleased to see you in my dear church, but know that your own chapel is the true pilgrim shrine, it is there you have the Blessed Virgin, there she manifested herself to you.——"

The Miraculous Medal, as revealed to Sister Catherine, bears on the reverse the Sacred Hearts of Jesus and Mary, the first crowned with thorns, the second pierced by a sword. These are symbols which all comprehend. Are they not, at the same time, a prophetic sign?

We are permitted to recognize here a foreshadowing of that devotion which would be rendered by the Archconfraternity of Notre Dame des Victoires, to the most Holy and Immaculate Heart of Mary.

We may likewise see pre-figured, that later development in our day, of devotion to the Sacred Heart of Jesus, a devotion born in France, and which the entire nation wishes to proclaim amidst pomp and grandeur, by the construction of a splendid monument, that from the heights of Montmartre, shall overlook all Paris.

Thus, by a mysterious gradation, the medal of the Immaculate Conception has conducted us to the Immaculate Heart of Mary, and the Heart of the Mother has introduced us into the Heart of the Son, the adorable Heart of Jesus, that Heart which has so loved men, and which saves nations as well as individuals.

## IV.

## Graces Obtained from 1838 to 1842, in Greece, America, China, etc.

### CURE WROUGHT IN SANTORIN (GREECE)—1838.

Letter of M.N., Priest of the Mission, in Santorin:

"Mme. Marie Delenda, wife of M. Michel Chigi, son of the Vice-Consul from Holland to Santorin, for seven years had suffered most excruciating pains, inducing such a state of nervous sensibility, that she was unable to bear the least excitement. She had had several children, but they all died before birth and receiving baptism. The physicians consulted, declared unanimously, that her disease was incurable, and that none of her children would ever come into the world alive. Greatly distressed at such a sad prospect, she had recourse to the Miraculous Medal, and obtained from it what medical skill was unable to effect; her next child, born not long after, was a fine, live, healthy one. Her husband, as pious as herself, was transported with joy and gratitude. 'Behold!' said he to the attendant physician and conducting him to an image of the Immaculate Mary, 'Behold our Protectrice, our Liberatrix, the Mother of our child!' The physician knelt, said a prayer and retired. Since then, the mother's health is good; at least she has had no relapse of her former apparently incurable disease, which recovery is sufficient to attest the protection of Mary Immaculate. Full of gratitude, the two spouses have never ceased to urge the erection of the altar and inauguration of the image of Mary Immaculate, in fulfillment of their promise.

"Several other miraculous cures have also been wrought there through the invocation of Mary Immaculate. I am assured of this; four of them are well attested, and marvelous. The bishop, the clergy, the people of Santorin, are all ready to affirm my assertions, and not one of them but would be more likely to exaggerate than detract from my account. When Monseigneur went to visit the Chigi family after the birth of their child, he asked to see the image, and looking at it, said: 'This is the second miracle wrought in Santorin by the Immaculate Virgin. The first is known to me through the confessional, and consequently, I cannot divulge it.'

"It was on the 28th of May, the inauguration of the image of the Immaculate Conception took place. Monseigneur himself officiated in the translation, after the High Mass and procession terminating the Forty Hour's Devotion at the cathedral. The image was placed upon an altar prepared for the purpose, in the courtyard of the donor's house. From the altar to the outer door, a very prettily decorated arched pathway was formed by means of drapery, and upon the threshold, was a triumphal arch. All the pavement, not only in the court but even to our church, was covered with flowers and fragrant grasses. Monseigneur, preceded by the clergy, and followed by all the Catholics and several Greek schismatics, repaired to the place where the image was exposed. Having incensed it, he intoned the Ave, Maris Stella, and the procession began to move. The clergy with the cross at their head commenced to defile. Then came two young girls bearing each a banner of white silk, whereon was depicted the spotless Virgin, these were suspended diagonally at the entrance of the sanctuary. Next, were two more young girls holding extended, the front of the altar representing the reverse of the medal, and finally, the image borne by the donor and one of his nearest relatives. Monseigneur walked immediately after, and behind him, Mme. Chigi holding her child in her arms and accompanied by her sister. The people were not in the ranks of the procession, but ranged along each side, that they might readily see the image and kiss it as it passed, which they did with so much eagerness and enthusiasm that there was considerable danger of its meeting with an accident. This, however, we averted by many precautions, and at length reached the church. At the entrance, another very beautiful triumphal arch had been erected, surmounted by a large representation of the reverse of the medal upon a floating banner, bearing the inscription: 'Ave, Maria Immaculata.' The church door was decorated with drapery, likewise the interior of the walls, which were also hung with flowers, verdant crowns and garlands. The image was now placed upon a temporary throne, which had been prepared until a more suitable one could be erected. Another High Mass was celebrated, at the end of which the children chanted alternately with the choir the 'Te Mariam laudamus,' this being the first time it was ever heard in this country. The other individuals I have already mentioned as having been cured through the Immaculate Mary's intercession, made each one a votive offering to her image. One gave a veil, another a pretty golden cross, which decorated the Blessed Virgin's bosom during the ceremony; a third proposed having a silver crown made in fulfillment of her vow, but she was advised to give something else, since several others in unison had already promised a most beautiful golden crown."

## CURE OF MLLE. ÉLISE BOURGEOIS.

Letter of the Superior of the Daughters of Charity, in Troyes:

"Troyes, March 4th, 1842.

"In 1838, we had in our workroom a young woman, named Élise Bourgeois, aged eighteen years, who, after great suffering, was attacked by an anchylosis in the knee. For seven months and a half she suffered excruciatingly, and her malady had reached the crisis. Her limb had shrunk up about two inches, and she could not walk without the aid of a cane or someone's arm. On the 8th of April, which was Monday in Holy Week, one of our young Sisters told me that the Notice contained an account of a Christian Brother, whose foot on the point of being amputated, was cured by the sole application of the Miraculous Medal, one night when his sufferings were greater than usual. I now reproached myself for having allowed this poor child to be so long afflicted, without our once thinking of having recourse to Mary for her recovery; and ascending to the work-room, I related to the children this account of the Christian Brother, and told the young woman to arouse her faith, to put all her confidence in Mary Immaculate, to apply the medal to her knee, and commence a novena with her companions. All Tuesday night her sufferings were great indeed, she said it seemed as if all her bones were dislocated. Nor was she able to obtain a moment's repose the next day. There now issued from a little hole which had formed in her knee, a quantity of serous matter. The day following, she arose with much difficulty, and was taken to the chapel where she heard Holy Mass. At the elevation, she placed her sound knee upon the bench, saying most fervently to the good God: 'Since Thou art present, deign to cure me, that I may be entirely Thine.' She immediately felt something like the touch of a hand, which replaced the bones in their natural position, and lengthened the shrunken limb; but she did not yet dare rest upon it, for fear of injury. At the end of Mass, she knelt to receive the priest's benediction, and despite herself, she rested her weight upon the afflicted knee. She remained in the chapel with her companions to say her prayers and thank the Blessed Virgin for the great favor just obtained. From that time, she has never suffered the slightest pain in the limb, and it appears perfectly sound.

"As soon as the children perceived that she was cured, they declared it a miracle, and all hearts were filled with the deepest emotion and gratitude. Élise now asked permission to go to the cathedral to confession; a request I granted reluctantly, although she assured me, she was not suffering in the slightest, yet she had not been out for seven months and a-half, and I could scarcely realize her recovery. Several Masses of thanksgiving were said in our chapel, during the first of which we had the Blessed Sacrament exposed, and the Te Deum chanted. The noise of this miracle soon spread throughout the city, and several people came to see the healed one. She also requested permission to go to the house of one of her uncles, who had a very impious neighbor, that had been informed of her miraculous recovery, but who had also been told that he need not believe until he had seen Élise for himself. He was perfectly convinced, acknowledged it beyond denial, and said that in thanksgiving, a Te Deum should be chanted in the cathedral.

"I forgot to say, that our physician had seen this young woman two months before her recovery and pronounced the disease incurable. I had also had her examined by a surgeon, who ordered much blistering, but without expecting a cure."

Accompanying this letter are the signatures of seven Sisters of Charity and twenty-three other individuals, witnesses of the miracle.

### A TRAIT OF PROTECTION. (TEXAS).

The following was sent to us by Mgr. Odin, Vicar Apostolic of Texas, in a letter dated April 11th, 1841.

"I had, in the city of Nacogdoches, an opportunity of witnessing how Mary Immaculate loves to grant the prayers of those who put their trust in her. A Maryland lady, on leaving her native State to settle in Texas, had received a Miraculous Medal; her confessor, on giving it to her, exacting the promise, that she would never omit the daily recitation of the little prayer, 'O Mary! conceived without sin, pray for us who have recourse to thee!' and assuring her at the same time that this good Mother would never allow her to die without the last consolations of religion. She faithfully complied with her promise. For four years she was confined to her bed, and often, it was thought, at the point of death, but her confidence in Mary, always inspired her with the hope of receiving the last Sacraments ere leaving this world. As soon as she heard of our arrival, we were summoned to her bedside; she received the Holy Viaticum and Extreme Unction, and expired a few days after, filled with gratitude for her celestial Benefactress.

### CURES AND INCIDENTS OF PROTECTION. (CHINA).

In a letter of July 1838, Mgr. Rameaux, Vicar Apostolic of the provinces of the Kiang-Si and Tché-Kiang, in sending us the invocation of the medal translated into Chinese, says, that the Chinese have a great devotion to this little prayer, and always follow the Ave Maria by a recitation of it. He also informed us, that Mgr. de Bézy, Vicar Apostolic of the Hou-Kouang, and M. Perboyre, Missionary Apostolic, would transmit to us several accounts of miraculous marks of protection. We received these accounts some months later, and quote them as follows:

"1st. In the province of the Hou-Kouang, a Christian had been racked by a terrible fever for two months, accompanied by constant delirium. Three physicians had attended to him, but in vain. Finding himself on the verge of death, he sent for me to administer the Last Sacraments. I gave him the Holy Viaticum, but deferred Extreme Unction, seeing that my duties would retain me in that locality some time longer. I gave him a present of the medal, and advised a novena, assuring him, that if it were for the benefit of his soul, he would be restored to health. He began the novena; on the seventh day, the fever left him, and on the eighth he had recovered his usual strength. On the ninth day of the novena, he came to see me, and assured me that he was perfectly well. I reminded him of thanking the Blessed Virgin for so great a favor, and he promised to recite with his friends the Rosary in her honor. But our Christian, pre-occupied with various affairs that his sickness had interrupted, forgot the promise. Five days after, he had a relapse. This made him conscious of his fault; he approached the Sacraments again and began another novena. Though he continued to grow worse from day to day, I still had great hopes that the Immaculate Mary would come to his assistance, and I assured him of his recovery before the end of the novena. My confidence was not deceived; he recovered entirely, to the great astonishment of all the Christians. This time his gratitude was effectual, and the fever did not return.

"2nd. In Tien-Men, a village of the same province, the Christians, numbering about two hundred, are distinguished for their piety and a great devotion to the Blessed Virgin. For eight years, successive inundations had reduced these Christians to extreme poverty; but this year, at the first sign of an overflow, they had recourse to Mary Immaculate by means of the medal, and soon the waters retired without doing the slightest harm to the Christian territory, whilst that of the pagans was devastated. And our Christians now return most grateful thanks to their good Mother for the abundant harvest they have just gathered.

"3rd. The following account was sent us by M. Perboyre, in a letter of August 10th, 1839. The reader will learn, with interest, that this is the same missionary who, arrested a month after for his religion, so generously confessed the Faith one whole year amidst the most frightful tortures, and at last consummated the sacrifice by his glorious martyrdom, September 11th, 1840.

"Whilst I was giving a mission to the Christians of the Honan province, November 1837, they brought to me a young woman who had been afflicted with mental aberration for about eight months, telling me she was very anxious to confess, and, though she was incapable of the Sacrament, they begged me not to refuse her a consolation she appeared to desire so earnestly. Her sad condition of mind precluded all ideas of her deriving any benefit from the exercise of my ministry, but I heard her out of pure compassion. In taking leave of her, I placed her under the especial protection of the Blessed Virgin—that is, I gave her a medal of the Immaculate Conception. She did not then understand the value of the holy remedy she received; but, from that moment, she began to experience its beneficial effects, her shattered intellect improving so rapidly that, at the end of four or five days, she was entirely changed. To a complete confusion of ideas, to fears that kept her ever in mortal agony, and which, I believe, were the work of the demon, succeeded good sense, peace of mind and happiness. She made her confession again, and received Holy Communion, with the liveliest sentiments of joy and fervor. This especial instance of Mary's generosity will doubtless surprise you little, you who know so well that the earth is filled with her mercy; but your hearts will be excited anew to fervent thanksgiving for this favor, which is the principal reason of my acquainting you with it."

1st. Letter from a Missionary of Macao, dated August 25th, 1841:

"A widow who had but one son, reared like herself in paganism, saw him suddenly fall under the power of the demon; his paroxysms were so furious that all fled before him, and he ran through the fields uttering the most lamentable cries. Anyone that attempted to stop him was immediately seized and thrown to the ground. His poor mother was in despair, and almost dying of grief, when Divine Providence deigned to cast upon her a look of compassion. One day when he was unusually tormented, the young man fled hither and thither like a vagabond, not knowing where he went; everyone tried to stop him, but he brutally repulsed all who lay hands on him. The most merciful God permitted a Christian to be among the number of those who witnessed this spectacle. Animated with a lively faith, and touched at the unfortunate creature's sufferings, the Christian told all who were pursuing the demoniac to desist, that he unaided could arrest him, that he would quiet him, and restore him docile and gentle to his mother. This language astonished the pagans, but they did as requested, although thinking the Christian ran a great risk. Our good Christian wore the Miraculous Medal of the Immaculate Mary; taking it in his hands he approached the possessed and showing it to him he commanded the demon to flee and leave the young man in peace. The demon obeyed instantly, and the young man seeing the medal in the Christian's hands, humbly prostrated himself before the miraculous image, without knowing what it was. The pagans, watching from a distance, were greatly astonished. The Christian now commanded the young man to rise and follow him, and still holding in his hand the medal, which was as a magnet attracting the young pagan, he thus conducted him to his mother. 'Mother,' he exclaimed, to her great consolation, as soon as he saw her, 'Do not weep any more, I am freed from the demon; he left me as soon as he perceived this medal.' Imagine the poor mother's joy, on hearing these words! She was perplexed to know whether it was a dream or a reality! The Christian reassured her, and recounted all that had passed, adding, that her son would never be possessed again, if she renounced her idols and became a Christian. She promised sincerely, and they immediately began to divest their altar of its false gods. Then the Christian, feeling assured they would be faithful when instructed in the truths of religion, withdrew, laden with the thanks of both mother and son for the inestimable service he had just rendered them."

2nd. Extract of a Letter from M. Faivre, Priest of the Mission in the Province of Nankin, May 6th, 1841:

"The two great means God uses for the accomplishment of good in this Mission are our Lord's cross and the Immaculate Mary's protection. As to the most powerful protection of Mary conceived without sin, we have experienced it so often, and in so especial a manner, both as regards ourselves and the welfare of the Mission, that it would be tedious to recount in detail, even if I wished to do so, all the favors we have received at her maternal hands.

"Seeing the Blessed Virgin's clemency towards us and our Christians, we have done all we could to honor her and advance her honor among the Christians, by seeking to inspire them with the liveliest confidence in this good, holy Mother. On the Feast of the Assumption, 1839, we consecrated this Mission to her, and ever since it has been called Mary's Diocese. We have given as a rule to our virgins especial devotion to the Immaculate Conception. We have established Mary Immaculate patroness of the seminary Providence has created in this Mission. (This seminary now numbers six scholars who lead lives of regularity and edification and make rapid progress in the study of Latin.) One of our virgins, already advanced in age, had been for several years confined to her bed, without the slightest hope of recovery, the thirteen physicians who had been successively consulted having declared her malady incurable. Seeing her end approach, she asked for the missionary, that she might receive the Last Sacraments. He came, and administered the Sacraments of the dying, exhorting her to accept death in a spirit of conformity to the will of God. She replied that she was fully resigned to His holy will and had no hope of deriving any benefit from human means, but she felt convinced that if she could get a Miraculous Medal, her health would be restored. The missionary, seeing so much faith and confidence, gave her the one he wore, having no other convenient just then, and recommended her to make a novena in honor of the Immaculate Conception of the Blessed Virgin. All the family joined her in making the novena, and from the fifth day she was entirely cured. The attending physician, who was a pagan, coming to see her at the end of the novena, was utterly surprised to find her so well, and he eagerly inquired what extraordinary remedy had been employed to effect such a change. She replied that she had used no remedies, but the Lord of Heaven had restored her health. The physician returned, filled with veneration for the Lord of Heaven, who had displayed such great power; and the virgin, in expression of her gratitude to the Immaculate Mary, her august Benefactress, donated three hundred piastres to repair a chapel dedicated to Mary."

### CONVERSION OF M. RATISBONNE, AN ISRAELITE.

Rome, 1842.

M. Alphonse Ratisbonne belonged to a Jewish family of Strasburg, distinguished in the world as much for its social position as the universal esteem in which it was held; he himself was a member of a society for the encouragement of labor, contributing thus to the benefit of his unfortunate brethren. Towards the end of the year 1841, he became affianced to a young Jewess, who united in her person all those qualities calculated to assure his happiness. Before entering upon this new state of life, he decided to take a pleasure trip to the East, visiting on the way some of the most remarkable cities of Italy. There was nothing, he thought, interesting to him in the Eternal City, so from Naples he would direct his course to Palermo; but Divine mercy called him, though he did not recognize the voice; he is constrained, as it were, by a secret design of Heaven, to change his determination, and visit Rome. It was in this center of Catholic unity that the God of all patience and goodness awaited him, it was here that grace was to touch his heart. But what were his dispositions? Thou, O Lord, knowest them! ... His hatred of Catholicity was very far from suggesting a thought of his ever embracing it. He felt for our holy and sublime religion that violent animosity which could not contain itself, which chafed at anything reminding him of Christianity, and which had even grown more rancorous since his brother M. Theodore Ratisbonne's abjuration of Judaism and reception of Holy Orders. He could not pardon this desertion, and his implacable hatred increased with time. But the innocent object of his aversion never ceased to supplicate Heaven to shed a ray of divine light upon the deluded brother, who loaded him with indignation and contempt. Made sub-Director of the Archconfraternity of Notre Dame des Victoires, he often implored the associates' prayers for this brother's conversion.

Such were M. Ratisbonne's sentiments when he entered Rome. He had scarcely arrived ere he thought of leaving; everything he saw in the Holy City urged him to hasten from it, everything excited him to declaim against what shocked and vilified his belief.... He was not proof, however, against a species of emotion in visiting the church of Ara Coeli; but it was an emotion which lost all its influence, (if influence it could be said to have exerted upon this heart buried in the shades of death,) when he understood that it was the general effect produced by the first sight of this remarkable monument. So, far from giving way to it, he hastened, on the contrary, to affirm that it was not a Catholic emotion, but an impression purely religious. In traversing the Ghetto, his hatred against Christianity was still more inflamed at witnessing the misery and degradation of the Jews; as if the chastisement of that deicidal people had been inflicted by the children of the Church, as if this people had not called down upon itself the vengeance of innocent blood!

Before leaving Rome, M. Ratisbonne was to visit one of his childhood friends, an old schoolmate with whom he had always kept up an intimacy, although their religious belief was so widely at variance. This friend was M. Gustave de Bussière, a zealous Protestant, who several times had endeavored to profit by their intimacy, by persuading M. Ratisbonne to embrace Protestantism, but the latter was immovable, and the two friends, after useless discussions, usually ended by a renewal of their faith in two words, expressing most emphatically how invincible each deemed himself. "Headstrong Jew!" said one; "Enraged Protestant!" replied the other. Such was the result of these conversations, which never succeeded in shaking the opinion of either, or dissipating any of their deplorable errors. This opposition of principles, however, did not estrange their friendship. M. Ratisbonne called to see M. De Bussière and was admitted by an Italian servant. He inquired for M. Gustave de Bussière, but this gentleman was absent, and by a providential mistake the servant introduced him into the salon of M. Theodore Bussière, Gustave's brother, whom M. Ratisbonne had seen but once. It was too late to withdraw, and though somewhat disconcerted at the mistake, he stopped to exchange a few words of courtesy with his friend's brother. M. De Bussière had had the happiness of abjuring Protestantism, and he was a zealous advocate of the Faith he had so lately learned to prize. He knew that M. Ratisbonne was a Jew; he received him with affectionate eagerness, and the conversation naturally turning upon the various places of interest in Rome visited by the young French traveler, it soon drifted into a religious discussion. M. Ratisbonne did not disguise his real sentiments, he expressed his animosity against Catholicity, his inalterable attachment to Judaism and to the baron De Bussière's solid arguments, his only replies were the frigid politeness of silence, a smile of pity, or new protestations of fidelity to his sect, repeating that a Jew he was born and a Jew he would die!

It was then that M. De Bussière, not the least discouraged by M. Ratisbonne's emphatic language, and impelled by a secret impulse of grace, thought of offering him the Miraculous Medal. Doubtless this idea appears rash to many, and many would have banished it as a veritable folly, but the simplicity of faith teaches us to discern things by a very different light from that in which they are revealed to the world. Filled with this holy fearlessness of the Saints, M. De Bussière presents the young Jew a medal of the Immaculate Conception. "Promise me," said he, "to always wear this little image, I beg you not to refuse me." M. Ratisbonne, unable to conceal his astonishment at so strange a proposition, rejects it instantly with an expression of indignation that would have disconcerted any other than his new friend. "But," continues our fervent Catholic undismayed, "I cannot understand the cause of such a refusal, for, according to your view of things, the wearing of this object must be to you a matter of total indifference, whilst it would be a real consolation to me if you would condescend to my request." "Ah! I will comply, then, if you attach so much importance to it," replied the other with a hearty laugh; "I should not be sorry, moreover, to have an opportunity of convincing you that Jews are not so headstrong as they are represented. Besides, it will give me an interesting chapter to add to my notes and impressions of travel." And he continued to jest on the subject in a manner rather painful to the Christian hearts around him.

During this debate, the good father of the family had told his two little daughters (interesting children, whom an eminently religious education had already imbued with sentiments of piety), to put the precious medal on a cord. They did so, and gave it to their father, who hung it around the young Israelite's neck. Encouraged by this first success, he wishes to go still farther. He attempts nothing less than binding M. Ratisbonne himself to ask the favor and protection of Mary, of Mary whom he despises without knowing, Mary whose image he receives most reluctantly! M. De Bussière presents him a paper upon which is written St. Bernard's powerful invocation, the Memorare.... This time, the Jew can still less dissimulate his displeasure, it seems tried to the utmost; but the baron feels himself actuated by a secret impulse, that urges him to persevere in his solicitations, and conquer. He repeats his request, and even goes so far when he presents the prayer as to beg M. Ratisbonne to take a copy of it for him, as he has but one. M. Ratisbonne, convinced that resistance is useless, rather than repeating his refusal prefers acceding to the request, and thus ridding himself of such vexatious importunity. "Agreed," said he, "that you take my copy and I keep yours." And, hastening to this indiscreet zealot, he retired, murmuring to himself: "I really wonder what he would say if I were to insist upon his reciting the Jewish prayers? I must admit that I have, indeed, met a striking original!" It was thus he left this house of benediction and salvation, ignorant of the treasure he bore with him, the key of Heaven that had been given him; the image of the Mother of holy hope he wore upon his heart, and whose blessed effects he would so soon experience.

M. De Bussière, deeply grieved at the young Jew's levity, united with his family in conjuring the God of mercy to pardon the words of one who knew not what he said; and he recommended his dear children to lift up their hands to the Refuge of Sinners, supplicating her to obtain the gift of Faith for this poor soul in the shades of darkness and error! ... O Mary, your tender love graciously welcomed these prayers of the innocent, they penetrated your maternal heart, and soon obtained the object of their desires. The zeal of this devout servant of the Queen of Heaven was not confined within the narrow limits of his own family circle.... Going, that evening, according to a pious custom in Rome, to keep watch before the Blessed Sacrament with the prince B. and some other friends, he also engaged their prayers for the young Israelite's conversion.... Let us follow attentively all the details preceding the ever-memorable day which was to crown M. De Bussière's pious efforts. Let us not forget that a generous Christian, elevated by a lively faith above the vain prejudices of the world, and docile to the secret inspirations of grace, becomes the instrument of Providence in procuring God's glory and the salvation of a soul.

Meanwhile, M. Ratisbonne was making arrangements to leave Rome; he had already fixed it upon the day of his departure and had come to say good-bye to his friend and acquaint him with his intention of starting the next evening. "Going!" replied M. De Bussière; "do not think of it. I want you to grant me just eight days longer; our conversation of yesterday occupies my thoughts more than ever; let me entreat you to prolong your stay and let us go to the diligence office to countermand your order." It was in vain. M. Ratisbonne declined, saying he had already decided to go, and had no motive for deferring his departure. Under the pretext of a very imposing ceremony which was to take place at St. Peter's, M. De Bussière forced, rather than persuaded him to remain a few days longer.

We shall not here enter into a detailed account of what passed between them from the moment M. De Bussière's constancy gained the last triumph—that is, from the 16th of January to the 20th—inasmuch as there was not the slightest sign of the happy change, either in the language or conduct of M. Ratisbonne, towards the new friend divine Providence had given him, in spite of himself. He could not, however, avoid receiving this new friend's civilities, or refuse to be accompanied by him in visiting the various places of note in the Eternal City. M. De Bussière, full of hope against all human hope, allowed no opportunity to escape of enlightening his young friend; but not one consoling response could he obtain, M. Ratisbonne, by jest and raillery, always avoiding the arguments he would not take the trouble to refute, always ridiculing Catholicity, and thus afflicting the heart of the servant of Jesus Christ by responding coldly to the assiduity of his zeal, the serious nature of his propositions. "Make your mind easy; I will think of all this, but not at Rome. I am to spend two months at Malta; it will serve to while away the time." He was astonished at the imperturbable tranquility with which M. De Bussière persevered in trying to convince him; he could not understand that union of serenity (which religion alone inspires) with that ardent desire (that he doubtless attributed to obstinacy) of leading him to a new belief, for which, according to his own words, he felt more aversion than ever. To him this tranquility appeared incomprehensible. M. De Bussière did not hesitate to express his belief in the triumph of his cause; for instance, in passing the Scala Sancta with the young Israelite, as he pointed it out he bared his head respectfully and said aloud, as if in a voice of prophecy, "Hail, holy staircase! here is a man who one day will ascend your steps on his knees." This was on the 19th. M. Ratisbonne's only response was a disconcerting peal of laughter, and the two friends separated again, without the slightest religious impression having been made upon the Israelite, although, unknown to human ken, he was on the eve of the brightest day of his life.

During this short interval, M. De Bussière tasted the bitterness of losing one of his dearest friends. M. De La Ferronays died suddenly on the evening of the 17th, leaving to his family and all who knew him the sweet hope that he had bid adieu to this perishable life only to enter upon the joys of a blissful immortal one. Doubtless this event contributed to the young Israelite's speedy conversion, for whilst on earth M. De La Ferronays had prayed for him, and we have every reason to believe that he soon became his advocate in heaven. M. De Bussière had informed this dear friend of his hopes and the means employed for gaining the young Israelite to Jesus Christ, and he had received the consoling answer: "Do not be uneasy; if you have succeeded in making him say the Memorare, he is yours." ... Such was the admirable confidence of this fervent Christian in the powerful protection of the most compassionate Virgin Mary!

Yet notwithstanding the bitterness of the sacrifice Heaven had just demanded of the Baron De Bussière, he found it hard to part from this young man whom he longed to conquer to the Faith, and the resignation of his grief was a new prayer attracting the Divine mercy. Immediately after leaving him on the 19th, he went to prostrate himself beside the remains of his virtuous friend, begging that friend's assistance from the heights of heaven in obtaining what had been already recommended to his prayers on earth.

Thursday, 20th. —M. Ratisbonne's dispositions are not changed in the least; he never raises his thoughts above terrestrial things, the religious discussions of the preceding days have not even fixed his attention, or apparently not excited in his soul the slightest anxiety. As to his false belief, he never dreams of taking one step towards a knowledge of the truth; M. De Bussière is not with him to continue the conversation on religion, and he dismisses the subject from his mind. Leaving the café, he meets one of his fellow boarders; they discourse of balls and other frivolous amusements in such a way as to convince one that he was surely not engrossed with anything serious. It was then noon, and two hours later the young Jew had seen the light, two hours later he eagerly desired the grace of holy baptism, two hours later he believed in the Church!... Who is like to Thee, O my God? Who can thus, in an instant, triumph over human reason, and force it to render homage to Thy sovereign truth? ... Ah, it is Thyself, Thyself alone, Lord, it is the prerogative of Thy mercy to work such prodigies! Let us return to our Israelite.

It is one o'clock; M. De Bussière must repair to the church of St. Andrew delle Fratte to make some arrangements for the funeral ceremonies of M. De La Ferronays, which take place on the morrow. He sets out, and on the way happily meets M. Ratisbonne, who joins him, with the intention of taking one of their usual walks, when M. De Bussière had fulfilled the imperative duty that required his immediate attention.... But the moment of grace has come. They enter the church, where various decorations already announce the morrow's ceremonies; the Israelite inquires the meaning of them, and M. De Bussière, having replied that they were for the funeral obsequies of M. De La Ferronays, the intimate friend he had just lost, begs him to wait there an instant, whilst he goes into the house to execute a commission with one of the monks. M. Ratisbonne then glances coolly around the church, seeming to say by his air of indifference, that it is not worth his attention. We must remark that he was then at the epistle side of the altar. M. De Bussière returns after an absence of about twelve minutes and is surprised at not seeing his young companion. Could he have grown weary of waiting in a place that inspired only repugnance and disgust? ... He knew not and sought M. Ratisbonne. What was his astonishment at finding him on the left-hand side of the church, kneeling, and apparently wrapt in devotion! ... He could scarcely believe his eyes, and yet it was no mistake.... It was in the chapel of the archangel St. Michael that the prince of darkness had just been crushed.... A great victory already rejoiced all Heaven.... The young Jew was vanquished.

M. De Bussière approaches, but he is not heard; he touches his friend, but he cannot distract him; he touches him again, but still no response; he repeats it a third or fourth time, and at last M. Ratisbonne turns to answer, and his tearful countenance, his utter inability to express what has passed, his hands clasped most fervently, partly reveal the heavenly secret. "Oh! how M. De La Ferronays has prayed for me!" he exclaims. This is all he says. Never did M. De Bussière enjoy a more consoling surprise. The bandage of error blinding the young Israelite had fallen, and M. De Bussière's heart was filled with the liveliest gratitude to God.... He raises his young friend, who was completely overcome by this celestial visitation; he takes him and almost carries him out of the church.... He is all eagerness to know the details.... He asks M. Ratisbonne to reveal the mystery and begs him to say where he wishes to go. "Lead me," replies the new Paul, completely vanquished, "lead me where you will.... After what I have seen, I obey." ... And not being able to say more, he draws forth the unknown treasure he had been wearing upon his heart for four days. He takes the dear medal in his hands, he covers it with kisses, he waters it abundantly with tears of joy, and amidst his sobs escape a few words expressive of his happiness, but which a profound emotion almost prevents his articulating. "How good is God! What a plentitude of gifts! What joy unknown! Ah! how happy I am, and how much to be pitied are they who do not believe!" And continuing to shed torrents of tears over the miseries of those whom Faith has never enlightened, he already feels the holy desire of seeing the kingdom of Jesus Christ extended throughout the world. He can scarcely himself understand such a transformation, and amidst the various feelings surging through his heart, he interrupts his tears, his exclamations, and his silence, to ask M. De Bussière if he does not think him crazy.... Then answering his own question, "No," he continues: "I am not crazy.... I know well what I think and what passes within me.... I know that I am in my right mind.... Moreover, everybody knows that I am not crazy!" By degrees, these first transports of emotion give place to a more composed frame of mind; he can at last express his new desires, his new belief, and he asks to be conducted to the feet of a priest, for he craves the grace of holy baptism.... Already favored with the liveliest Faith, he aspires after the happiness of confessing his Divine Master amid torments and recalling the sufferings of the martyrs he had seen represented upon the walls of St. Étienne le Rond; he wishes to shed his blood in attestation of his Faith as a disciple of Jesus Christ.... Meanwhile, he has told M. De Bussière nothing of the sudden blow that vanquished him, and he refuses to tell except in the presence of God's minister; "for what he saw he ought not, he could not reveal except on his knees."

Father De Villefort, of the Society of Jesus, is chosen to receive the neophyte and hear this consoling secret, which will reveal the excess of Divine mercy towards the soul of the young Israelite. M. De Bussière himself conducts him to the Reverend Father, who welcomes him tenderly.... Then, in the presence of M. De Bussière, M. Ratisbonne takes in his hand the medal, the dear pledge of the Immaculate Mary's protection, and again covers it with respectful kisses, mingled with a shower of tears. He endeavors to overcome his emotion and exclaims in a transport of joy: "I have seen her! I have seen her!" Conquering his feelings, he continues his narration, interrupted from time to time by the sighs of an overburdened heart.

"I had been in the church but an instant, when suddenly I was seized with an inexplicable fear. I raised my eyes, the whole edifice had disappeared from my view, one chapel alone had, as it were, concentrated all the light, and in the midst of this effulgence there appeared standing upon the altar the Virgin Mary, grand, brilliant, full of majesty and sweetness, such as she is represented upon the medal—an irresistible force impelled me to her. The Virgin made me a sign with her hand to kneel, and she seemed to say: 'It is well.' She did not speak to me, but I understood all."

## APPARITION OF THE MIRACULOUS MEDAL

To M. Ratisbonne, January 20, 1842, in the Church of St. Andrew, delle Fratte, in Rome. "She did not speak one word to me," said M. Ratisbonne, "but I understood it all.
"

He ceased, but this short account eloquently revealed the abundant favors with which his soul had just been inundated. Reverend Father De Villefort and the pious baron listened with a holy joy, mingled with an involuntary feeling of religious awe, at thoughts of the infinite power which had just triumphed by such a striking manifestation of mercy.... The mystery was revealed, but M. Ratisbonne, now the disciple of the most humble of Masters, a God annihilated, expressed a wish to have the wonderful vision kept a profound secret; he even earnestly entreated that it should be, but Father De Villefort considered it wiser not to yield to the neophyte's modesty, God's glory, the Immaculate Mary's honor, demanding that such a miracle should be proclaimed. M. Ratisbonne's humility gave way to obedience. In the brief narration just quoted, one thing especially had struck the Reverend Father, "She did not speak to me, but I understood all!" What, then, had he understood, he who, having hitherto lived in the shades of darkness, found himself in an instant instructed in heavenly knowledge? What, then, had he understood, he who was suddenly recalled from the bosom of death which he loved, to a new life which but a short time previous he had solemnly declared he would ever ignore, 'a Jew he was born and a Jew he would die?' What had he understood, he the young Jew, so lately headstrong in his belief, an avowed enemy of Catholicity, but who now humbly prostrates himself at the feet of our Lord's minister to retract his words and renounce his own will, for he declares that, after what he has seen, he obeys? ... What has he understood? What has he seen? He has seen the Mother of divine grace, the bright aurora of the Sun of Justice; he has understood the gift of God, the eternal truth ... the unity of the Church, its infallibility, the sanctity of its morals, the sublimity of its mysteries, the grandeur and elevation of its hopes.... He has understood Heaven, and henceforth everything is changed for him, everything is renewed within him, he is no longer the same. His desires, projects, thoughts, earthly affections, where are they in the brilliancy of this celestial radiance? Vain prejudices of error, where are they? ... The Immaculate Mother of Jesus has rent asunder the band that veiled the young Israelite's eyes, and the shades of error are dissipated, the blind man sees the light, and his joy is inexpressible, for he knew not till then the true gifts, the blessings promised the children of the true Church.——

M. Ratisbonne had heretofore been completely ignorant of the truths of Catholicity, he acknowledges that he had never read even one book calculated to enlighten him on the subject, his hatred of Christianity kept him aloof from all that might change his views regarding it. He blasphemed without examining the object of his blasphemy, he judged without hearing, he despised without investigating.... And behold! despite himself, in an instant, in defiance of all his past protestations, he bends, he falls, he is conquered!

Rejoice, O Mary! for the dew of grace has not descended upon an ungrateful soil.... No; not in vain at your mysterious school has he learned all this privileged soul of your love, this heart that your incomparable beauty, your ineffable bounty has vanquished for Jesus Christ!

We see, indeed, that, from the moment his eyes are opened to the light, he adores the mysteries he formerly despised, loves what he hated, venerates what he ridiculed, and proves himself as humble and submissive to the Church as the most fervent Christian. That very day, he goes to the basilica of St. Mary Major, in tribute of gratitude to her who had just descended from Heaven, to bring him the gift of Faith, and its attendant blessings; thence he repairs to St. Peter's, to declare in that sanctuary dedicated to the Prince of the Apostles, his belief in the truths that Peter taught. M. De Bussière, who found a pious delight in offering to God this conquest of grace, accompanied him on his holy pilgrimage, and conversed intimately with him, they had but one heart and one soul. A new Paul, Ratisbonne, in what he experienced, now the Blessed Virgin gently forced him to prostrate himself at her feet, to receive the light of Heaven, recognized the strength of Him who vanquished His persecutors.... The profound emotion, the holy awe that filled the neophyte on entering a church, declared more fully the secrets that had been revealed to him.... Penetrated with the liveliest faith for the great Sacrament of love, he could not approach the altar, he was overwhelmed at the thought of the Real Presence of the God who resides in the Most Holy Sacrament. He considered himself unworthy to appear in this august Presence, as he was yet stained with original sin, and M. De Bussière relates, that he took refuge in a chapel, consecrated to the Blessed Virgin, exclaiming: "I have no fears here, for I feel myself under the protection of a boundless mercy." O Mary! you opened your maternal heart, and there he concealed himself, knowing that divine justice yields to mercy, when the guilty soul has found and invoked with confidence the Refuge of Sinners.... So great was the fervent neophyte's happiness when in the temple of the Lord, that he was unable to find words expressive of his happiness. "Ah!" said he in a holy transport, "how delightful it is to be here! How great reason have Catholics to love their churches and to frequent them! How zealous they should be in ornamenting them! How sweet to spend a lifetime in these holy places! They are truly not of earth but of Heaven!" Ah! are we not confounded and abashed by the fervor of him who has just been born into the truth! What would he think of the coldness, the levity, the ingratitude of the majority of Christians? ... Let us acknowledge it to our confusion; there is a Host who dwells in our midst, and whom we know not; we who eat at His table, who feed upon His own flesh, the Bread descended from Heaven, and behold! a young Israelite, instructed but a few hours in the wonders of God's love, teaches us how we must conduct ourselves in the presence of this Host, and with what sentiments our hearts should then be filled.

Next day, the news of this wonderful conversion had spread through Rome; everyone was anxious to learn something about it, and collected with pious curiosity the various statements in circulation; every one wished to see the newly converted and hear his account.... General Chlabonski even went to M. De Bussière's house. "So, you have seen the image of the Blessed Virgin," said he, accosting the neophyte. "The image?" answered the latter, "ah! it was no image, but herself I saw; yes, M. her real self, just as I see you now!" We must here remark that to the Church alone, appertains the power of judging and qualifying this vision; but everyone was impressed with the fact, that mistake or illusion seemed impossible, considering the young Israelite's character, education, prejudices, and horror for Christianity; moreover, in this chapel there was neither statue, picture nor any representation whatever of the Blessed Virgin. And we love to quote here the words of a wise man, who, referring to the event, says, "that without one grain of exaggeration, just as it happened, just as all Rome narrates it, the unexpected fact, the public fact of this conversion, considering all the circumstances, would of itself be a miracle, if a miracle had not caused it."

M. Ratisbonne reluctantly gave the details of what he had seen. When questioned closely as to what took place at the moment he found himself environed by this celestial effulgence, he answers ingenuously that he could not account for the involuntary impulse causing him to leave the right hand side of the church for the chapel on the left, especially as he was separated from it by the preparations for the morrow's ceremonies; that, when the Queen of Heaven appeared before him in all the glory and brilliancy of her immaculate purity, he caught a glimpse of her incomparable beauty, but immediately realized the impossibility of contemplating it, that urged by the desire, three times had he endeavored to lift his eyes to the face of this Mother of mercy, whose sweet clemency had deigned to manifest herself to him, and three times, in spite of himself, had his gaze been stayed at sight of the blessed hands, whence escaped a torrent of graces. "I could not," he told us himself after his arrival, "I could not express what I saw of mercy and liberality in Mary's hands. It was not only an effulgence of light, but it was also not rays I distinguished, words are inadequate to depict the ineffable gifts filling our Mother's hands, and descending from them, the bounty, mercy, tenderness, the celestial sweetness and riches, flowing in torrents and inundating the souls she protects."

In the first moments of his conversion, M. Ratisbonne gave vent to some of those thoughts which strongly pre-occupied him, those outpourings of a fervent heart which happily, are still preserved. "O my God!" he exclaimed in a transport of astonishment and gratitude, "I, who only half an hour before was blaspheming! I, who felt such violent hatred against the Catholic religion! ... Every one of my acquaintances knew full well, that to all human appearances, it was impossible for me ever to think of changing my religion. My family was Jewish, my betrothed, my uncle was Jewish. In embracing Christianity, I know that I break away from all earthly hopes and interests.... And yet I do it willingly; I renounce the passing happiness of a future which was promised me; I do so without hesitation, I act from conviction; ... for I am not crazy and have never been they well know it.... Who, then, could refuse to believe me, and believe in the truth? ... The most powerful interests enchained me to my religion, and consequently all should be convinced that a man who sacrifices everything to a profound conviction must sacrifice to a celestial light, which has revealed itself by incontrovertible evidence. What I have affirmed is true. I know it, I feel it; and what could be my object in thus betraying the truth and turning aside religion by a sacrilegious lie? ... I have not said too much; my words must carry conviction."

The Baron De Bussière had the consolation of entertaining at his own home the new son Heaven had given him; the young Jew remained there until the retreat preceding his baptism. It was right and just, indeed, that this friend should gather the first bloom of a heart refreshed by the dew of grace, that he should be the happy witness of the wonders wrought in that soul.... M. Ratisbonne himself had need of a confidant, some one that understood him thoroughly, and to whom he could communicate the emotions of his heart.... It was in moments of sweet intimacy, when alone with his friend, that he could give full vent to his feelings, and, in unison with him, admire the loving designs of divine Providence, and the means that had dissipated such deplorable errors. He bewailed the blindness in which he had lived! ... "Alas!" said he, "when my excellent brother embraced Catholicity, and afterwards entered the ecclesiastical state, I, of all his relatives, was his most unrelenting persecutor.... I could not forgive his desertion of our religion—we were at variance, at least; I detested him, though he had none but the kindest thoughts for me.... However, at the time of my betrothal, I said to myself that I must be reconciled to my brother, and I wrote him a few cold lines, to which he replied by a letter full of charity and tenderness.... One of my little nephews died about eighteen months ago. My good brother, having learned that he was seriously ill, asked as a personal favor that the child be baptized before its death, adding, with great delicacy, that to us it would be a matter of indifference, whilst to himself it would be a veritable happiness, and he hoped we would not refuse. I was infuriated at such a request!

"I hope, oh! yes, I hope that my God will send me severe trials, which may redound to His honor and glory, and convince all that I am actuated by conscience...." What generosity of heart! What knowledge! His eyes are scarcely opened to the truths of Catholicity, ere he embraces them in their full extent.... He knows already that the cross is the distinctive mark of the children of the Church, of God's elect, and this cross which so many Christians drag reluctantly after them, he greets, he awaits, he desires.... Moreover, it had been shown to him in a very mysterious manner; for he relates that the night preceding his conversion there was constantly before his eyes a large cross without the Christ, that the sight really fatigued him, although he considered it of no importance. "I made," said he, "incredible efforts to banish this image, but in vain. It was only later, when having, by chance, seen the reverse of the Miraculous Medal, he recognized the exact sign which had struck him.

Divine Providence, looking with a loving eye upon this young convert, directed his steps, and in these early days of his conversion, led him to a venerable Father who was to give him very precious counsel, upon the life of abnegation and perpetual sacrifice he had embraced. This servant of the Lord, immediately lay before him the importance of the step he had taken, the trials awaiting him, the temptation that would most assuredly beset his path, and without fearing to shake his constancy, he read him a few verses of the second chapter of Ecclesiasticus, upon the trials testing the virtue of the true servant and friend of God. With pleasure we quote here a part of this good priest's instructions:

"My son, when thou come to the service of God, stand in justice and in fear, and prepare thy soul for temptation. Humble thy heart and endure; incline thy ear and receive the words of understanding; and make not haste in the time of clouds. Wait on God with patience; join thyself to God and endure, that thy life may be increased in the latter end. Take all that shall be brought upon thee; and in thy sorrow endure, and in thy humiliation keep patience. For gold and silver are tried in the fire, but acceptable men in the furnace of humiliation. Believe God, and He will recover thee; and direct thy way, and trust in Him. Keep His fear and grow old therein."

M. Ratisbonne listened in respectful silence to these words of life; he cherished the remembrance of them, and the eve of his baptism, he asked the Reverend Father to put them in writing that he might meditate upon them the rest of his days.... It was accomplished, the joys of earth were sacrificed to the glory of bearing the cross of Jesus Christ.... He was initiated into heavenly secrets by reason of those favors the Immaculate Mary had conferred upon him.... He already felt the strength that God communicates to the soul, resolved to share the sorrows of its divine Master.

Ten days elapsed between the happy moment of the young Israelite's sudden comprehension of the truth, and his baptism. The Mother of Mercy had brought him from Heaven, the torch of Faith; in enlightening his intelligence, she had touched his heart; he sighed after the happy day, when the Church would admit him among the number of her children, and it was on the 31st of January, this tender Mother opened to him all her treasures, clothed him with innocence, called down upon him the plenitude of the gifts of the Spirit of love, and invited him to the banquet of Angels that she might give him the Bread of life.

The Gésu was the church selected for this solemn ceremony. Long before the appointed hour, it was filled with a devout, eager multitude, all anxious to get as near as possible to the holy altar. Nothing disturbed the beauty or serenity of the occasion, no cloud dimmed the brightness of this heavenly festival, which inundated truly Christian hearts with the purest joys.

M. Ratisbonne, clothed in the white robe of the catechumen, appeared around half-past eight, accompanied by the Reverend Father Villefort, (whose consoling duty it had been to prepare the neophyte for this beautiful day), and the Baron De Bussière, his godfather. They conducted him into the chapel of St. Andrew, where the touching ceremony was to take place. An object of the most profound curiosity, the fervent neophyte, wrapt in recollection, awaited with angelic serenity, the solemn moment.... The pious Romans gave vent to their feelings by words and gestures, kissing their chaplets in an effusion of grateful love for Mary Immaculate, the cause of our joy.... They pointed out one to another the zealous baron, whom divine Providence had chosen to give the Miraculous Medal to the young Israelite. "He is a Frenchman," they repeated, "He is a Frenchman! Blessed be God!"

His Eminence, the Cardinal Vicar, was to receive M. Ratisbonne's profession of Faith. He appeared at nine, clothed in his pontifical robes, and commenced the prayers prescribed for the baptism of adults.

The prayers terminated; His Eminence went in procession with the clergy to the foot of the church; the young Israelite was conducted to his presence. "What do you ask of the Church of God?" "Faith," was the immediate answer. "What name do you wish?" "Mary," said the neophyte, in a tone of tender gratitude; Mary, who had opened to him the path of salvation; Mary, who was to conduct him into the new life; Mary, who will one day introduce him into the City of the Saints, whence she descended to lead him to the divine fold.... Then followed his profession of Faith, his solemn promises.... He believes all, he promises all, he accepts all, he wishes to be a Christian, he is already one at heart.... His desires are gratified, the vivifying waters are poured upon his head, the grace of holy baptism has invested him with all the rights of his eternal heritage, the spirit of darkness is confounded. Behold the child of God, the brother of Jesus Christ, the new sanctuary of the Spirit of love, the favorite of the Queen of Heaven, the friend of Angels and the well-beloved son of Mother Church!

It was on this occasion that the Abbé Dupanloup, who happened to be in Rome at the time, celebrated before an immense audience the infinite mercies of God and the Immaculate Mary's miraculous protection of a child of France. We cannot refrain from inserting here a few fragments of the account printed at Rome. It is well calculated to increase devotion to Mary:

"How admirable are the thoughts and ways of divine Providence, and how deplorable the lot of those who neither comprehend nor bless them. For such, the life of man is only a sad mystery, his days a fatal series of events, man himself a noble but miserable creature, cast far from Heaven upon this land of tears, to live here in perpetual darkness, to die in despair, oblivious of a God who heeds neither his virtues nor his sorrows.... But, no; Lord, Thou art not forgetful of us, and life is not thus; despite our infinite misery, thy

Providence watches over us, it is far above the heavens, more boundless than the sea—it is an abyss of power, wisdom and love. ——

"Thou hast made us for Thyself, Lord, and our hearts are never at rest until they repose in Thee! We feel an insatiable need, which stirs the depths of our being, which consumes us, and when we yield to it, we inevitably find Thee!

"I bless Thee especially, I adore Thee, when from the depths of Thy eternity, Thou dost remember compassionately the lowliness of our being, the dust of which we are fashioned; when from the heights of heaven, Thou dost cast a glance of pity and love upon the most humble of Thy children; when, according to the Prophet's expression, 'Thou dost move heaven and earth,' and work innumerable marvels to save those who are dear to Thee, to conquer one soul!

"O, you, upon whom, at this moment, all eyes are bent with inexpressible emotion, with the tenderest love; for it is God, it is His mercy we love in you, in you whose presence in this holy place inspires these thoughts, tell us yourself what were your thoughts and ways, by what secret mercy the Lord pursued and reclaimed you?

For who are you? What do you seek in this sanctuary? What are these honors you seem to bear? What is this white robe in which I see you clothed? Tell us whence you came and whither you were going? What obstacle has suddenly changed your course? For walking in the footsteps of Abraham, your ancestor, whose blessed son you are this day, like him, blindly obedient to the voice of God, not knowing whither your journey tends, you suddenly find yourself in the Holy City.... The Lord's work was not yet accomplished; but it is for you to describe to us the rising of the Sun of truth and justice upon your soul, for you to picture its brilliant aurora.... Tell us why you enjoy, like ourselves, perhaps more keenly than ourselves, the good word, the virtues of the future and all our most blessed hopes.... Tell us, for we have the right to know, why you enter possession of our goods as your heritage? Who has introduced you among us, for yesterday we knew you not, or rather we knew you.... Oh! yes, I shall tell all; I know the joy that will fill your heart at my revealing your miseries as well as the celestial mercies. ——

"You did not love the truth, but the truth loved you. To the purest and most ardent efforts of a zeal that sought to enlighten you, did you oppose a disdainful smile, an indifferent silence, a subtle response, a haughty firmness, and sometimes blasphemous pleasantries. O patient God! O God, who loves us despite our miseries! Thy mercy has oftentimes a depth, a sublimity, a tenderness and, allow me to say it, a power and delicacy that are infinite!

"Suddenly a rumor is circulated throughout the Holy City, a rumor that consoles all Christian hearts, he who blasphemed yesterday, who this morning even ridiculed the friends of God, has become a disciple of Christ; celestial grace has touched his lips, he utters now only words of benediction and sweetness, the most vivid lights of the evangelical law seem to beam from his eyes; we may say that a celestial unction has taught him all things. Whence does he receive this enlightenment of the eyes of the heart, that heart which sees all, which has understood all? O God! Thou art good, infinitely good, and I love to repeat those sweet words, so lately on the blessed lips of him, whose memory is henceforth ineffaceably impressed upon our hearts. We wept over him a few days ago, we still regret him, but we have dried our tears. 'Yes, thou art good, and the children of men have truly called Thee the good God!' (Last words of M. de La Ferronays.) Thou dost set aside the laws of nature, thou dost account nothing too much to save Thy children! When Thou dost not come Thyself, thou dost send Thy angels! ... O God! shall I here relate all? I ought to enjoin reserve upon my speech.... But who is she? Quæ est ista? I cannot say the word, and yet I cannot be silent.

"Hail Mary! You are full of grace; Ave, gratia plena, and from the plentitude of your maternal heart, you love to bestow your gifts upon us. The Lord is with you, Dominus tecum, and it is through you He is pleased to descend to us! And now to praise you worthily, I must borrow the images of Heaven or speak the inflamed language of the prophets! For, O Mary! your name is sweeter than the purest joys, more delightful than the most exquisite perfumes, more charming than the harmony of angels, in corde jubilus; more refreshing to the faithful heart than honeycomb to the wearied traveler, mel in lingua; more encouraging and cheering to the guilty but repentant heart than the evening dew to the leaves parched and shriveled by the mid-day sun, ros in herba. You are beautiful as the orb of night, pulchra ut luna; you, who guide the bewildered traveler; you are brilliant as the aurora, aurora consurgens; fair and pure as the morning star, stella matutina; and it is you who precede the dawn of the Sun of Justice in our hearts.

"O Mary! I can never portray all your loveliness and grandeur, and it is my joy to succumb beneath the weight of so much glory! But since I speak in the midst of your children, your children who are my brothers, I shall continue to proclaim your praises from the depths of my heart's affection.... At your name, O Mary, Heaven rejoices, earth quivers with joy, hell fumes with impotent rage.... No, there is no creature so sublime or so humble, that invoking you, will perish. Those august basilicas, erected by the piety of mighty nations, those golden characters, those rich banners worked by royal hands, likewise the modest offerings of the sailor in your lowly chapels, in the crevices of the rock, on the shores of the sea, or even your humble picture which martyr's hands have traced upon the catacombs, all attest your power in appeasing the tempests of divine wrath, and attracting upon us heavenly benedictions.

"O Mary, I have seen the most savage wilds of nature smile at your name and blossom into beauty; the pious inhabitants of the deserts celebrate your glory, the mountain echoes, the torrent billows, vie with one another in repeating your praises. I have seen great cities bring forth and cherish, under the shadow of your name, the purest and most noble virtues. I have seen youth, with generous impulse, confident ardor, and the inexpressible charm of virtue irradiating its countenance, prefer your name and the happiness of celebrating your festivals to all the enchantments of the world and its most brilliant destinies! I have seen old men, after a godless life of sixty or eighty years, rise upon their couch of pain, to remember at the sound of your name the God who had blessed their early infancy; you were to them as a pledge of security and of peaceful entrance into the Eternal City! O Mary, who are you then? Quæ est ista? You are the Mother of our Savior, and Jesus, the fruit of your womb, is the God blessed from all eternity. You are our Sister, soror nostra es; though a child of Adam like ourselves, you have not participated in our sad heritage, and our woes excite your deepest and most tender compassion.

"O Mary, you are the masterpiece of the Divine power! You are the most touching invention of God's goodness! I could not say more—you are the sweetest smile of His mercy! O God, give eyes to those who have them not—eyes that they may see Mary and understand the beautiful light of her maternal glance; and to those who have no heart give one, that they may love Mary; for from Mary to the Word Eternal, to the Beauty ever ancient and ever new, to that uncreated Light which strengthens the feeble sight and appeases every desire of our souls, from Mary to Jesus, from the Mother to the Son, there is but a step!——

"Our dearly beloved brother—and I am happy to be the first to call you thus—behold under what favorable auspices you enter this new Jerusalem, the tabernacle of the Lord, 'the Church of the living God, which is the pillar and ground of truth. But before delivering your heart to these emotions of joy, there is one severe lesson it should learn this day; and since I am destined to be the first to announce to you the words of the Gospel, I shall conceal from you nothing of the austerity it inculcates. 'You have understood all,' you say; but let me ask if you have understood the mystery of the cross. Ah! be careful, for it is the foundation of Christianity. I speak now not only of that blessed cross which you lovingly adore, because it places before your eyes Jesus crucified in expiation of your sins, but borrowing the emphatic language of an ancient apologist of our Faith, I shall say to you: 'This is no question of the cross that is sweet for you to adore, but of the cross to which you must soon submit.' Ecce cruces jam non adorandæ, sed subeundæ. Behold what you must understand if you are a Christian and what baptism must disclose to you! ... Moreover, in vain would I endeavor to dissimulate the truth, by saying that your future may reveal no crosses; I see them in store for you. No doubt, we must venerate them from afar off, but it is infinitely better to bend beneath their weight when laid upon us, and courageously carry them. I shall be mistaken, if the evangelic virtues are not increased and fortified in your soul by patience. And blessed be God for it! You have been introduced into Christianity through Mary and the Cross! ... It is an admirable mode of introduction! And again, I repeat, blessed be God for it! For I say to you, He has given you ears to hear and a heart to feel this language! Son of the Catholic Church you will share your Mother's destiny! Look at Rome, Rome where you have just been born into the Church; her heritage here below, is always to combat and always to triumph. Moreover, nothing astonishes her; and after eighteen centuries of combats and victories, it is here, in the center of Catholic unity, at the foot of the Apostolic See, that focus whence daily emanate the most vivid and purest rays of Faith, piercing the shades of paganism, error and Judaism, that the Church has poured over your forehead the beneficent water of celestial regeneration. What do I say? It is Peter himself, the Moses of the new law, worthily represented by the first Vicar of his august Successor, who has struck for you the mysterious rock, the immovable stone. Petra erat Christus, whence gush forth those waters springing up unto eternal life.

"But I have said enough; I retard your happiness. Heaven, at this moment, regards you with love, the earth blesses you and Jesus Christ awaits you; go forward then; angels have commenced the feast, and the friends of God continue it with you here below! And even he who seems dead in our eyes, and whose heart is living in the hand of the Lord! you know him, his supplications and prayers have been poured forth in your behalf; the solemn moment has now arrived! Abraham, Isaac, Israel, the patriarchs, and prophets from their heavenly abode encourage you, and Moses blesses you, because the law in your heart has developed into the Gospel; mercy and truth sustain you, justice and peace attend you, repentance and innocence crown you.... And finally, it is Mary who receives and protects you!

"O Mary! it is a necessity and a duty for us to repeat once more this prayer, this cherished prayer, and I know that not one of all the multitude here assembled but will fervently repeat it with me: 'Remember, O most pious Virgin Mary, that no one ever had recourse to thy protection, implored thy aid or sought thy mediation, without obtaining relief. Groaning under the weight of our sins, we come, O Virgin of virgins, to cast ourselves in thy arms, and do most humbly supplicate thee. O Mother of the Eternal Word, to remember the just, remember sinners, remember those who know thee, and those who know thee not; remember our woes and thy mercy.' I shall not say remember this young man, for he is thy child, the sweet and glorious conquest of thy love, but I shall say, remember all those dear ones for whom he offers this day, the first prayers of his Catholic heart; restore them to him in time and eternity. ——

"And since I am a stranger here (no, let me recall my words, no one is a stranger in Rome, every Catholic is a Roman), but since we were both born on the soil of France, I think my prayers find an echo in the hearts of all who hear me, when I say: remember France, she is still the home of noble virtues, generous souls, heroic love.... Restore to the Church in France her pristine beauty."

The Holy Sacrifice terminated the imposing ceremony. Our new Christian, overwhelmed beneath the weight of so many favors, had to be assisted to the Holy Table, where he received the Bread of Angels as the seal of his celestial alliance. Inundated with happiness, the tears gushed from his eyes, and after receiving, it was necessary to assist him to his place.... Several pious Christians participated in the divine banquet, to which the Church so tenderly invites all her happy children, and the admirable spectacle of a blessed union with their new brother, was another edifying episode of this memorable day.

The Te Deum which followed, that most fervent hymn of gratitude, arising from every heart and mingling with the sound of all the bells, was no less impressive. "I pray God," wrote a witness of this ceremony, "never to let the memory of what I experienced during these three hours be effaced from my heart; such an impression is, beyond doubt, one of the most precious graces a Christian soul can ever receive."

Clothed with innocence, enriched with the gifts of Heaven, admitted to its joys, buried in the sweet transports of gratitude and love, M. Ratisbonne could not relinquish immediately his dear solitude. He had made one retreat, as a preparation for the reception of these three grand Sacraments, and he was filled with ineffable consolation; feeling now the necessity, the imperative duty of returning thanks to his Benefactor, he wished to commence a second retreat, so that afar from the world, he might be deaf to the confused noises of its frivolous joys, and amidst the silence of a sweet peace, celebrate the Lord's magnificence, chant hymns of gratitude, taste in secret and at leisure the gifts which had been imparted to him, and the new treasures he possessed.

Another grand consolation was in store for him. He sighed after the happy moment when he could prostrate himself at the feet of the Sovereign Pontiff, and there testified his submission to and love for that holy Church who had just admitted him into the number of her cherished children. An audience was granted him. The two friends, M. Ratisbonne and the Baron de Bussière, were conducted into the presence of His Holiness by the reverend Father General of the Society of Jesus. Having bent the knee three times before the Vicar of Jesus Christ, they received in unison, that holy and desirable benediction, which many pious Christians esteem themselves happy in obtaining, after long and wearisome journeys. They were welcomed with truly paternal tenderness by the venerable Pontiff, who conversed some time with them, and loaded them with tokens of his favor. M. Ratisbonne knew not how to express his admiration for the great simplicity, humility and goodness of this worthy Successor of the Prince of the Apostles. "He was so exceedingly kind," has M. Ratisbonne told me several times since, "as to take us into his chamber, where he showed me near his bed, a magnificent picture of my dear medal, a picture for which he has the greatest devotion. I had procured quite a few Miraculous Medals. His Holiness cheerfully blessed them for me, and these are the weapons I shall use in conquering souls for Jesus Christ and Mary."

The Holy Father crowns all his favors, by presenting M. Ratisbonne a crucifix, a precious souvenir which the young Christian will ever cherish, clinging to it in his combats and his sorrows, as a weapon that must assure him the victory over hell. A new soldier of Jesus Christ, he needs no other arms than the cross and Mary Immaculate, signal protectors that will guide him in the ways of justice, and one day, usher him into the light of eternal felicity.

Shortly after his second retreat, M. Ratisbonne prepared for his return to France, and bade adieu to the Holy City, though not without the sweet hope of again offering there his tribute of fervent thanksgiving. We have seen and conversed with him many times. The first emotions of a boundless and almost unparalleled happiness are past, but the fruits remain; daily does the precious gift of Faith strike deeper root into this soul regenerated by the waters of holy Baptism; and the divine life, which was communicated to him on the day of his baptism, our new brother nourishes by the frequent reception of the Holy Eucharist, and a withdrawal from all worldly society; for whilst awaiting the manifestations of the Lord's will in regard to his future, he feels the necessity of preserving, in the secrecy of a peaceful and recollected life, the treasures he has received.

M. Ratisbonne's conversion, publicly styled a miracle, excited too much interest and comment for the Holy See to allow it to pass unnoticed. The Sovereign Pontiff ordered a canonical examination according to the rules of the Church. The Cardinal Vicar prescribed an investigation. Nine witnesses were examined; all the circumstances weighed, and after a favorable conclusion, the most eminent Cardinal Patrizzi, "pronounced and declared the 3rd of June 1842, that the instantaneous and perfect conversion of Alphonse Marie Ratisbonne, from Judaism to Catholicity, was a true and incontrovertible miracle, wrought by the most blessed and powerful God, through the intercession of the Blessed Virgin Mary. For the greater glory of God and the increase of devotion to the Blessed Virgin Mary, His Eminence deigns to permit the account of this signal miracle, not only to be printed and published but also authorized."—A picture commemorative of the apparition of the Blessed Virgin to M. Ratisbonne, a representation of the Virgin of the medal, was placed in the chapel of St. Andrew's Church, where the miracle had taken place.

A few days after his return to France, M. Ratisbonne, in token of his gratitude, and with the intention of obtaining his family's conversion, felt urged to erect a chapel under the invocation of Mary Immaculate, in the Providence orphanage of the Faubourg St. Germain, Paris. The laying of the corner stone took place May 1st, 1842, and the sanctuary was finished and dedicated May 1st, 1844, with great solemnity, in the presence of the founder of the house, M. Desgenettes, curé of Notre Dame des Victoires, the Baron de Bussière, M. Étienne, Superior General of the Priests of the Mission and daughters of Charity, M. Eugène Boré, then a simple layman, but afterwards M. Étienne's immediate successor, the abbé de Bonnechose, later an Archbishop and Cardinal, and many other distinguished persons.

The pious convert often repaired to this sanctuary to mingle his prayers with those of the Daughters of Charity and their dear orphans; and many times has he also enjoyed the ineffable consolation of celebrating the Holy Sacrifice and thanking his celestial Benefactress, before the beautiful picture of the Immaculate Conception placed above the high altar, as a souvenir of the miracle of St. Andrew delle Fratte, for M. Ratisbonne is now a priest. Not content with leading a pious life in the world, he has renounced forever the joys and hopes of time to embrace the ecclesiastical state, which consecrated him unreservedly to God. For several years he has been associated with his beloved brother Theodore in the order of Our Lady of Sion, the object of which congregation is the conversion of Israelites.

## V.

## Graces Obtained from 1843 to 1877, in France, Germany, Italy, America.

### CURE OF A LITTLE GIRL (PARIS)—1843.

This account was sent to us in the month of January, 1877, by the very person who was cured:

"About the 15th of December 1843, a little girl, Zénobie de M., just one year old, was attacked, at the same time, by water on the chest, a disease of the bowels, and cerebral congestion. Dr. Flandrin, a friend of the family, was called in immediately, and gave the child every attention, but his skill was powerless, and the family was plunged in the deepest grief. The child's eldest sister alone cherished a faint hope in the depths of her heart; she had intended consecrating herself to God in a religious state and had always regarded the birth of this little one as a gift of Providence, sent to take her place in the family, and console her afflicted parents. God will not, she thought, take back the child. In her room was a picture representing the apparition of the Miraculous Medal; she knelt before it, begging the child's recovery, and renewing her promises of embracing a religious life should the petition be granted. This generous offering, she kept a secret. A little while after, the doctor came and declared the child's case hopeless, and moreover, its recovery not desirable as it would remain imbecile, paralyzed, or blind. He proposed, however, a consultation with M. Blache, physician of the Necker hospital, who prescribed energetic treatment, but said, 'this child cannot live.'

The poor mother, deeming it inadvisable to cause the little creature unnecessary suffering, gently laid it in the cradle, saying with the faith and resignation seen in none but a Christian mother: 'The Lord gave it to me, the Lord wishes to take it away, may His holy will be accomplished!' In the afternoon, one of the aunts came to accompany the elder sister to church, and whilst their prayers ascended to the Most High, more for the mother than the child, this mother obeys spontaneously a supernatural impulse, and taking the Miraculous Medal as a last hope, she applies it to the body of the child, and repeats with confidence the invocation: 'O Mary! conceived without sin, pray for us who have recourse to thee!' The plaintive cries ceased, and when M. Flandrin came that evening to see if the little one was still alive, he was greatly surprised to perceive a faint improvement since morning, the whole body covered with a gentle perspiration, and the little paralyzed arm able to move in any direction. 'But what a pity,' said he, 'the child will be blind,' which indeed it seemed to be already, as a light passed several times before its eyes produced no effect whatever.

"The mother who had not yet mentioned her secret, waited until all had left the room, then taking her dear medal, she lay it upon her infant's eyes and repeated the invocation. After a sound sleep of about twenty-four hours, little Zénobie awoke, recognizing all around her, and smiling upon all, her sight was restored!

"The child's father, penetrated with faith and piety, said: 'Assuredly, God alone has restored our child to us; henceforth, she shall be called Marie, that she may ever bear in mind to whom she is indebted for life.' An attack of measles now supervened and finished the work, according to the doctor, by absorbing the water on the brain, and throwing out upon the surface of the skin the heretofore internal malady. A small gold cross, having engraved upon it the memorable date of this miraculous cure, was hung around the neck of little Marie, who is now a Daughter of St. Vincent de Paul."

## CONVERSION OF A CAPTAIN IN THE AUSTRIAN ARMY.

Letter from the Superioress of the Daughters of Charity, at the Hospital of Gratz (Austria), 1860:

After the war in Italy, a Polish regiment passed through Gratz; the captain, attacked by a violent hemorrhage, was obliged to stop at the general hospital, in charge of the Daughters of Charity. Their constant and unremitting attentions did not retard the progress of the disease, and his life was in imminent danger.

Full of consideration, gratitude, and politeness for those who nursed him, he nevertheless expressed great displeasure whenever they approached him on the subject of religion; he had requested to be spared the visits of the chaplain of the regiment, and as to the hospital chaplain, he dared not present himself. It was necessary to keep the patient very quiet, and avoid all worry, for the least excitement might cause a mortal hemorrhage.

A Sister, who had been watching by his couch one night, left, in mistake, a little book containing an account of favors obtained through the Blessed Virgin's intercession. The sick man took the book and read a few pages; another Sister coming into his room, he showed her a passage, and said, putting his hand to his forehead with a significant gesture:

"Here, Sister, just read this nonsense; as for myself, I cannot understand how anyone can write such books—if I may dare, let me beg you to take this away."

Vain was every effort to reach his heart by pleasant distractions, by engaging his attention or his interest; he was insensible to all. A few days after the occurrence just mentioned, a Sister ventured to offer him a medal of the Blessed Virgin suspended to a cord, so that he might wear it if he wished. He was too polite to refuse the present, but he let it remain just where the Sister had put it. His servant, though a devout Christian, dared not speak to him of receiving the Sacraments, and, although the patient expected to leave the hospital soon, it was very evident to all else that the fever was daily sapping his strength and rapidly conducting him to the tomb. Much grieved at his condition, and especially his impenitence, the Sisters determined to make one last effort to save this soul. And what was it? They wrote the Blessed Virgin a note, as follows: "Grant that, by some means, most holy Mother, he may accept your medal, prepare him yourself to receive the Sacraments, and assist him at the hour of death. O Mary! conceived without sin, pardon our temerity, we attach this note to your statue, and leave it there till you deign to hear our prayers."

The chief physician of the hospital said, one day, to the Sister on leaving this patient's room: "The captain will die without the Sacraments, he seems inflexible." "Oh! as to that," she replied, "the Blessed Virgin will not fail to overcome his obstinacy." Three or four days elapsed; one morning the sick man requested the Sister to put the medal around his neck, which she did most joyfully. In the afternoon, he called her again: "Sister," said he, "I beg you to send for the chaplain of my regiment to hear my confession, so that to-morrow I may receive the Holy Eucharist and Extreme Unction." The worthy priest was happy to answer the summons; he remained a long time with the sick man, and next morning, after celebrating Mass at the altar of the Immaculate Conception, he administered to him the Holy Viaticum and Extreme Unction. We were all edified at the dying man's piety. He cherished his medal with religious fidelity, often asking for it and kissing it tenderly. A few days after receiving the Last Sacraments, he rendered his soul to God, saved, as we have every reason to hope, by the intercession of Mary conceived without sin.

## CONVERSION OF A HARDENED SINNER.

A letter from the Superioress of the Daughters of Charity at Issoudun, 1862:

In the month of August 1862, a young man aged twenty-nine, and who had been married several years, was dying of consumption. Vainly did his friends endeavor to turn his thoughts to eternity; every idea of religion seemed extinguished in his heart, and he positively refused to see the priest. A pious acquaintance informed the Sisters of his deplorable state; one of them went immediately to see him. She met with a cool reception, but was not the least disconcerted, and spoke to him very kindly, proposing to send him a physician, and adding that she would supply all necessary medicines and nourishment. "I need neither doctors nor medicines," was the reply, "I am going to die, and I ask only that you will let me die in peace." His poor wife, who was present, holding their little child in her arms, said to him with tears: "Accept Sister's offer, and perhaps you will recover," but he made no answer; and the Sister now turning to his wife, endeavored to console her, by promising to send the doctor and return soon herself. The doctor came and met with no better reception. In a few days the Sister presented herself again, and was received as before, all her advances eliciting no response save a frigid silence; but naught discouraged, she returned day after day, though her reception was always the same. As the young man grew worse, the Sister's prayers increased, and she felt inspired to offer him a medal of the Immaculate Conception, still hoping that the good God would lead back to the fold, this poor strayed sheep. "I accept a medal!" he exclaimed vehemently, "and what do you wish me to do with it? It would suit my wife or child well enough, but as for myself, I want no medals!" The Sister withdrew from the contest for the time, but not discouraged, she returned to the charge next morning. "Ah," said she pleasantly, "you are going to take the medal to-day?" "You know what I told you yesterday," he answered, "besides, Sister, I am afraid of becoming imbued with your sentiments should I accept it, for I perceive that you are much more unhappy than I care about being." A ray of happiness illumined the Sister's countenance, for she knew that he who fears is already conquered. After plying her with questions about religion, he concluded thus: "After all, death will be a great relief to me; I have twice made an unsuccessful attempt at committing suicide. I suffer so much that I desire nothing but to die as soon possible." Next day, the Sister asked her Superioress to visit him and offer him the medal. She did so, and he not only accepted it, but at last consented to see the priest. When our Sister next saw him he was completely changed, and expressed his joy at the priest's visit, and his desire of seeing him soon again. "Sister," said he, "I am too miserable, I wish to be like you." The priest did not delay his second coming, and the poor, suffering creature, having made his confession, asked for Holy Communion, which he had not received for many years, but this favor was denied him, his throat being so inflamed that he could swallow only a few drops of liquid. His last days were sanctified by the most admirable resignation; no one ever heard him utter a complaint, he asked for one thing only, the visits of the priest and Sister, which alone seemed to afford him any consolation. And on the Feast of All Saints, evincing every mark of a sincere conversion, he breathed his last.

## CONVERSION OF A MALEFACTOR.

A Letter from the Superioress of the Daughters of Charity, at the Hospital of Beuthen (Prussian Poland)—1865:

There was brought to our hospital, a young man of notoriously bad character. He entered our doors blaspheming, and as the physician had told the Sister that he had but a few days to live, she essayed a few words of piety and consolation, to turn his attention to the state of his soul; but he answered her by malediction. At last, one day she said to him, "My friend, since you will not listen to me, I will ask my Superioress herself to come." "Let her come," was his reply, "if she were to tell me to hang myself, I would obey her, but as for confession, she may talk about that as much as she pleases, I shall never yield." These words were followed by so many blasphemies, that it was with a very heavy heart the poor Sister sought her Superioress. "Have you given him a medal?" said the latter. "A medal!" was the reply, "he would throw it away." "Ah, well, we must put one under his pillow and trust to prayer, for it is useless to talk to him; tell him only that I say he is not worthy of going to confession, and I forbid his doing so."

As soon as the Sister who was nursing him left the presence of her Superioress, the latter threw herself upon her knees and began to repeat that beautiful prayer, the Remember. In a very few minutes the Sister returned, this time shedding tears of joy. "Ah, Sister," said she, "he wishes to confess; as soon as I had put the medal under his pillow and recited the Remember for him, I delivered your message." "Indeed!" said he, rising from his seat, "Well, I would just like to see the person that could prevent it; tell your Superioress that to-morrow morning at eight o'clock, I am going to pay the curé a visit."

The Sisters felt a little troubled concerning a confession apparently dictated by the spirit of contradiction, but their fears were dissipated when the penitent returned bathed in tears. He had just been to Holy Communion; asking the Sisters' pardon for his past misconduct, he begged them to implore the Blessed Virgin to let him live eight days longer, that he might weep for his sins. This favor was granted him, and daily did he bedew his pillow with tears. At the end of the eight days he died, blessing God, and pressing the medal to his lips.

## CONVERSION OF AN ACTRESS.

A letter from the Superioress of the Daughters of Charity, at the Hospital of Beuthen (Prussian Poland), 1865:

Some years ago, a young Protestant woman, belonging to a troupe of comedians, arrived in Beuthen with her company. The good God permitted that she should find lodgings in a Catholic family, with whom she soon essayed a controversy. "Mademoiselle," said the master of the house, "it would be better for you to go see the Sisters about these things; the Blessed Virgin has wrought wonders in their establishments, I am sure you would return fully enlightened on the subject you have been discussing." The young girl laughed at such a proposition; but a few days after, impelled by curiosity, she repaired to the hospital and asked for the Sister-Servant. "Invite her in," said the latter, who had already heard of the young actress; "no doubt, the Blessed Virgin has something in store for her here." After a few formalities of etiquette, our visitor introduced the subject of religion, and attempted to enter into a controversy with the Sister. "Alas! Mademoiselle," replied the latter, "the poor Daughters of Charity have neither the time nor learning necessary for a discussion of these subtle questions, but they have other arms with which to vanquish you;" and, smiling, she presented her disputant a little medal of the Blessed Virgin. "Promise me to wear this slight souvenir, it will be a constant reminder that we are praying for you." She allowed the Sister to put the medal on her neck, and retired rather pleased with her visit.

From this day, the Sisters at the hospital began to recommend the young actress to Mary conceived without sin. Not many weeks after, the curé said to the Sister-Servant: "Do you know, Sister, that Mademoiselle M., who spent most of her time promenading with gentlemen and smoking cigars, now comes to me for religious instruction? In a little while she will make her abjuration." And, indeed, it was not very long before she repaired to the hospital. "Sister," said she to the Sister-Servant, "I am going to confession to-day, and to-morrow I make my First Communion. On my first visit here, I was enraged at you. I could have fought you and cast to the winds this medal that I now kiss. From the very moment you put it on my neck, an unaccountable change was wrought in me." Next day, the church was filled with Protestants and Jews, all anxious to witness a ceremony which had excited so much comment. After her reception into the Church, the young convert, on the eve of her departure, paid another visit to the Sister Servant, and the latter saw by her very countenance what great changes grace had wrought in this soul. "Well," said the Sister, just to try her, "here is a silver medal to replace yours which has become very black." "Oh, no," was the earnest, prompt reply, as she tenderly pressed her own medal, "I would not exchange this for any other in the world, for it is since I began to wear it my soul has awaked to a new life."

Some years later, the Sister received a letter dated from Rome, it was from the young convert, who wrote to her as follows: "Sister, Providence has led me to Rome, and it is no longer Mlle. M. you must address, but Sister St.—— of the B. convent. Your desires are accomplished; I now belong entirely to God, as I once did to the world; the Blessed Virgin vanquishes souls with other arms than those of controversy."

We must add, to the praise of the young actress, that her moral character was always irreproachable.

The Superioress of the hospital at Beuthen, in narrating these facts, adds: "I could mention, for the greater glory of God and honor of the Immaculate Mary, numberless incidents of this kind, but lack of time and my weak eyes prevent my giving the details. I will say, however, and that without the slightest exaggeration, that not a week passes but the Blessed Virgin bestows upon our patients at the hospital some new proof of her maternal bounty. The medal, so dear to us, is miraculous, and the instrument by which we snatch from destruction souls that have cost Our Lord so much. Ah! how numberless, in this unhappy land, the snares of the enemy of our salvation to entrap souls; but to vanquish him, I everywhere circulate the Miraculous Medal (you know what numbers we get), and my confidence in Mary is never deceived."

### CONVERSION OF A PROMINENT FREE MASON.

New Orleans (United States), 1865.

Among the patients at the great Charity hospital, New Orleans, was a very prominent Free Mason. His hatred of religion was displayed in a thousand ways; not only did he interdict the Sister who nursed him any allusion to his salvation, but he even habitually repaid by harsh and injurious words her kindness and attention to his physical sufferings. If others ventured to mention the subject of religion to him, they were received with jeers and banters. Several times was he at the point of death, and yet, sad to relate, his dispositions remained the same. At last, when the Sister saw that he had but a few hours to live, she stealthily slipped a Miraculous Medal under his bolster, and said interiorly to the Blessed Virgin: "My dear Mother, you know I have spared no effort to touch this poor man's heart, but in vain; now I abandon him to you, it is you who must save him; I leave him entirely in your hands, and shall try to divest myself of all anxiety concerning him." That evening, in making her rounds, she glances at him and learns from the infirmarian that ever since her (the Sister's) last visit, he had been very calm and apparently absorbed in thought. On inquiring of the patient, himself how he felt, she was astonished at his polite answer, but remembering that she had entrusted him entirely to the Blessed Virgin's care, she did not venture a word about his soul, and bidding him good night, she left the room.

About nine o'clock, he called the infirmarian, and asked for a priest; knowing his former bitterness, the infirmarian thought it a joke and treated it accordingly; the patient repeated his request, but with no better success. Then he began to weep and cry aloud for a priest; all the other patients were mute with astonishment, and the infirmarian unable to resist such entreaties went for the chaplain and the Sister. The dying man requested Baptism, which was administered immediately, as well as Extreme Unction, and before morning he had rendered his account to the Sovereign Judge. His body was interred with Masonic rites, but his soul, thanks to the powerful protection of Mary Immaculate, had been carried by angels to the bosom of its God.

## CONVERSION OF A SICK PROTESTANT.

New Orleans (United States).

At the same hospital in New Orleans, a Sister for a long time had vainly endeavored to convince a Protestant of the most essential truths of religion, that he might receive Baptism, but he was deaf to all her persuasions. One day she showed him a Miraculous Medal and related its origin. He appeared to listen somewhat attentively, but when she offered it to him, "Take it away," said he, in a tone of great contempt, "this Virgin is no more than any other woman." "I am going to leave it on your table," was the Sister's reply, "I am sure you will reflect on my words." He said nothing, but to put it out of sight, placed his bible over it. Every day, under the pretext of arranging and dusting his room, the Sister assured herself that the medal was still there. Several days elapsed, during which the patient grew worse; one night, whilst lying awake racked with suffering, he perceived a brilliant light around his bed, though the rest of the room was enveloped in darkness. Greatly astonished, he succeeded, in spite of his weakness, in rising and turning up the gas, to discover if possible, the cause of this mysterious light. Finding none, he returned to bed, and a few minutes after, he perceived that the luminous rays escaped from the medal. He then took it in his hands and kept it there the remainder of the night. As soon as the Sisters' rising bell rang (which was four o'clock), he called the infirmarian, and begged him to tell the Sister he desired Baptism. The chaplain was immediately informed. "Impossible!" he exclaimed, for having had frequent conversations with the sick man, he was well aware of his sentiments, and could scarcely believe him in earnest. Nevertheless, he obeyed the summons, and finding the patient really disposed to profit by his ministry, he administered the Last Sacraments, and shortly after receiving which the poor man died, blessing God and the Blessed Virgin for the graces bestowed upon him.

## CONVERSION OF A PROTESTANT GIRL.

New Orleans, (United States).

A poor young Protestant girl, brought to our hospital to be treated for a grave malady, had so great a horror of our holy religion, that at the very sight of a Catholic near her, she acted like one possessed. The presence of a Sister was especially irritating, and one day she even went so far as to spit in the Sister's face, but the latter, nothing dismayed, and ever hoping that the God of all mercy would change this wolf into a lamb, continued her kind attentions, the more disrespectful her patient, the more gentle and considerate the Sister. The latter was at last inspired with the thought of slipping a Miraculous Medal between the two mattresses; she acted upon the inspiration, and the following night the Immaculate Mary's image became an instrument of salvation and happiness to a guilty soul. Pitching and tossing upon her bed by reason of a high fever, the patient, in some unaccountable manner, found the medal, and the Sister's astonishment next morning at seeing her clasping it in her hands, and covering it with kisses, was second only to that she experienced on perceiving the wonderful transformation grace had wrought in this poor creature's soul. A supernatural light had revealed to her the sad state of her conscience; her criminal life filled her with horror, and penetrated with regret for the past, she sighed only for holy Baptism. After the necessary instruction, she was baptized; and, during the remainder of her sickness, which was long and tedious, her patience and fervor never faltered. She persevered in these edifying sentiments, until a happy death placed the seal upon the graces, she had received through the intercession of Mary Immaculate.

## CONVERSION OF A PROTESTANT.

New Orleans (United States).

A Protestant gentleman had spent four years at the hospital, sometimes in one hall, sometimes another. As his malady had not been very serious, no one had considered it necessary to speak to him concerning his soul. However, when his condition became more aggravated, the Sister, after invoking the Blessed Virgin's assistance, told him the physician considered his case dangerous, and she thought he ought to receive Baptism, without which no one could be saved. He listened attentively, then turning to her, said: "Sister, if I were to ask you to become a Protestant, would you comply with my request?" "No," was the decided answer. "Well, then," he continued, "rest assured that it is just as useless for you to attempt persuading me to become a Catholic."

Despite this positive refusal, she let no occasion pass without enlightening him, were it ever so little, upon some of the truths of religion. One day, showing him a Miraculous Medal, she told him he would confer a great favor on her by reciting the little invocation: "O Mary! conceived without sin, pray for us who have recourse to thee!" "What, Sister! a Catholic prayer! that is impossible, I cannot!" She said no more, but slipped the medal under his pillow, and there it remained untouched for several days, during which time she redoubled her attentions to the physical necessities of the poor patient, who gradually grew weaker. At last, one evening she said to him: "Well, Henry, are you not going to do what I asked you?" "Yes, Sister, I most earnestly desire to become a Catholic." The chaplain was called immediately; he had barely time to administer Baptism and Extreme Unction, ere the dying man's regenerated soul was carried by angels to the abode of the blessed.

## CONVERSION OF A YOUNG METHODIST.

St. Louis (United States), 1865.

A young man, a Methodist, arrived at the hospital in an extremely weak condition. The physician at once pronounced his case hopeless, and said he had but a few days to live. Consequently, the Sister's first care was for his soul. Questioning him, she soon learned that he believed neither in the efficacy nor necessity of Baptism, and all her efforts to induce him to receive this Sacrament were unavailing. He had no desire for any conversation on the subject, and his invariable reply to all her arguments was: "I believe in Jesus, that suffices; I am sure of being saved." The Sister redoubled her prayers, for in them lay her only hope, and time was precious. A good priest visited him every day; once, after a much longer visit than usual, he told the Sister on leaving the room it was impossible to do anything with that man, unless God wrought a miracle in his favor, and they must entreat Him to do so. The poor man persisted, indeed, in refusing all spiritual succor, though receiving gratefully the attentions bestowed upon his body. His strength diminished day by day, and he calmly awaited death; one thought alone disquieted him, that of never seeing his mother and dying afar from her. Perceiving himself on the brink of the grave, he called one of his companions whom he begged to be with him at that fearful moment and wrote the particulars of it to his mother. Whilst he made this request, the Sister slipped a Miraculous Medal under his pillow, confidently believing that Mary would not let this soul entrusted to her perish; yet he was already in his agony. Two Sisters watched beside his bed till midnight, when obliged to retire, they left him in charge of an infirmarian and the young man who had promised to be with him at the hour of death. Apparently, he had not more than half an hour to live, so next morning when the infirmarian came to meet the Sister, she was prepared for news of the patient's death, but to her astonishment the infirmarian exclaimed: "Come Sister, come see him, he is restored to life!" He then told her that the patient, to all appearances, had been dead an hour; that the friend and himself had rendered all the last duties to the body, having washed and dressed and prepared it for the grave; then the young man went to bed, and he alone remained with the corpse. After watching near it some time, he approached to bandage the jaws, but what was his fright whilst thus engaged, to see the dead man open his eyes! The Sister heard no more, but eagerly hastened to the spot, and found the man still breathing. With a great effort he said: "Oh! what a blessing that you have come!" In reply, she exhorted him to receive Baptism, and told him that he was indebted to the Blessed Virgin for this prolongation of his life. "I wish to be baptized," said he, and when the Sister replied that the priest would come, "Oh! that will be too late!" was his pitiful answer. The other patients now joined their entreaties to his, and the Sister, after reciting aloud the acts of faith, hope, charity and contrition, which the dying man endeavored to repeat, with hands clasped and eyes raised to Heaven, baptized him. Whilst the regenerating waters flowed upon his soul, transports of love and thanksgiving escaped his lips. Half an hour later, he closed his eyes, never to open them here below. All that the infirmarian related of his first death, was confirmed in the most positive manner, by the Protestant friend who had assisted in preparing him for the grave.

## CONVERSION OF M. F——

St. Louis, (United States).

A Protestant named F—— was brought to our hospital in an advanced stage of consumption. He detested the Catholic religion most heartily and received the Sisters' services with extreme repugnance. His physical strength diminished perceptibly, but his mind retained its energy and clearness. By degrees, the odor escaping from his decayed lungs, became so intolerable that all abandoned him. M. Burke, a missionary priest and the Sisters, being the only persons who had the courage to go near him, and pay any atten- tion to his comfort. Yet neither priest nor Sister dare mention religion. They contented themselves with putting a Miraculous Medal under his pillow, and invoking her, who so often deigns to display her power in favor of those who deny it. She did not delay in granting their petition. A few days later, as the Protestant minister left the ward, after making his usual distribution of tracts, the sick man said to the Sister, "Sister, it is done; I am converted." "Ah," said the latter interiorly, "our good Mother has accomplished her work." And it was indeed true; for the patient requested a priest, was instructed, and in a few days received the Sacraments of Baptism, the Holy Viaticum and Extreme Unction, with inexpressible fervor. The very expression of his countenance was changed; the happiness that inundated his heart beaming from every feature. "Ah!" said he, "my sufferings are great, but I feel that I am going to Heaven; the truth has made me free." In these happy dispositions, he expired, promising that in heaven he would pray for all who had been instruments of his conversion.

### CONVERSION OF AN UNBAPTIZED PATIENT.

St. Louis, (United States).

A patient brought to the hospital in a hopeless condition, openly manifested his hatred of Catholicity. Yet, as he was in imminent danger of death, the Sister, profiting by a moment in which he seemed a little better disposed than usual, ventured to ask him if he would be baptized; he answered roughly, "No, that he scarcely believed in baptism, and not at all in Catholic baptism, that in case of his recovery, perhaps he would receive baptism by immersion, and become a member of some church, but that would never be the Catholic Church." "At any rate," added he, "I am not going to torment myself now about such things." The poor Sister having no other resource than the Blessed Virgin, and seeing that the young man approached his end, stealthily slipped a medal under his pillow. Next morning it was picked up by the infirmarian, who, thinking the Sister had dropped it accidentally, was about to return it, but the patient opposed him; the little image pleased his fancy, and he wanted to keep it himself. To quiet him, the infirmarian was obliged to ask Sister if the patient might have it. The request was granted. Towards evening someone came to the Sister with a message from the patient, he wished to see her. "Sister," said he as soon as she approached, "you have told me I could not be saved without Baptism; let me be baptized, for I wish to be saved." Filled with joy at this news, she began to instruct and prepare him for the ceremony. It took place next morning, and during the day, this soul, now the child of God, went to repose in the bosom of its celestial Father, to bless and thank Him for all eternity for His mercies.

### CONVERSION OF A YOUNG GIRL.

Buffalo (United States).

A young Protestant girl about twenty years of age came to the hospital, covered from head to foot with a disgusting itch, which the physician pronounced incurable. The Sister who dressed her sores, told her that the Blessed Virgin could obtain her recovery, and would do so, if she wore the medal and relied upon the Blessed Virgin's intercession. The poor girl knowing her case was deemed hopeless by the physician, answered bluntly: "I do not believe in your Blessed Virgin, and I want no medal." "Very well," replied the Sister, "then you may keep your sores." A few days after she asked for a medal herself, put it on her neck, received instruction and was baptized, and in a short time she left the hospital perfectly cured, greatly to the astonishment of the physicians, who had all pronounced her malady incurable.

### CONVERSION OF A SINNER.

Hospital of Gratz (Austria).

An artist whose life had been far from edifying, was an inmate of our hospital. One morning the Sister was greatly surprised at his expressing a desire to confess. Perceiving her astonishment, he said: "This morning, Sister, the chapel door was slightly open, and from my bed I could see the Blessed Virgin's statue." (It was that of the Immaculate Conception.) "It appealed so strongly to my heart, that I have had no peace since. I must put my conscience in order." He did go to confession, not once, but several times, and he often expressed great regret for his past life. "Ah!" he would say, "what a life I have led, and how sad the state of my soul when Mary came to my aid." When asked what he supposed had attracted Mary's compassion, he answered: "I was merely looking at the statue, no thought of religion was in my mind; when suddenly, recollections of my past life filled me with fear, and Mary at the same time inspired me with a horror for sin." In this instance, repentance and reparation were the immediate consequences of the Immaculate Mary's merciful and maternal glance.

### CONVERSION OF A GREEK SCHISMATIC.

Hospital of Gratz (Austria.)

A Greek schismatic, attacked by a mortal malady, was brought to the hospital. He declared his intention of remaining attached to the errors in which he had been educated, and the Sisters, seeing his determination, entrusted him to the Blessed Virgin, consecrating him to her by placing under his pillow a medal, which for him proved truly miraculous. One day, a Franciscan Father visited the sick, and the young man asked the Sister to bring the good Father to see him. He conversed a long time with the latter but manifested no intention of becoming a Catholic. Meanwhile, he grew worse, and, one day, when taken with a hemorrhage, he asked for this Father, "because," said he, "I wish to embrace the Catholic religion." The Sister was surprised, for she had said nothing to persuade him, but the Blessed Virgin had accomplished her work without earthly assistance. He confessed and made his abjuration; he even requested the Reverend

Father to announce, in a loud voice, to the other patients that he entered the Church of his own free will. His attacks of vomiting made the priest hesitate to give him the Holy Viaticum, but he insisted so strongly, and had so ardent a desire to receive, that the good God permitted these spells of vomiting to become less frequent, so that he could make his first and last Communion at the same time, which he did with inexpressible fervor and consolation. Interrogated about his conversion, he answered: "For a long time I felt that everything earthly was of little value, and I sought for the true and lasting." During the delirium of his last moments, he spoke continually of a white robe. The grace of Baptism had clothed his soul in spotless raiment, and to Mary's intercession was he indebted for it.

## CONVERSION OF AN APOSTATE.

Austria, 1866.

In one of the prisons confided to the care of the Daughters of Charity, was a young man belonging to a respectable Catholic family, whose shame and disgrace he had become. After a short stay, he fell sick, and his condition necessitated removal to the infirmary; faithful to his principles of impiety, he absolutely refused all spiritual succor, and whenever he saw one of the chaplains pass, he either turned away his head or concealed it under the bedclothes. All the Sisters begged the Superioress to make one last effort for his soul. She paid him a visit, and was received politely, but to rid himself of her importunity, he avowed himself a Protestant, and related how he came to forsake the Faith, after making the acquaintance of several very bad characters, his companions in crime and his counselors in advising him to become a Protestant. The Sister asked him if he felt no remorse for such conduct, but he became enraged and exclaimed aloud: "I am a Protestant, and I wish to live and die a Protestant!" Seeing it impossible to do anything with the miserable creature, she interiorly recommended him to the Refuge of Sinners, and merely asked him to accept the medal she offered, to wear it and sometimes kiss it. He seemed quite pleased to get rid of her so easily, and placing all her confidence in Mary, she withdrew.

The poor man passed a sleepless night, our Blessed Mother touched his heart, and very early next morning he sent word to the Sister that he wanted a priest to receive his solemn profession of Faith, in reparation of his scandalous apostasy and crimes. But his reputation was such that the prison chaplain doubted his sincerity and would not go to him except upon repeated solicitations of the Superioress. He was deeply affected at witnessing the change grace had wrought in this soul, and the consequent compunction with which the prodigal confessed his sins. The dying man then made a public abjuration of his errors, and expired a few minutes after, in the grace of God and under the protecting smile of Mary.

## CONVERSION OF A SOLDIER AT THE HOSPITAL OF CAVA.

Cava, (Italy), 1866.

A young soldier suffering from disease of the chest, was brought to the Military Hospital of Cava. His first question was to ask if the Sisters had charge of that hospital; on receiving an affirmative answer, he said to himself: "They will bother me about going to confession, so I shall call myself a Jew to get rid of them," and Jew he was designated on the card of admission. Perceiving the serious nature of his malady, the Sisters to whose especial care he had been confided, visited him as often as possible. One of them offered him a medal of the Immaculate Conception; regarding it with a smile of pity, he said: "I accept it, because it would not be polite to refuse, but believe me, I consider it a mere plaything and nothing more."

Every time the chaplain visited the hall, to speak a word of consolation to one and another, the poor Jew covered his head. The Sister sometimes ventured a few words to him about the good God, but he would never reply, and her approach was the signal for his feigning sleep. One evening when he appeared worse than usual, two Sisters went to see him just before they retired for the night. On hearing them approach, he exclaimed: "O Sister, a priest!" The chaplain was immediately summoned to his bedside, the poor dying man repeating all the while: "A priest! a priest!" As soon as the chaplain came, the patient made his profession of Faith in a very audible voice; he then confessed, and just as the priest, in administering Extreme Unction, was anointing the ears, the penitent rendered his soul to God, leaving us the consoling hope that it had found mercy in its Maker's sight.

## CONVERSION OF A WOUNDED SOLDIER.

Palermo (Italy), 1866.

In 1866, at the Military Hospital of Palermo, was a poor man who had just undergone the amputation of his left arm. His impiety was so great, that the Sister felt constrained to remove a large crucifix that had been placed near his bed, for he covered it with invectives. The miserable man's bodily infirmities were as hopeless as his spiritual, yet no one could succeed in inducing him to give any attention to his soul, or even to listen to a word about the good God. What could be done in such an extreme situation? The poor Sister was in great distress, when one day whilst dressing his wounds, she was inspired to slip a medal of the Immaculate Conception between the bandages around the stump of the amputated member. Next morning, on witnessing the great change that had been wrought in her patient's spiritual condition during the night, she was less astonished than happy, for she had confidently relied upon the Blessed Virgin. He asked for a priest, who came immediately; he confessed, publicly repaired the scandals of his past life, and received with piety the Holy Viaticum and Extreme Unction. His few remaining days were spent in blessing that God who had shown him such boundless mercy. "Oh! how good God is!" did he repeat incessantly to his companions, "I have committed manifold sins and He has pardoned me all!"

### CURE OF AN AUSTRIAN OFFICER.

Hospital of Gratz (Austria), 1867.

An officer in the garrison at Gratz, suffered from a serious wound in the right arm. He was brought to the general hospital, so that he might be more conveniently under the especial treatment of M. Rzehazeh, a very eminent surgeon. The latter exhausted all his skill, but in vain, and after a few weeks he saw the necessity of amputation to save the officer's life. Learning the doctor's decision, the patient was deeply grieved, and his oppressed heart sought refuge in piety. He who had never spoken of God, who had accepted a proffered medal only from courtesy, now appeared to experience a genuine satisfaction when the Sisters told him they would implore the Blessed Virgin in his behalf. During the few days immediately preceding the operation, he felt inspired with great confidence in his medal, and frequently repeated the invocation engraved upon it: "O Mary! conceived without sin, pray for us who have recourse to thee!" The danger was now imminent, and the amputation, which must not be delayed, was to take place tomorrow. One of the Sisters, perceiving that the young officer's confidence expressed itself in continual prayer, suggested that evening that he lay the medal upon his afflicted arm, and let it remain all night, a suggestion which was joyfully received. Next morning, she hastened to ascertain her patient's condition, and get the medal. He had spent a quiet night, his sufferings being less severe than usual; and the Sister, whilst attributing his improvement to the anodynes prescribed, understood full well that the precious medal had also been instrumental in procuring relief, and that Mary had looked compassionately upon him; but she did not yet realize the full extent of the blessing. The surgeon came a few hours after, and whilst awaiting his assistants, he carefully examined the wounded arm, he touched it, he probed it, and to his great astonishment, perceived that amputation was not necessary. The other doctors on arriving confirmed his opinion of this surprising change. The officer was mute with happiness, and not until he found himself alone with the chief surgeon did he impart to the latter, as a secret, his opinion as to the cause of this wonderful change. On leaving him, the surgeon (notwithstanding the injunction of secrecy), could not refrain from saying to the Sister: "I believe the Sisters of Charity have engaged the good God in this case."

The officer's arm was entirely healed; a few weeks later he left the hospital, taking with him the precious medal as a memento of gratitude and love for Mary Immaculate.

### CONVERSION OF M. N—— AT LIMA.

Letter from a Daughter of Charity in Lima (Peru), 1876:

M. N—— had been suffering a long time from hypertrophy of the heart, the physicians having vainly exhausted all the resources of their skill, were forced to tell the family that he was beyond the power of human aid, and should look to the state of his soul, sad news for this father of a family, and a man devoid of religion. In vain did his relatives and friends, with all possible delicacy, endeavor to turn his thoughts to religion and induce him to receive the Sacraments; he would hear nothing on the subject; a priest, who was an intimate friend of the family, attempted to second their efforts, but he met with no better success; the sick man became exasperated at all allusions to religion, he blasphemed everything relating to it, sparing not even the Blessed Virgin.

One day, after listening to an account of the conversion of M.——, of Lima, our patient's relatives expressed a desire of having recourse to similar means for their dear one's conversion. "It is very simple," said the person addressed, "you have only to ask Sister N., of St. Anne's Hospital for a medal, she got one for M. Pierre, she will not refuse you." One of his nephews was immediately repaired to the hospital and returned with a medal. A niece offered it to him; "Mamma," said she, "sends you this medal and begs that you will wear it." "Certainly," was the reply, "I will wear it for her sake, but I want everybody to understand that I have no notion of confessing."

He spent a quiet night and was quite pleased next morning to find himself somewhat better. "Euloge," said he, to one of his nephews, "what preparation should a person make who intends taking a long journey?" Euloge, who thought he certainly must be in a dream to hear his uncle speak thus, inquired to what journey he alluded. "Ah!" was the answer, "I speak of Eternity." The poor young man, delighted at such a happy change, replied that the best preparation was to put one's conscience in order by making a good confession. "I will do so, send me a priest," said his uncle. As soon as the clergyman arrived and heard his confession, he administered the Holy Viaticum. All the assistants were overcome with emotion when they saw the sick man, almost in his last agony, supported by his children, to receive on bended knee, the God who had just pardoned all the sins of his life. A few moments after, he blessed his children, gave them his parting counsel, and died in sentiments of piety rivaling his past irreligion. His family was deeply grateful to Mary Immaculate for this token of her favor.

## CONVERSION OF AN UNBELIEVER.

Letter from a Sister of Charity in Lima, Peru, 1877:

An old lady whose youth had been pious, having lost her Faith by reading bad books, had not frequented the Sacraments for thirty-five years. The Sister with whom she lived was carried to her grave, after an illness of only five days, and it was natural to suppose that the Christian death of one so dear would have softened her heart; on the contrary, it embittered her the more, and she vented her grief in blasphemies. A Sister of Charity witnessing this scandal, and not being able to soothe the poor creature, was inspired with the thought of giving her a medal of the Blessed Virgin; the old lady accepted, and wore it for several days, during which she appeared greatly pre-occupied, and somewhat less confident in her skepticism; but having yielded to a diabolical suggestion, that urged her to lay the medal aside, doubtless because grace tormented her conscience with keen remorse whilst the medal was on her person, she fell back into an habitual hardness and melancholy that she styled peace. The Sister perceived this, and inquired if she still wore the medal; on receiving a negative answer, our good Sister represented the danger to which her soul was exposed without it, and the old lady promised to put it on again. Many prayers were offered up for her, and at the end of fifteen days, the Sister, who was greatly interested in this poor woman's soul, paid her another visit; perceiving no change in her sentiments, she inquired immediately if the medal had been resumed. The poor woman, who was very uncouth, dared not speak, but made a sign with her head which revealed all. "What have you done with it, and where is it?" asked the Sister. The old lady replied that it was in her wardrobe, and she had made several ineffectual efforts to put it on again. The Sister understands that this miserable soul is under some diabolical influence, holding her aloof from aught calculated to reclaim her to God; she feels that now is the moment for prompt action, and in a tone of severity, says: "Very well, since you will not wear the medal, I abandon you entirely." These words produced the desired effect; the old lady ran to the wardrobe, and taking up the medal, put it around her neck this time to remain. Soon experiencing the sweet and powerful influence of Mary Immaculate, so justly called the Gate of Heaven, in a few days she assisted at the Holy Sacrifice and listened to the instruction, and from that time was entirely changed; she confessed and made her Easter Communion, and the deepest compunction and gratitude are now the abiding sentiments of her heart. She wished to remain at the church door, feeling herself unworthy of penetrating further into the sacred edifice, and it was with the greatest difficulty her friends could prevail upon her to accept a place nearer the altar. She never ceases to thank God and Mary; and she told the Sister that, from the moment the medal was on her neck, she knew neither peace nor rest till she had returned to her duties, so great are the power and love of that Virgin who is the sovereign Terror of demons.

## CONVERSION OF A SCANDALOUS SINNER.

Moirans, 1877.

The Superioress of the Sisters of Charity at Moirans, relates as follows a very consoling conversion, redounding to the glory of Mary Immaculate:

"The most important manufacturer of our village, who employed from four to five hundred men and women, has just died, and contrary to all expectations, his death was penitent and consoling. He had been impious and immoral, and the profligate characters in his workshops were a curse to the surrounding country. His rudeness was such that everybody trembled before him. His wife and two daughters, pious Christians, silently bewailed his misconduct; and as for myself, I had barely sufficient acquaintance with him to render justifiable my calling upon him in any urgent need.

"One morning I received a message in great haste; this person was very sick and wished to see me. I went at once, but the disease was of so serious a character and its progress so rapid, that I saw the poor man on the verge of the grave ere I could find a means of turning his thoughts to eternity. I had told his wife and daughters to give him a medal of the Immaculate Conception, but he refused to accept it, and we were reduced to the necessity of stealthily putting it under his pillow. On the third day, as I was about to leave, after rendering him all the care and attention in my power, he wished, in the effusion of his gratitude, to shake hands with me. I profited by the opportunity to tell him how much pleasure he could give me by consenting to receive the curé, who had just come to see him. He made a sign in the affirmative and with a smile that very rarely parted his lips. We went out of the room, leaving him alone with the priest, whom he had welcomed cordially. In half an hour the latter returned blessing God, for the sick man had made his confession. He now consented to wear the medal, and that evening he received Extreme Unction, but not the Holy Viaticum, as he had spells of suffocation. I asked his wife to let his employees see him, that they might be edified at their patron's conduct. The request was granted, but not many came, as the workshops were closed at this hour; those who did come prayed a few minutes beside him. Next morning his family was greatly rejoiced at his apparent physical improvement, but their hopes were deceived, and very soon his last agony began. He was recommended to the prayers of the parish; the whole village manifested a touching interest in his condition, and his employees all came to see him. The throng around the dying man was renewed every quarter of an hour, and we recited the Chaplet aloud, a most appropriate devotion for this occasion, the last moments of one whom the Blessed Virgin had snatched from eternal misery. Amidst this concert of praises to Mary, he expired. The Christian Brothers, to whom he had been very hostile, willingly aided us in rendering to him the last duties of religion."

# PROGRESS OF THE DEVOTION TO MARY: CROWNED BY THE DEFINITION OF THE IMMACULATE CONCEPTION.—I. OUR LADY OF LA SALETTE.—II. THE CHILDREN OF MARY.—III. THE DEFINITION OF THE IMMACULATE CONCEPTION

### I.—Our Lady of La Salette.—1846.

In her first manifestation to Sister Catherine, July 19, 1830, the Immaculate Virgin announced the disasters which threatened France; grief was depicted upon her countenance, tears stifled her voice, she earnestly recommended prayer to appease the wrath of God.

Sixteen years later, this Mother of mercy, appearing to two little shepherd children upon one of the summits of the Alps, repeated, in a most solemn manner, the same warnings and the same counsel. The first apparition remains in obscurity, but knowledge of the second has been spread throughout the world, and with most consoling results. The miracle of La Salette has greatly increased devotion to the Blessed Virgin and given Christians a clearer idea of the important duties of penance and prayer, which, in reality, are the embodiment of all practical piety.

We quote the best authenticated account of La Salette, that of the Abbé Rousselot, who himself received it from the mouths of the children.

"Two peasant children, Mélanie Mathieu, aged fourteen years, and Maximin Giraud, aged eleven, both simple and ignorant, as might naturally be expected of their age and condition, were together upon the mountain of La Salette, which overlooks a village where they were at service under different masters. Their acquaintance was very slight, their first meeting having been only the day before the occurrence we are about to relate.

When the Angelus announced the hour of noon, they went to soak their hard bread in the water of a spring. After this rural repast, they descended a little farther, and laying down their crooks beside another spring, then dry, they seated themselves a slight distance apart, upon a few stones which had been piled up there, and went to sleep.

"It was Saturday, September 19th, 1846, and eve of the day on which fell the Feast of Our Lady's Seven Dolors.

"'After taking the cows to water, and eating our lunch,' says Maximin, 'we went to sleep beside a stream, and very near a spring which was dry. Mélanie awoke first and aroused me to hunt our cows. We crossed the stream, and going in an opposite direction, saw our cows lying down on the other side, and not very far off.'

"'I came down first,' says Mélanie; 'when I was within five or six steps of the stream, I perceived a light like that of the sun, but even more brilliant and not the color of sunlight, and I said to Maximin: Come quick to see the bright light down here.' 'Where is it?' inquired Maximin, coming towards me. 'I pointed with my finger in the direction of the spring, and he stood still when he saw it. Then the light seemed to open, and in the midst of it appeared a Lady, she was seated, and her head resting upon her hands.' 'We were both frightened,' continues Maximin, 'and Mélanie, with an exclamation of terror, let fall her crook.' 'Keep your crook,' said I, 'as for me, I am going to keep mine. If it does anything to us, I will give it a blow with my crook.' And the Lady arose. She crossed her arms, and said to us: 'Come to me, my children, do not be afraid. I am here to tell you something very important.' All our fears vanished, we went towards her and crossed the stream, and the Lady advancing a few steps, we met at the place where Mélanie and I had fallen asleep. The Lady was between us, and she wept all the time she was talking. 'I saw her tears flow,' adds Mélanie.

"'If my people,' said she, 'do not humble themselves, I shall be forced to let them feel the weight of my Son's uplifted arm. I have stayed it heretofore, but it now presses so heavily that I can scarcely support it much longer. And all the while I am suffering thus for you, I must pray without ceasing if I wish to prevent your abandonment by my Son. And, moreover, you do not appreciate it.'

"'In vain will you pray, in vain will you strive, never can you recompense what I have undergone for you. I have given you six days of the week wherein to work, the seventh I reserved for myself, and even that is denied me! It is this which weighs down my Son's arm.'

"'Even those who drive carts must curse and mingle my Son's name with their oaths.'

"'These are the two things that weigh down my Son's arm.'

"'If the harvest fails, it is for no other reason than your sins. I tried last year to make you see this in the failure of the potato crop. You took no account of it. On the contrary, when you found the potatoes rotted, you swore and mingled my Son's name with your maledictions. The potatoes will continue to rot, at Christmas there will be none.'

"I did not know what this meant," said Mélanie, "for in our part of the country we do not call them potatoes. I asked Maximin what they were, and the Lady said to me:

"'Ah! my children, you do not understand me, I will use other language.'

"The Blessed Virgin now repeated the preceding in patois, and the remainder of her discourse was also in patois. We give the translation as follows:

"'If you have wheat, it must not be sown, the animals will devour what you sow; and should any remain, it will yield naught but dust when threshed.'

"'There will be a great famine. Before the famine comes, little children under seven years of age will be seized with fright and die in the arms of those who are holding them. Some will do penance by reason of famine. Even the nuts will fail and the grapes rot.'

"After these words, the beautiful Lady continued to speak aloud to Maximin. Though seeing the motion of her lips, Mélanie hears nothing. Maximin receives a secret in French. Then the Blessed Virgin addresses herself to the little girl, and Maximin ceases to hear her voice. She likewise confides to Mélanie a secret in French, but a lengthier secret it appears than that entrusted to Maximin. Continuing her discourse in patois, and to be heard by both, she adds: 'If they turn aside from their evil ways, the very rocks and stones will be changed into heaps of grain, and potatoes will be found scattered over the fields.'

"The Queen of Heaven then addressed herself more directly to the children.

"'Do you say your prayers with devotion, my children?'

"'Oh, no, Madame,' they both answered, 'we say them with very little devotion.'

"Our divine Mother continued: 'Ah! my children, you must say them fervently evening and morning. When you have not the time, and cannot do better, say an Our Father and a Hail Mary; and when you have the time you must say more.

"'No one goes to Mass, except a few aged women; all the rest in summer spend Sunday working, and in winter, when at a loss for something to do, they go to Mass only to ridicule religion; and during Lent they frequent the shambles as if they were dogs.'

"After a few more words, reminding Maximin that he had already seen the failure of the grain, the august Queen finished in French as follows: 'Ah! my children, tell this to all my people.' And before leaving them, she repeated the command.

"The two children add: 'Then she ascended about fifteen steps, to the place where we had gone to look after our cows. Her feet barely touched the surface of the verdure, which did not even bend beneath her, she glided over the surface as if suspended in the air and impelled by some invisible power. We followed her, Mélanie a little ahead, and I two or three steps from the Lady's side. The beautiful Lady was now gently elevated to about the height of a yard,' said the children. 'She remained thus suspended in the air for a moment. She glances up to Heaven and then at the earth, her head disappears from our view, next her arms, and lastly her feet. She seemed to melt away. There remained a brilliant light that gleamed upon my hands, and the flowers at her feet, but that was all.'

"At the first words of his son's narration, Maximin's father began to laugh, but very soon recognizing the marks of incontestable sincerity, he hastened to comply with his Christian duties, so long neglected. The neighboring inhabitants followed his example, there were no more blasphemies, no more profanation of Sunday, the whole country was soon transformed, even maternally. Like those of Jonas to Nineveh, the prophetic warnings of the divine Messenger were conditional. They were fulfilled in general, as can still be remembered."[23]

The apparition of La Salette, as is the case with all extraordinary events, was variously appreciated even among Catholics, some receiving the account with enthusiastic confidence, others strongly contesting the reality. But for a long time, doubts have ceased, Providence having, by numberless miracles, confirmed the faith of those who believed; and the mountain sanctified by Mary's presence, has never ceased to be visited by [pilgrims from the most distant countries. Mgr. De Bruillard, Bishop of Grenoble, anxious to prevent illusion on so important a question, nominated a commission composed of most competent persons, to examine and pass judgment upon this apparition. The result being in the affirmative. His Grace, in a circular of September 19th, 1851, declared as follows:

"We assert that the apparition of the Blessed Virgin to two little peasants, the 19th of September, 1846, upon one of the peaks of the Alps, situated in the parish of La Salette, of the archpresbytery of Corps, bears every mark of truth, and that the faithful are confirmed in believing it indubitable and certain.

"Wherefore, to testify our lively gratitude to God and the glorious Virgin Mary, we authorize the devotion to Our Lady of La Salette."

The circular, before publication, was submitted to the Holy See, whose approval it received, and Mgr. De Bruillard's two successors have always endorsed his appreciation of the apparition.

Consequently, this devotion is invested with every guarantee of authenticity that the severest criticism could exact.

A church of the Byzantine style and graceful appearance is erected upon the holy mountain, near where the apparition took place. The identical spot remains uncovered, and the grass still grows upon the soil hallowed by Mary's sacred footsteps; a series of crosses, fourteen in number, to which are attached the indulgences of the via crucis, indicate the path she took. The spring, formerly intermittent, has been inexhaustible since the apparition, and its waters have worked miracles. Near the church, a convent has been built to accommodate the numberless pilgrims, who daily resort hither in the favorable season. Numerous chapels, dedicated to Our Lady of La Salette, are scattered throughout Christendom, and abundant graces repay the faith of those who in these sacred shrines invoke her intercession.

## II.—The Children of Mary.—1847.

Rome, the guardian of our Faith and Catholic traditions, has given municipal privileges to the Children of Mary, in consecrating to them a chapel in one of her most celebrated churches, St. Agnes Beyond the Walls. The Italian sodalities are all inscribed there and represented by a group of the children of Mary surrounding this young Saint, who in the third century was martyred for her virginity. They seem to say to her, "Agnes, you are our eldest Sister, the well beloved of Jesus Christ and His Mother."

This place of honor, this representation proclaims most eloquently, that the Children of Mary form in the Church, a family as ancient as Catholicity itself.

Nearly nineteen centuries ago, Jesus, our Redeemer, was in the agony of death upon the tree of the cross, which his love had chosen as the instrument of our redemption; "seeing," says the Evangelist, "that all was consummated" for our salvation, He wished to place the seal upon His work, by making His last will and testament.

Looking first at Mary, His Mother, and then at John, the beloved disciple, he made John a Child of Mary in these memorable words: "Ecce Mater tua, ecce filius tuus: Behold thy Mother, behold thy son."

Such is the origin of the Children of Mary. We believe with the holy Church, that the eternal Word, after becoming incarnate to render men redeemed with His blood, the Children of His heavenly Father, gave them also, at the hour of His death, His own Mother to be theirs. We know likewise, that among the children of every family, there is always one most tenderly attached to the mother, for instance, Jacob and Rebecca; John and Mary.

Even so, in the bosom of the great family of Catholicity, do we find, in all ages, souls jealous of rendering to Mary the most intimate filial devotion, selecting her in an especial manner, for their model and protectress.

Such are the religious orders particularly devoted to her service, also, the confraternities established for the same purpose in many parishes. The Society of Jesus, which was founded in the sixteenth century, laboring zealously to extend the glory of God among the youth under its charge, found no means so effectual in forming hearts to virtue and piety, as that of placing them under Mary's protection; and the celebrated Association of the Prima Primaria, canonically erected by Pope Gregory XIII, in 1584, became the parent stem of all the congregations, subsequently found in honor of the Mother of God.

It was reserved for our age, to give full development to this fruitful devotion, by popularizing and thus making it a powerful means of salvation. In placing themselves under the patronage of the Immaculate Conception, the Children of Mary cannot fail to obtain from their divine Mother the most abundant and precious benedictions.

In 1830, the Immaculate Virgin had uttered a prophecy which resounded incessantly in the heart of the missionary, to whom was confided the account of the apparitions of the medal. "The Blessed Virgin wishes you to found a congregation, of which you will be the Superior, a confraternity of Children of Mary; the Blessed Virgin will bestow many graces upon it as well as upon yourself, indulgences will be granted it. The month of Mary will be celebrated with great solemnity; Mary loves these festivals; she will require their observance with abundant graces."

But why this command and this prediction of the Queen of Heaven to her servant, in regard to something which was not all new?

Sodalities of the Children of Mary already existed among the numberless youths educated by the Fathers of the Society of Jesus. And following their example, the Ladies of the Sacred Heart had formed similar associations among their scholars, and in 1832, had even established them for ladies in the world, under the invocation of the Immaculate Conception. It would seem then that the new work was superfluous.

It is true, Associations of the Children of Mary already existed and accomplished much good, but they were confined to a few isolated places, and recruited from a chosen class, they were not popular; and Mary designed as elements of the future work, that multitude of young girls in the ordinary walks of life, surrounded by all the trials, exposed to all the dangers of the world, who to-day form her blessed family, whose innocence she guards, whose modest virtues she encourages, and from whom she receives in exchange, a tribute of love, praises and a visible service acceptable to her heart. Let us speak a word concerning its establishment. When the apostolic heart of M. Aladel received Sister Catherine's consoling predictions, he did not fully comprehend how he, a simple missionary, should accomplish the designs of the Queen of Heaven.

Whilst quietly awaiting the propitious hour and means foreseen by Providence, he seized every opportunity to speak to the children and young people of Mary's bounty and the happiness of belonging to her. His simplicity and animation, when discoursing upon this his favorite theme, attracted all hearts; his listeners hung entranced upon the good father's words; and the unction of grace sustaining the ardor he had enkindled, the associations were formed by way of trial, in the houses of the Daughters of Charity, where M. Aladel had officiated.

Such were those of the Providence Orphanage in Paris, of the House of Charity of St. Médard, of the Madeleine; also, those of St. Flour, Mainsat, Aurillae, established from 1836 to 1846. The young girls, who were externs, very soon rivaled the inmates of the establishments in obtaining similar favors; several new associations were begun in the year 1846, those of St. Vincent de Paul, St. Roch, St. Paul, St. Louis, in Paris, and others in Toulouse, Bruguière, etc., in the province.

Whilst in Rome in 1847, M. Étienne, Superior General of the Priests of the Mission and Daughters of Charity, obtained from the Sovereign Pontiff a rescript dated June 20th, empowering him and his successors to establish among the scholars attending the schools of the Daughters of Charity a pious confraternity, under the title of the Immaculate Conception of the Most Blessed Virgin, with all the indulgences accorded the Congregation of the holy Virgin established at Rome for the scholars of the Society of Jesus.

Three years later, the Sovereign Pontiff extended a similar favor to the youths educated by the Priests of the Mission; also, to the little boys in charge of the Daughters of Charity.

The Miraculous Medal adopted as the Livery of the Children of Mary.

From this time, 1847, thanks to the benediction of Pius IX, the Sodality of the Children of Mary, spread rapidly in all quarters of the globe, wherever the Daughters of Charity were established. A manual containing the rules of the Association, its privileges, and obligations, was compiled by M. Aladel, the Director of the work. The livery naturally adopted by the Children of Mary was the Miraculous Medal, suspended from a blue ribbon.

The new Association from its very origin gave a wonderful impulse to youthful piety; humble girls, earning their daily bread, practiced the most heroic virtues, under the influence of a desire to become faithful Children of Mary; and, sustained by the same spirit, the poorest courageously resisted temptation, and complied with those duties so little esteemed at the present day—filial devotion and self-denial.

To these precious fruits are also joined some beautiful flowers of devotion; how eagerly the Children of Mary repair to re-unions of the Association, especially on all their Mother's feasts, chanting her praises and exciting one another to fervent piety.

But the death of these young girls is still more admirable than their life; many of them stricken down in the very bloom of youth, fortified with their medal and ribbon as with a precious talisman, smile at death and defy hell.

Thirty years have passed since the grain of mustard seed was confided to the earth, and it has now become an immense tree, whose branches overshadow the most distant countries. Europe numbers nearly a thousand of these Sodalities, about six hundred being composed of externs, or mixed associates. They amount, in other portions of the world, to nearly two hundred. This displays the visible effects of the benediction of St. Peter's Successor; the promises made in 1830 were not realized until they had received the approbation of the Vicar of Jesus Christ, Pius IX, whose name will always be dear to the Children of Mary.

The Associations vary in number from ten to three hundred sodalists, which gives us an average of eighty thousand young girls, courageously holding themselves aloof from satan's snares and pomps, and leading a life of purity and piety amidst the seductions of a corrupt world.

Surely this must be a miracle of God's right hand and Mary's bounty!

### III.—Definition of the Immaculate Conception.

We have observed several times in the course of this work, that the principal end of the apparition of 1830, was to popularize belief in the Immaculate Conception. The facts we have related prove most conclusively that, thanks to the Miraculous Medal, this object has been fully attained.

As a preparation for the accomplishment of this great design, Providence placed in St. Peter's chair, a Pontiff animated with the most filial tenderness for Mary, and inspired him from the beginning of his pontificate, with the desire of glorifying the most holy Mother of God, by proclaiming the Immaculate Conception an article of Faith. And this hope, this desire, had Pius IX, in the ninth year of his reign, the happiness of realizing amidst the universal applause of the Catholic world.

We quote below from M. Villefranche's beautiful History of Pius IX, the account of this memorable event:

"By an Encyclical dated from Gaëta, Pius IX had interrogated the Episcopacy of the Universal Church, on the subject of the belief in the Immaculate Conception. The answers received were six hundred and three in number. Five hundred and forty-six Bishops earnestly entreated the doctrinal definition, a few hesitated, though only as to whether it was an opportune moment or not for the decision, for the sentiment of the Catholic world was in unison as regards the belief itself.

"To assist at this solemnity, Pius IX summoned to his presence, all the Bishops who could repair to Rome. They came five hundred and ninety-two in number, and from all quarters of the globe except Russia, where they were held in check by the suspicious despotism of the Emperor Nicholas. These prelates put the finishing touch to the work of the commission charged with preparing the Bull; but at the very moment of making the final pause in its rendition, it was asked if the Bishops assisted there as judges, to pronounce the definition simultaneously with the Successor of St. Peter, and if their presence must be mentioned as judges, or, if the supreme judgment should not be attributed to the word of the Sovereign Pontiff alone. The debate terminated suddenly, as if by the inspiration of the Holy Spirit. 'It was the last sitting,' says Mgr. Audisio, an eyewitness; 'the hour of noon had just been sounded, every knee was bent to recite the Angelus. Then each one resumed his place, and scarcely had a word been spoken, when there arose a universal acclamation to the Holy Father, a cry of eternal adherence to the Primacy of St Peter's See, and the debate was ended:' 'Petre, doce nos; confirma fratres tuos! (Peter, teach us; confirm thy brethren!)' And the instruction these pastors asked of the supreme Pastor was the definition of the Immaculate Conception.

"The 8th of December, 1854, was the grand day, the triumphal day, which, according to the beautiful words of Mgr. Dupanloup's circular, 'crowns the hopes of past ages, blesses the present age, evokes the gratitude of future generations, and leaves an imperishable memory; the day that witnessed the first definition of Faith, which was not preceded by dissension and followed by heresy.' All Rome rejoiced. Immense multitudes, representing every tongue and nation on the globe, thronged the approaches to the vast Basilica of St. Peter's, far too small to accommodate all who came. Soon, the Bishops were seen forming into the line of march, ranged according to their seniority, and followed by the Cardinals. The Sovereign Pontiff, amidst the most brilliant surroundings, appeared last, whilst the chant of the Litany of the Saints, wafted to Heaven, invited the celestial court to unite with the Church militant in honoring the Queen of Angels and men. Seated upon his throne, Pius IX received the obeisance of the Cardinals and Bishops, after which the Pontifical Mass began.

"When the Gospel had been chanted in Greek and Latin, Cardinal Macchi, Dean of the Sacred College, accompanied by the Dean of the Archbishops, and the Dean of the Bishops present, with an Archbishop of the Greek rite and one of the Armenian, presented themselves at the foot of the throne, and supplicated the Holy Father, in the name of the universal Church, to raise his Apostolic voice and pronounce the dogmatic decree of the Immaculate Conception. The Pope replied that he willingly granted this prayer, but ere doing so he would invoke once more the assistance of the Holy Spirit, and now, every voice united in the solemn strains of the Veni Creator. When the chant had ceased, the Pope arose, and in that grave, sonorous, majestic voice, to whose profound charm millions of the faithful have borne testimony, commenced reading the Bull.

"He established: first, the theological motives for belief in Mary's privilege; then he adduced the ancient and universal traditions both East and West the testimony of religious orders and schools of theology, of the holy Fathers and the Councils, and finally, the pontifical records, ancient as well as modern. His countenance, as he pronounced the words inscribed upon these pious and magnificent documents, betrayed his emotion. Several times he was so overcome that for a few moments it was impossible for him to proceed. 'And consequently,' he adds, 'after having offered unceasingly in humility and fasting, our own prayers and the public prayers of the Church to God the Father through His Son, that He would deign to direct and confirm our thoughts by the inspiration of the Holy Spirit, after having implored the assistance of all the celestial court, ... in honor of the holy and indivisible Trinity, for the glory of the Virgin Mother of God, for the exaltation of the Catholic Faith and the increase of the Christian religion, by the authority of Our Savior, Jesus Christ, the blessed Apostles, Peter and Paul, and our own.——'

"Here his voice was stifled with emotion, and he paused an instant to wipe away the tears. The assistant, deeply affected as well as himself, but mute with respect and admiration, awaited in profound silence the continuation. In a clear, strong voice, slightly elevated by enthusiasm, he proceeded:

"'We declare, profess, and define, that the doctrine affirming that the Blessed Virgin Mary was preserved and exempt from all stain of original sin, from the first instant of her conception, in view of the merits of Jesus Christ, Savior of men, is a doctrine revealed by God, and for this reason, all the faithful must believe it with firm and unwavering faith. Wherefore, if anyone should have the presumption, which God forbid, to allow a belief contrary to what we have just defined, let him know that he wrecks his faith and separates himself from the unity of the Church.'

"The Cardinal Dean, prostrating himself a second time at the feet of the Pontiff, supplicated him to publish the Apostolic letters containing the definition; the Promoter of the Faith, accompanied by the Apostolic Prothonotary also presented themselves, to beg that a verbal process of the decree be prepared. And now the cannon of the castle of St. Angelo and all the bells of the Eternal City, announced the glorification of the Immaculate Virgin!

"In the evening, Rome, enwreathed in illuminations, and crowned with inscriptions and transparencies, resounded with joyous music, and was imitated at that very time by thousands of cities and villages all over the face of the globe. If we were to compile an account of the pious manifestations relating to this event, it would fill, not volumes, but libraries. The Bishops' responses to the Pope before the definition were printed in nine volumes; the Bull itself, translated under the care of a learned French Sulpitian into every tongue and idiom of the universe, filled about ten volumes; the pastoral instructions, publishing and explaining the Bull, and the articles on the subject in religious journals, would certainly require several hundred, especially if we add thereto the poems, scraps of eloquence, and descriptions of the monuments and fêtes. We should not omit mention here of the spontaneous and incomparable periodical illuminations at Lyons, each time the course of the year brings round the memorable 8th of December."

Pius IX knew that the Catholic movement leading to the definition of the Immaculate Conception had originated in France, and he was happy to see the French people enthusiastically welcome the Pontifical decree of December 8th and celebrate with unparalleled magnificence Mary's glorious privilege. Henceforth, the love he bore that country was firmly rooted in his heart, and her misfortunes had but increased his tenderness and compassion. It consoles us to insert here the prayer to the Blessed Virgin which he composed, and recited daily to obtain for her the protection of the Queen of Heaven:

"O Mary! conceived without sin, look down upon France, pray for France, save France! The greater her guilt, the more need of your intercession. Only a word to Jesus reposing in your arms, and France is saved."

"O Jesus! obedient to Mary, save France!"

# THE MIRACULOUS MEDAL AND THE WAR

The wars which have taken place since the year 1854, the epoch of the definition of the Immaculate Conception, have presented a spectacle to which the world was unaccustomed. Not only were priests called upon to administer to the spiritual necessities of the soldiers in camps and ambulances, but Sisters also were charged with the care of the sick and wounded. The priest's cassock and the robe of the religious, became almost as familiar to the eye as the military costume itself! Sisters of Charity accompanied the armies in the wars of the East, in 1854; in Italy, in 1859; in the United States, in 1861; in Mexico, in 1864; in Austria and Prussia, in 1866; in France and Germany, in 1870; and we find them ministering to the Russian army and the Turkish ambulance in 1877. For them no enemies existed; the camps of both belligerents claimed their attention, they were equally devoted to all who needed their ministry of charity.

During the hardships and dangers of war, chaplains and Sisters could not fail to invoke the Blessed Virgin, and the Miraculous Medal naturally became the sign of the soldier's devotion and the pledge of our merciful Mother's protection, against the moral and physical dangers war brings in its train. The medal was profusely distributed; it was accepted and worn with confidence; even Protestants and Schismatics asking eagerly for it; officers as well as private soldiers attaching it to their uniforms when they set out for the combat; the sick employed it to obtain recovery, or at least, an alleviation of their sufferings; the dying kissed it with love; many attributed to it their preservation in battle, and a still greater number were indebted to it for their eternal salvation.

In proof of the above, we shall present some facts, selected from the thousands related in the correspondence of the missionaries and Sisters who followed the several armies.

## WAR IN THE EAST, FROM 1854 to 1856.

"On the Feast of the Assumption, we shall have at Varna, a beautiful religious ceremony, at which the whole army will assist. I have brought from Constantinople a banner of the Blessed Virgin; this we will set up, and confidently invoking Mary, we know she will obtain the cessation of the cholera, and success of our arms." [24]

"The inmates of our hospital of Péra, at Constantinople, number about twelve hundred, including sixty officers. These gentlemen receive the Miraculous Medal with joy and gratitude. Endeavor to find some good souls who will send us a large supply of these pious objects." [25]

"The three patients whose confessions I heard were poor Irish. They manifested great resignation in their sufferings; all three asked for, and gratefully received, a medal of the Immaculate Conception. An English officer (a Catholic), who wore with pious confidence the medal of Mary, told me that several of his colleagues, though Protestants, had accepted the medal and preserved it respectfully, and that the cholera and balls of the Russians had, so far, spared them." [26]

"Even amidst the turmoil of war, and despite the multitude of sick and wounded, the Catholics of Constantinople celebrated solemnly the definition of the dogma of the Immaculate Conception. Mr. Boré wrote as follows, March 22d, 1835: 'The triduum of thanksgiving for the declaration and promulgation of the dogma of the Immaculate Conception was fixed for the Feast of Saint Joseph. We have endeavored to unite, in the expression of our joy, with that of the faithful throughout the Catholic world, and to imitate, to the best of our ability, those magnificent and most consoling manifestations that have taken place in France, who in this has shown a true love for the Mother of God, a love already repaid by a new development of national strength and vigor. The zeal and skill of our dear Sisters in charge of the adjoining establishment have greatly contributed to the splendor of the feast. The good taste and experience of one of them suggested to her the idea of substituting for the large picture over the main altar a figure of the Immaculate Conception; the Blessed Virgin was crowned with golden stars, her dress and drapery were rich and radiant in a glory of gauze, the whole framed in lilies. The head, borrowed from the portrait of a Circassian lady, and the golden crescent under her feet, were happy indications, both in color and emblem, of the events transpiring around us. A Catholic Armenian lady lent a set of diamonds, which flashed back the myriad flames of tapers and candles contained in candelabras, hidden in the abundance of lilies. This illumination, improvised by our pupils in imitation of those they knew would take place throughout France, was indeed an honor to their taste and piety.'"

"We sometimes meet with sick persons, who, through human respect, ignorance, or indifference, are prevented from receiving the succors of religion. We give them a medal of the Immaculate Conception, and the Blessed Virgin charges herself with their conversion. Nearly always, without any other inducement, and, as it were, of themselves, they ask for the priest and prepare to receive the Sacraments, manifesting the liveliest sorrow for having offended God and abused His benefits. I could cite examples by thousands."

"Numbers of soldiers wear the Miraculous Medal, the scapular, a reliquary, a cross, or sometimes not one but all of these, and those who do not possess these articles are happy to receive them. In a word, the army is, in a great measure, Catholic, and knows how to pray."

"A soldier wounded in both legs at the battle of Alma, received for more than two months, the unremitting attention of the physicians and Sisters though without experiencing any relief. Having despaired of saving his life otherwise, the surgeons decided upon amputation. They began by the limb which was most shattered. Next day the patient was in a hopeless condition; there was no question of further amputation. Recourse was then had to supernatural remedies; a novena was made to the Immaculate Mary, and in a few days the patient showed signs of improvement. He is now cured, and his piety and good example are the admiration of his comrades." [27]

"A patient who was brought in yesterday, refused to go to confession. I placed under his pillow a medal of the Blessed Virgin, and left him quiet, continuing to give him assiduous care. This morning he called me, and in a resolute tone, inquired if people here died like dogs. 'I am a Christian, and I wish to confess.' 'Yesterday I proposed confession,' said I, 'but you objected, and even sent the priest away.' 'It is true,' he replied, 'but I am sorry for having done so; I wish now to see him as soon as possible.' Since his confession he is completely changed; and calmly awaits the approach of death." [28]

"Among the Russian prisoners brought to Constantinople after the battle of Tchernaïa, many wore the medal of the Immaculate Conception. By this I understood at once that they were Catholics and Poles." [29]

"A young lieutenant in the eighty-fifth regiment, had been wounded in the skull, and when brought to the hospital, his throat was gangrened, and he could scarcely speak. A secret sympathy attracted us towards each other, and he accepted gratefully the services I rendered him. As he was evidently sinking, I spoke to him of the Blessed Virgin, and alluded to the medal he wore around his neck. He smiled and replied by pressing my hand. When his confession (during which he regained his voice and strength) was finished, he said: 'Monsieur abbé, I have a favor to ask of you.' 'What is it, my friend? tell me; I am anxious to gratify you.' 'Be so kind,' said he, 'as to inform Father Boré that I am here and am very ill.' These words pierced my heart; however, I was able to answer him: 'Father Boré is he who now speaks to you.' Raising his eyes moistened with tears, and, again pressing my hand, he added: 'I am the brother-in-law of your dear friend, Mr. Taconet, and also brother of the captain of zouaves, whom you assisted a year ago at Varna.' I then recognized in him Mr. Ferdinand Lefaivre; he had been recommended to me by a pressing letter from Mr. Taconet, but this letter reached me only after my young friend's death. Mr. Taconet wrote that, on the eleventh of May, the lieutenant with his family had heard Mass at the church of Notre Dame des Victoires, and that he did not doubt but the Blessed Virgin would watch over a life so precious. His hope was not misplaced, for the Blessed Virgin called him to herself, fortified with the Sacraments, on the day of her triumph." [30]

"While we were invoking our Immaculate Mother, on the eve of a combat, in which one of our young soldiers was to take part for the first (and perhaps last) time, he arose and went to Mary's altar; kneeling an instant, he arose again, and hung around the statue's neck a silver heart, in which were inscribed his name and the names of his parents. I feel, as St Vincent has forcibly expressed it, that he did not perform this act of devotion without tearful eyes and a sobbing heart." [31]

"A serious fire had broken out in the city of Salonica. The flames soon appeared opposite the Sisters' house, the buildings on the other side of the street, a few yards distant, being seized and devoured by the fire, which the wind continued to fan into activity. Already the Sisters' roof and that of the adjoining house were covered with dense smoke. I cast therein several Miraculous Medals. There was no prospect of human succor, as the rumor of there being powder in the vicinity had caused everyone to seek safety in flight. I also retired, deeming it useless to expose myself longer; and besides, I was obliged to go to the assistance of a poor man, who, partially intoxicated, persisted in remaining near the fire. I returned shortly after, expecting to see our houses in flames; I doubted not but they would be wholly consumed. As I approached, a young man stopped me on the way, and said: 'Your property is saved, sir; the Sisters' house is not even in danger.' Only on reaching the scene could I be convinced that he had spoken truly. It would be impossible to express my emotion at the sight. I sent to inform our dear Sisters of the fact and they could scarcely credit this marvelous preservation. It suffices to add, that all Salonica is unanimous in pronouncing it a miracle." [32]

"In an ambulance crowded with Russians was a young Pole, severely wounded and suffering intolerable pain; he earnestly invoked the sweet and merciful Virgin Mary. By his side lay a Russian Protestant, wounded also, and attacked by violent dysentery. So offensive was the odor from his disease, that both patients and nurses complained. He appeared utterly indifferent to everything concerning religion. He took no notice of the Sister as she passed and repassed; he never even deigned to look at her. The young Pole, on the contrary, called her frequently, and gratefully received her care and consolations. One evening our young Catholic was suffering more than usual; the pain drew tears from his eyes; his groans and cries were incessant. He called the Sister and begged her to help him, saying his patience was exhausted; he was in despair; his sufferings were excruciating. The Polish Sister, consoling and encouraging him, bade him have confidence, and gave him a medal to apply to the wounded limb. The young man followed her suggestion; and laying his hand on the medal to keep it in place, he soon fell asleep. Our Protestant appeared unconscious of what was going on, yet he had seen and examined all. Some days after, he called our Polish Sister to him, (she was the only one who could understand him) and said: 'Sister, please give me what you gave this young man that did him so much good, for I suffer greatly!' 'My friend, she replied, I desire nothing better than to relieve you also; but you lack what effected his cure, faith, and confidence. You Protestants deny the power of the Blessed Virgin; you do not acknowledge her as your Queen, your Advocate, your Mother. So, what can I do? It was a medal of Mary that so speedily relieved your neighbor, the young Pole.' 'Give me one also, Sister,' he answered, 'I believe all that you tell me; you do good to everyone, why should you deceive me?' 'But,' said the Sister, 'have you confidence in Mary, the Mother of God? Do you believe in her mercy and her power?' 'I believe all that you believe, Sister, since Mary hears the prayers of the unfortunate, and brings relief to the suffering, she cannot deceive us!' The Sister, much consoled at hearing these words, gave him a medal, and our admirable talisman affected in his soul the most gratifying results. He asked to receive instruction from a priest, and after some days employed in studying the holy doctrines of the Church, and in assiduous prayer to Mary he abjured his errors. As he had been separated from the other patients, on account of the unpleasant odor we have mentioned, he was at full liberty to act as he wished. After his baptism, and the reception of the holy Eucharist, being unable to restrain his transports, he exclaimed: 'Oh, how happy I am! My heart has never known such joy! I am content to die, and I do not regret having been struck on the battlefield! To my wound do I owe my salvation. Oh! how we poor Protestants are deceived! By what lies are we led astray! How good God is to rescue me from error! May the sweet and holy Virgin be known and loved always and everywhere!' And in these beautiful dispositions, he expired." [33]

"A sergeant advanced in years had been suffering for three months from a severe dysentery; one morning the Sister who was visiting the sick found him in tears. 'Ah! my brave soldier,' said she, 'what is the meaning of all this grief?' 'O Sister,' he exclaimed, 'lend me patience, for mine is exhausted. I am in despair; I can endure my sufferings no longer; I feel that I am going to die, and just at the time I was to receive a pension—at the very moment I hoped to return to my country with honor and see my family once more. Must I die afar from home and leave my bones in a strange land?' Groans were mingled with his words, and his gestures had all the violence of despair. The Sister who relates the fact says: 'My heart ached at witnessing the grief of this brave man, with his white hairs and numerous scars. However, as my tears would not have dried his, I tried to rouse his courage by other means, and I promised him a perfect cure if he would unite in prayer with our little family at the hospital. Giving him a Miraculous Medal, I recommended him to God and Mary with my whole heart. We made a novena to the Immaculate Virgin, and ere its termination our sergeant was entirely cured." [34]

"Every evening our soldiers assembled around the Sisters in charge and sang pious canticles; they even composed music and words suited to the occasion. These they intoned, uniting their deep, sonorous voices with the Sisters'. In unison and harmony of mind as of voice, they repeated in chorus the sacred names of Jesus and Mary as a rallying cry of hope, confidence, and triumph—a chant of love, a united echo of heaven and country. Then their hearts thrilled with joy inexpressible, and they were filled with pride and happiness at the thought of belonging to that France who imparts to her children the heroism of courage and the virtue of the perfect Christian. During the month of May our military concerts were multiplied; all were rivals in zeal. The altars were adorned with admirable piety and taste, notwithstanding our extreme poverty. Entire trees were felled to assist in concealing the dilapidated state of the barracks, which had been converted into chapels. Had our soldiers been free to do so, they would have despoiled the gardens of the Turks to adorn the sanctuary of the Queen of Heaven.

"In the ambulances of Péra some of the most zealous soldiers, both officers and privates, wished to present Mary a solemn homage of their devotedness and gratitude. They chose a heart as the symbol of their sentiments. All the balls extracted from their wounds were collected to compose the offering. But a soldier suddenly exclaimed with enthusiasm: 'Comrades, what are we doing? Shall we offer the Blessed Virgin a schismatical heart? All

these balls are Russians!' 'True,' replied another, 'these balls are Russian; we must have French balls. Let us ask the Russians for those we sent them.' 'Stay,' said a third, 'you have forgotten that these Russian balls are stained with our blood!' 'Well, then, let us use them,' suggested a fourth, 'the French balls will form the center.' They went immediately to ask the Russians for the French balls. These were willingly given. The heart was prepared; their names inscribed on it with the designation of the regiment, and the offering was presented to Mary amid the most lively acclamations and transports of joy and gratitude."
[35]

## ITALIAN WAR, 1859.

Letter of Sister Coste:

Gaëta, December 18th, 1860.

During the siege of Gaëta, the Sisters of Charity willingly remained in the city, to assist the sick and wounded Neapolitans. They felt that there was no greater security against the dangers to which they were exposed, than that of recommending themselves and their abode to the protection of the Blessed Virgin, by means of the Miraculous Medal. Their Superioress, Sister Coste, wrote December 18th, 1860: "Frequently the cannon roars in our ears; bombs whiz around us, but divine Providence is our shield. The first night of our sleeping at the palace, we were saluted by the Piedmontese, who sent us a multitude of bombs; one of them burst just outside our room, and you might have supposed a thunderbolt had fallen. Yet, the precious medal of our Immaculate Mother, which we had placed at all the doors and windows, shielded us from danger. A large piece of iron detached itself from the bomb mentioned above, and remains in the wall, a visible testimony of Mary's protection. This circumstance reanimated our confidence, and we hesitate not to pass through the streets, notwithstanding the whizzing of projectiles."

## UNITED STATES.

Extracts of letters written by Sisters of Charity during the War of Secession, from 1861 to 1865:

"Military Hospital (House of Refuge),}

"St. Louis, Missouri.}

"Many of our poor soldiers scarcely knew of the existence of God, and had never even heard baptism mentioned. But, when the Sisters explained to them the necessity of this Sacrament, and the goodness of God, who, by means of it, cleanses us from the original stain, and adopts us as His children, they were filled with the deepest emotion, and often shed tears. On one occasion, a patient said: 'Sister, do not leave me; tell me more about that good God whom I ought to love. How is it that I have lived so long and have never heard Him spoken of as you have just done? What must I do to become a child of God?' 'You must,' replied the Sister, 'believe and be baptized.' 'Well, baptize me,' was his answer. The Sister persuaded him to await the arrival of Father Burke, who would be there the next morning. The patient consented reluctantly. 'Ah!' said he, 'it is very long to wait, and I am so weak; if I die unbaptized, I shall not go to Heaven.' To relieve his anxiety, the Sister promised to watch near him and administer baptism, should she perceive any unfavorable change in his condition. 'Now,' said he, 'I am satisfied; I rely on you to open for me the gates of Heaven; it is through your intervention I must enter.' He spent a quiet night. Next morning, Father Burke admitted him into the Catholic Church, by the Sacrament of Baptism, which he received with admirable piety. A crucifix was presented to him; grasping it eagerly, he kissed it, saying as he did so: 'O my God! I did not know Thee or love Thee before coming to this hospital!' Then, turning to the Sister, he said: 'Sister, I have forgotten the prayer you taught me;' and he repeated after her several times, 'My Father, into Thy hands I commend my spirit, sweet Jesus, receive my soul.' He died pronouncing these words."

"The precise number of baptisms cannot be ascertained; there were probably seven hundred during the two or three years of our residence in the hospital. Five hundred Catholics who had led careless or sinful lives returned sincerely to God and resumed the practice of their religious duties. A great number of these had received no other Sacrament than that of Baptism, and they made their first Communion at the hospital. The majority of the newly baptized died; the others on leaving asked for medals and catechisms, saying they desired to instruct themselves and their families."

"A soldier named Nichols fell dangerously ill, and in a few days was reduced to the last extremity. Vainly did we strive to touch his heart and awaken him to a sense of religion. His sufferings were terrible; both day and night was he denied repose, and he could scarcely remain a moment in the same position. His condition was most pitiful. Many of his companions, knowing that he had never been baptized, and having perceived the beneficial effects of baptism upon others, begged the Sisters to propose to him the reception of this Sacrament, thinking it might be a comfort to him, and not being aware of the many efforts that had already been made to induce him to believe in its necessity and efficacy. However, we redoubled our efforts, and placed a Miraculous Medal under his pillow. His comrades regarded his sufferings as a visible chastisement of his impiety. We could not induce him to pronounce the name of God, but he implored the physician, in the most heart-rending accents, not to let him die. Four days passed without the least change, when one of his companions, who appeared the most deeply interested in his welfare, said to him, with eyes filled with tears, how much he regretted to see him die thus, utterly bereft of a hope for the future. The other soldiers had engaged this man to acquaint the patient with his danger, and persuade him to make his peace with God, for they saw that human respect alone prevented his showing any signs of repentance. This last effort of charity was crowned with success; he called for the Sister, and when she came, said to her: 'Sister, I am ready to do all you wish.' After instructing him in what was necessary for salvation, and feeling convinced of the sincerity of his dispositions, she asked him by whom he wished to be baptized. 'By any one you please,' was his answer. But to be sure that he did not desire a Protestant minister, she said: 'Shall I send for the priest who attends this ward?' 'Yes,' he replied, 'it is he I wish to baptize me.' The priest was sent for without delay, and we had the inexpressible consolation of seeing this poor sinner admitted into the number of the children of God by the very person who, a few days previous, had been an object of his raillery. He became perfectly calm, and expired shortly after, invoking the holy name of Jesus."

"Among the patients was a poor young man named William Hudson, who for a long time refused to receive baptism. The Sisters, however, nowise discouraged, explained to him the Sacrament of Baptism, and instructed him in the mysteries of our holy religion, and the Sister, under whose immediate charge he was, hung a medal around his neck. Finally, he asked to speak to good Father Burke; was baptized, and expired in the most edifying dispositions, pronouncing the holy name of Mary. Several others followed his example and made their peace with God before death."

"Mr. Huls, a man of thirty-five, though convinced of the necessity of baptism, postponed the reception of it from day to day. Knowing that he had but little attraction for our holy religion, I forbore to mention the subject too frequently. Nevertheless, seeing that death was rapidly approaching, I placed a medal under his pillow and begged the Blessed Virgin to take charge of his salvation. The next day, just as I was turning away after giving him a drink, he called me and said: 'Sister, what ought I to do to prepare for the next world?' I told him that it was necessary to repent of his sins, because sin is the greatest of evils, and it had caused the sufferings and death of our Lord Jesus Christ; that God's goodness and mercy towards sinners are infinite, and that He is always ready to pardon us, even at the last moment, if we sincerely return to Him. I urged him to cast himself with confidence into the arms of this merciful Father, who earnestly desired to open for him the gates of the Eternal City, and I added that it was necessary to be baptized. He assured me that he believed all I had said to him; he then repeated with fervor the acts of faith, hope, charity, contrition, and resignation to the will of God. Seeing that he was entering into his agony, I baptized him; the Sacraments appeared to revive his strength. He began to pray and made such beautiful aspirations of love and gratitude to God, that one might have said his good angel inspired them, particularly the act of contrition. I remained with him to the last, praying for him, when he had not strength to do so himself; if I paused a moment through fear of fatiguing him: 'Go on Sister,' he would say in dying accents, 'I can still pray.'"

"Another soldier, William Barrett, scarcely twenty years of age, was almost in a dying condition when brought to the hospital. After doing all I could for the relief of his poor body, I inquired very cautiously as to the state of his soul. Alas! it was deplorable; not that he had committed great crimes, but that he was entirely ignorant of everything relating to his salvation. He had never said a prayer, and he hardly knew of the existence of a God. My first conversation with him on the subject of religion, was not altogether pleasing to him, for he did not understand it; but when I had briefly explained the principal articles of Faith, he listened very attentively, and begged me to tell him something more. When I told him that our Lord had loved us so much as to become man and die on a cross for our salvation, he could not restrain his tears: 'Oh!' said he, 'why did no one ever tell me that? Oh! if I had only known it sooner! How could I have lived so long without knowing and loving my God!' I now prepared him to receive the Sacrament of Baptism and tried to make him sensible of God's great mercy, in bringing him to the hospital, that he might die a holy death. He understood this and much more, for grace had spoken to this poor heart, so truly penetrated with sorrow for sin. 'I wish to love God,' said he, 'but I am such a miserable creature! I would like to pray, but I do not know how. Sister, pray for me, please.' I promised to do so, and offering him a medal of the Blessed Virgin, I told him that by wearing it, he would secure the intercession of the Mother of God, who is ever powerful with her divine Son. He gladly accepted the medal, put it around his neck, and repeated, not only the aspiration, O Mary! conceived without sin, pray for us who have recourse to thee, but other prayers, to obtain the grace of a happy death. He then asked me when I would have him carried to the river, for he was under the impression that he could not be baptized without being immersed. I explained to him the manner in which the Catholic Church administers this Sacrament, and the dispositions necessary for receiving it. Listening eagerly to every word I uttered, 'Pray with me, Sister,' said he, 'come nearer, that I may hear you better, for I do not know how to pray.' He repeated with great fervor all the prayers I recited and thought only of preparing himself for his baptism which was to take place on the following day. From that time, he wished to converse with the Sisters only. If his companions or the attendants came to him, he answered them in a few words, evidently showing that he desired to be alone with his God. One of the officers asked him if he wished any one to write to his family. 'Do not speak to me of my family now,' said he, 'the Sisters have written to my parents. I wish for nothing but to pray and to be baptized.' And the words ever on his lips, were these: 'O God, have mercy on me, a sinner.' Towards evening he became so weak that I thought it best to remain with him. At three o'clock in the morning, fearing that he was in his agony, I administered the Sacrament of Regeneration; he lived till seven o'clock. The fervor with which he united in the prayers was truly edifying; even when scarcely able to speak, he tried to express his gratitude to God for His goodness and mercy to him. He was most anxious to quit this world, that he might go to that Father, who had admitted him into the number of His children, and whom he so earnestly desired to see and know."

"A soldier, advanced in age, told me one day, that in his country the prejudices of the people were so strong against our Faith, that they would refuse hospitality to a traveler did they know him to be a Catholic; as to himself, he had never met with a Catholic previous to his coming to the hospital; but what he had seen here (nothing comparable to which had he ever witnessed among Protestants), was sufficient to convince him of the truth of Catholicity; that he had belonged to the Presbyterian Church, but he would remain in it no longer, and desired to be instructed in our holy religion. I gave him a catechism and some other books, which he read with great attention. Perceiving that his end approached, he asked for a priest and was baptized. 'If it were the will of God,' said he, speaking of his property, which was considerable, 'I should like to live a little longer and enjoy my fortune; but if the Lord wills otherwise, I am ready to leave all.' He was ever repeating these words: 'Not as I will, O Lord, but as Thou wilt.' From the moment of his baptism, he applied himself most diligently to a profitable disposition of the remainder of life, that he might prepare for his journey to eternity. At times, when he felt a little stronger, he studied the catechism; and when he could no longer hold a book, he prayed and meditated in silence. One day as I was giving him a drink, he showed me his medal. 'Ah!' said he, tears of gratitude streaming down his cheeks, 'behold! my Mother. I kiss her every hour!' He prayed constantly, even when he could neither eat, drink, nor sleep. Once when he was extremely weak, the attendants having changed his position, he fainted, and rallied only with great difficulty. On perceiving that I was trying to restore him: 'Ah! Sister,' said he, 'why did you not let me go?' He also remarked to the attendants that he feared the Sister would prolong his life for a month, but his fears were not realized; in a few days he slept the sleep of the just.

"One of the soldiers, who had been a long time in the hospital, having fallen very ill, I tried to persuade him to make his peace with God, before going to meet that God as his Judge. My efforts met with little success; he did not admit the necessity of baptism, and he was not in the least concerned about his salvation. But he accepted a medal, and without being aware of it, he swallowed some drops of holy water. Then I recommended him very earnestly to the Blessed Virgin, and in a few days after he asked to be instructed and was baptized. We could not give him greater pleasure than to pray beside him. He received Extreme Unction with deep and sincere devotion and expired in the happiest dispositions."

"In the hospital was a soldier named Sanders, who, though not very ill, was unable to join his regiment. He had no idea of religion. I remarked that he observed us very closely, as if examining our conduct; nothing escaped him. Before leaving, he came to bid me goodbye and thank me for the care I had bestowed upon him. I was somewhat surprised, as I had had no occasion of serving him; but, seeing he was so well disposed, I profited by the opportunity to offer him a medal and a book explaining the Catholic Faith. He accepted them with gratitude and returned to his regiment. A year later, he came again to the hospital, hastening to inform me of his conversion, and seeking a priest, by whom he was gladly instructed and received into the fold of the Holy Church. 'I owe my conversion,' said he, 'to the intercession of the Immaculate Mary and your prayers, and it has been my happy lot to bring other souls to God.' This was, indeed, the case; employed in a military hospital, where he was the only Catholic, by his zeal and solicitude he instructed many poor sick, called a priest, had them baptized, and enjoyed the consolation of procuring eternal happiness for many his fellow-soldiers."

"In 1862, a Sister of the hospital at New Orleans gave a medal to one of the attendants on the point of setting out for the army, and she advised him to keep it always about him. Sometime after, he returned, having received a slight wound on the head. On seeing the Sister, he exclaimed: 'Sister, here is the medal you gave me; it has saved my life! Just in the midst of battle, the string by which the medal hung around my neck broke, and whilst the cannons were roaring around us, I attached it to a button of my uniform; all my companions fell, and I escaped with this slight contusion.'"

## Military Hospital of Philadelphia.

"A soldier was brought to the hospital grievously wounded. A few questions which the Sister put to him on the subject of religion revealed the fact that not only was he not baptized, but also most ignorant of the truths essential to salvation. The Sister then began to instruct him, and with all requisite prudence, gave him to understand that the physicians despaired of his recovery. From this moment he listened with the deepest interest to explanations of the catechism; and, one day, when Sister had spoken to him of the necessity of that Sacrament which renders us children of God and heirs of heaven, he joined his hands and said in the most beseeching tone: 'Oh! do not let me die without baptism!' The Sister then asked him from what minister he desired to receive this Sacrament and he replied: 'From yours; from him who says Mass in the Sister's Chapel.' Before the close of the day, Father MacGrane had satisfied the sick man's pious desire, and the new Christian, filled with joy, incessantly repeated acts of love and gratitude. The physician, making his evening visit, found him so ill that he directed the attendant to watch him all night, saying he might die at any moment. Before retiring, the Sister gave him a medal of the Blessed Virgin, and briefly narrating to him how this tender Mother had often wrought miraculous cures by means of her blessed image; she encouraged the dying man to address himself to Mary with entire confidence.

"Next morning, she was surprised to find him better; but he was much troubled about 'his piece,' which he could not find; he feared it had been taken away. The Sister soon found and restored it to him; receiving it most joyfully, he asked for a string and placed the medal over his wound. When the physician came, which was soon after, he was no less surprised than the Sister at perceiving the change in his patient's condition. The patient, (Duken by name), continued to improve, and in a few weeks, he could walk with the aid of crutches. His first visit was to the chapel; from that day, whenever we had Mass, he rose at five o'clock in order to attend it; and so eager was he for Father MacGrane's instructions, that the intervening time from one Sunday to another seemed to him very long. He attributed his cure to the Blessed Virgin, and it was indeed most remarkable; for he was out of the physician's hands long before many other soldiers of the same ward whose wounds were less dangerous, and who had received the same attentions, were able to leave their beds. He asked for a furlough that he might visit his wife, whom he was very anxious to see a member of the true Church, but 'knowing her prejudice against Catholics, he dared hope for such a happiness.' It was, nevertheless, granted him; she consented to be baptized with her children, and Duken returned to the hospital, blessing God and the holy Virgin for the wonderful graces bestowed on his family.

"Our Sisters of the South, like those of the North, were in great demand wherever sufferings and miseries claimed relief, and they responded to the call with holy courage and eagerness.

"In these divers localities was the Miraculous Medal the instrument God frequently employed in delivering souls from the yoke of Satan. How often have we seen Mary's image kissed respectfully by lips which had formerly uttered only blasphemies against the Mother of God! Everyone asked for a medal; some, no doubt, urged by curiosity or the desire of possessing a souvenir of the Sisters, as they themselves acknowledged; but, even so, they could not carry upon their person this sweet image, without growing better and experiencing the effects of Mary's protection. In nearly every case, what rendered the triumph of grace still more remarkable was the fact of its acting upon men who were not only ignorant, but fanatical, hating the name of Catholic, and excited to fury at the sight of a priest. A Sister relates that she ventured, one day, to ask a soldier, who was in the threshold of eternity, if he had been baptized. 'No,' was the reply, in a voice of thunder; 'no, and I have no wish to be plunged in water just now. Let me alone!'

"'Recommending him to Mary,' says the Sister, 'I left him. Towards evening, I heard a noise in the ward in the direction of his bed, and the attendant came in haste to say that the patient had sent for me.' 'Ah!' said the latter, in a tone very different from that of his morning's speech; 'I am dying, baptize me, I beg of you.' 'Giving him briefly the necessary instruction, I administered the holy rite, and a few hours later he peacefully expired.'

"Rarely did these poor soldiers complain of their fate; though but little accustomed to the rigors of military life, they bore them with admirable patience. However, there was one exception to the general rule, that of an old soldier, who murmured continually and accused God of afflicting him unjustly. Arguments were worse than useless, they served but to aggravate the evil. Failing in this means to bring him to a better state of mind, I offered him a medal of the Blessed Virgin. By degrees, his complaints ceased, his countenance became composed and serene, and I had the consolation of seeing him expire in the most edifying dispositions."

## THE WAR BETWEEN PRUSSIA AND AUSTRIA, 1866.

Letter of Mr. Stroever, Priest of the Mission, July 1st, 1867:

"The wounded arrive in great numbers, and all our houses are filled. Everyone wishes to have a medal; I inquired of one, who had begged for a medal at any price, if he were a Catholic. 'No,' was the answer; 'I am a Protestant, but I would like to have it as a souvenir of yourself;' and he received it most gratefully.

"We observe a certain degree of piety among the soldiers, and the sick are most eager to receive the Sacraments. The Protestants show a remarkable inclination to Catholicity. Not only the private soldiers, but even persons of distinction, wishing to have medals, scapulars, or a crucifix. They take no measures to conceal these objects of devotion, and no one seems surprised at seeing them on their persons."

## REMINISCENCES OF THE COMMUNE, PARIS, 1871.

Notes of a Sister of the Hospital d'Enghien:

"During the siege, we had placed Miraculous Medals over all the doors and windows of the house. As one of our Sisters expressed the intention of concealing them, Sister Catherine exclaimed: 'No, no; they must be seen; put them in the middle of the principal entrance.'

"During the few days immediately preceding our departure from the house, the federal national guards said to one another: 'Let us go and ask the venerable Sister Catherine for medals; she has given some to our comrades who have shown them to us, we would like to have them too.' 'But you, poor creatures,' replied a Sister, 'you have no faith, no religion, what good will the medal do you.' 'Very true, Sister,' said they, 'we have not much faith, but we believe in the medal; it has protected others, it will also protect us, and when we go to battle, it will help us to die as brave soldiers.' Good Sister Catherine gave medals to all who presented themselves, and many, who belonged to the enemy, sent their comrades to procure them.

"After the army had entered Paris, thirty of the wounded insurgents, before being brought to trial, were sent to the Hospital d'Enghien to be nursed by the Sisters. The house was already transformed into an ambulance, and we were obliged to take one of the dormitories of the orphans for the newly arrived patients. The appearance of these men was so frightful, that Sister Eugenie who had been appointed to attend them, had not the courage for the first two days to make any suggestions to them concerning religion; but finally, feeling that she must comply with her duty, and urged by the advice of a companion, she went to Sister Catherine and asked for medals for the insurgents. Sister gave them cheerfully and encouraged her to use this powerful means of inspiring these unfortunate men with Christian sentiments. Animated by this thought, Sister Eugenie repaired the ward, and much affected, proposed to say evening prayers. 'Yes, Sister,' answered some among them. Trembling, she began; but at the Creed, overcome by excitement and terror, she wept like a child, and was obliged to pause. When she recovered her voice, it was not to continue the prayers, but to tell the prisoners how much she felt at the thought that on the morrow, they would be judged and perhaps condemned; then making them a brief exhortation, inspired by the circumstances, she offered to give each one a medal of the Blessed Virgin, begging them to retain it about their person, happen what might. The proposition was accepted immediately, but Sister Eugenie was too frightened to give the medal into their hands; in the middle of the night, when all seemed to be asleep, she quietly placed a medal under each one's pillow. How great was her joy next morning, to see all these poor insurgents with the medal around their neck.

"The Superioress came into the hall where the men were collected and asked if they wished a priest to come and hear their confessions. All consented with unequivocal signs of gratitude. A good priest, one of the hostages of the Commune, came and heard their confession. On leaving them he seemed much consoled, and said he had every reason to hope for their salvation. The unfortunate men left the house at seven o'clock and were conducted to Versailles; they were calm and resigned, and when about to leave, showed the Sisters the medal they wore. Doubtless, God accepted the sacrifice of their life in atonement for their faults."

# Recent Apparitions of the Blessed Virgin in France, Italy, and Germay

## THE CONFIDENCE WITH WHICH THESE APPARITIONS SHOULD INSPIRE US.

The definition of the dogma of the Immaculate Conception, has, in our age, brought to its climax, devotion to the Blessed Virgin. Divine Providence employed twenty-four years in preparing the world for this great event; we have seen in the preceding chapters, how much the apparition of 1830, contributed thereto, and how powerful the influence of the Miraculous Medal in propagating this devotion. Since this time a second period of twenty-four years has elapsed, during which devotion to the Immaculate Mary has shone as a radiant star in the firmament of the Church, spreading everywhere the light of truth and the warmth of true piety; and, by a gentle yet efficacious impulse, producing unanimity of mind and heart in the great Catholic family.

Since the definition, as well as before it, France continues to be the privileged country of Mary; nowhere else are miracles so numerous, or graces so abundant. Whence arises this glorious prerogative. So far as we are permitted to penetrate the secrets of God, it appears to us, to our understanding: France who has wrought so much evil by disseminating philosophical and revolutionary doctrines, is to repair the past by propagating truth, and Mary desires to prepare her for this mission. Everyone knows, moreover, that the French character possesses a force of expansion and a power of energy that render the French eminently qualified to maintain the interests of truth and justice. Then, again, is not France the eldest daughter of the Church, since she was baptized in the person of Clovis, the first of the Most Christian Kings; and in virtue of this title, is it not her duty to devote herself under the patronage of her Mother in heaven to the defense of her Mother on earth?

Be the motives of Mary's predilection for the French nation what they may, the fact is incontrovertible. Nevertheless, the Blessed Virgin has not forgotten other Catholic countries; they also have had their share in the singular favors she has so generously dispensed in our days.

## OUR LADY OF LOURDES.—1858.

Four years after the definition of the Immaculate Conception, Mary vouchsafed to manifest herself anew to the world, and this time, as if in token of her gratitude, she took the glorious name the Church had just decreed her: "I am the Immaculate Conception." It was in France that the vision of the medal took place, preparatory to the act of December 8th, 1854; it was also in France, at Lourdes, in the diocese of Tarbes, at the base of the Pyrenees, that Mary came in person, to testify and proclaim that privilege which she prized above all others. In 1830, she chooses a young, unlettered Sister for her confidant; in 1846, she addressed herself to two poor peasant children; in 1858, she also selects one in the humblest ranks of life as the depository of her merciful designs.

Bernadette Soubirous, born at Lourdes in 1844, of poor parents, was a young girl of weak and delicate health; she could neither read nor write; she knew no prayers but her Chaplet, and she could speak only the patois of the country. "On February 11th, 1858," says she, "my parents were in great perplexity for want of wood to cook the dinner. I put on my hood and offered to go with my younger sister Marie and our friend, the little Jeanne Abadie, to pick up some dead branches." The three children repaired to the bank of the Gave, opposite the grotto of Masabielle; in which were collected the sand and branches of trees drifted there by the current. But to reach the grotto, it was necessary to wade through the shallow bed of the river. Marie and Jeanne took off their shoes without hesitation; Bernadette delayed and feared crossing, as she was suffering from a cold. Whilst thus deliberating, she was astonished by a rushing wind, instantly repeated, though the trees near the river were motionless. One vine was only slightly agitated, an eglantine, which grew in the upper part of this natural grotto. This niche and the wild rose within reflected a most extraordinary brilliancy; a Lady of admirable beauty appeared in the niche, her feet resting on the eglantine, her arms gracefully bent, and her hands joined; with a sweet smile, she saluted the child. Bernadette's first emotion was one of fear; she instinctively grasped her chaplet, as if seeking defense in it, and she tried to raise her hand to make the sign of the cross, but her arm fell powerless and her terror increased. The Lady also had a Chaplet suspended from her left wrist; taking it in her right hand, she made a very distinct sign of the cross, and passed between her fingers the beads (white as drops of milk); but her lips did not move. She smiled upon the shepherdess, who, reassured from this moment, recovered the use of her arm, made the sign of the cross and recited the Chaplet. The little Bernadette remained on her knees nearly an hour, in ecstasy. At length, the Lady made her a sign to approach, but Bernadette did not move. Then the Lady, extending her hand, smiled, and, bowing as if bidding farewell, disappeared. Returned to herself, Bernadette thought of rejoining her companions, who, having seen nothing, were at a loss to understand her conduct. She entered the water, which she found, to her surprise, of a gentle warmth. On reaching home, she imparted the secret to her sister, and then to her mother, who did not credit it.

However, the child being tormented by an earnest desire to behold the apparition again, her parents granted permission for her return to the grotto with several companions; the same manifestation took place and the same ecstasy. On Thursday, February 18th, she again repaired to the grotto; the apparition was visible for the third time, and the Lady requested Bernadette to come there daily for a fortnight. Bernadette promised. "And I," replied the Lady, "promise to render you happy not in this world, but the next."

On the succeeding days, the young girl went to the grotto, accompanied by her parents and an ever-increasing crowd. None of them saw or heard anything. The transfiguration of the countenance of Bernadette announced the presence of a supernatural being, who urged the child to pray for sinners.

On the sixth day of the fortnight, the august Lady revealed to Bernadette three secrets, forbidding her to communicate them to anyone. She taught her a prayer and charged her with a message. "You will go," said she, "and tell the priest that a chapel must be built here, and that the people must come here in procession."

Bernadette communicated this order to the curé, but he hesitated to believe the child, and told her to ask the Lady for a sign which might confirm her words, for example, to make the wild rose which winter has divested of its leaves, break forth into blossom, then the month of February.

The Blessed Virgin did not judge proper to grant the miracle, but she tried Bernadette's obedience, by commanding her to kiss the ground on several occasions, and to climb the rock on her knees, praying meantime for sinners. One day she enjoined her to go and drink at the fountain of the grotto, to wash therein, and to eat of a certain herb which grew in that place. Bernadette saw no fountain, and no one had ever heard of one in the grotto, yet on a sign from the Lady, the docile child dug the earth with her fingers, and discovered a muddy water which, notwithstanding her repugnance, she used as commanded.

At the end of several days, the little thread of muddy water had become a limpid and abundant spring, and what was still more marvelous, it wrought innumerable prodigies. On February 26th, using this water, a man who had gone blind twenty years previous, by the explosion of a mine, recovered his sight, and on the last day of the fortnight, a child dying, or as was supposed, dead, regained life and health in the waters of this fountain.

We will not dwell here upon the persecutions directed against Bernadette by the magistrates, or upon the vexations besetting the pilgrims who flocked hither from all parts of the world. Everyone has read these details in the work of M. Lasserre, who so ably depicts the dignity and firmness displayed in the affair by the parish priest, M. Peyramale.

The apparition of March 25th has a special significance. Bernadette, on several occasions, inquired about the Lady's name. At this question, the vision, on the day mentioned, unclasped her hands, the chaplet of golden chain and alabaster grains sliding on to her arm. She opened her arms and directed them towards the earth, as if to indicate that her virginal hands were filled with benedictions for the human race; then raising them towards the celestial country, whence descended on this day the divine messenger of the Annunciation, she clasped them with fervor, and looking towards heaven with an indescribable expression of gratitude, she pronounced these words: "I am the Immaculate Conception." Having said this, she disappeared, and the child found herself and the multitude in the presence of a bare rock.

The Immaculate Virgin appeared to Bernadette twice again, on Easter Monday, April 5th, and July 16th, the Feast of our Lady of Mount Carmel.

The following 28th of July, the Bishop of Tarbes named a commission of inquiry, composed of ecclesiastics, physicians and learned men. July 18th, 1862, he published a decree concerning the events that had taken place at Lourdes; it was couched in the following words:

"We judge that the Immaculate Mother of God did really appear to Bernadette Soubirous, Feb. 11th, 1858, and on succeeding days to the number of eighteen times in the grotto of Masabielle, near the city of Lourdes; that this apparition bears all the characteristics of truth, and that the faithful may rely upon its reality."

Mary had petitioned that a chapel be built upon the spot. The first stone was laid in the month of October 1862, the piety of pilgrims furnishing the necessary funds for the erection of the edifice, and on the 21st of May 1868, the Holy Mass was celebrated there for the first time, in the crypt which was to bear the new sanctuary. The connection existing between the apparitions of 1858 and 1830 is indicated by two painted windows in the sanctuary, one of which represents Bernadette's vision, the other that of Sister Catherine.

The pilgrimage to Lourdes has assumed vast proportions; thanks to the railroads, the pilgrims each year number hundreds of thousands, coming from every quarter of the globe, and countless miracles recompense the faith of those who seek in this sanctuary the merciful power of the Immaculate Mary.

The grotto of Lourdes, reproduced in a thousand places, has become one of the most popular objects of devotion.

As to Bernadette, the interest and veneration attached to her have not in the least affected her candor and simplicity. She has retired to the convent of Sisters Hospitallers of Nevers, and nothing distinguishes her from the humblest of her companions.

## OUR LADY OF PONTMAIN (DIOCESE OF LAVAL).—1871.

"France, having been invaded by the Prussians, was conquered; Paris was besieged and suffered the horrors of famine, aggravated by the rigors of an extremely cold winter. It was at this period the Blessed Virgin vouchsafed to appear, bringing words of hope and consolation to the people of her predilection. The place favored with this apparition was the little town of Pontmain, situated about four leagues from Fougères, on the confines of the dioceses of Laval and Rennes. It was Monday, January 17th, 1871, about six o'clock in the evening; Eugène Barbedette, a child aged twelve years, looking from the door of the barn where he was occupied with his father and younger brother, Joseph, aged ten years, perceived in the air, a little above and behind the house of the family of Guidecoq, which was opposite him, a tall and beautiful Lady, who smiled upon him. He called his brother, his father, and a woman of the village who was talking to him at the moment. But his brother was the only one except himself who saw the vision, and both gave exactly the same description of this wonderful being. The Lady was clothed in a wide-sleeved blue robe, embroidered with golden stars. Her dress descended to the shoes, which were also blue, fastened with a clasp of gold-colored ribbon. She wore a black veil, covering a portion of her forehead and falling behind her shoulders to the girdle. Upon her head was a golden circle like a diadem, and with no ornament but a red line passing through the middle. Her face was delicate, very white, and of incomparable beauty.

"In a little while, quite a crowd had collected around the barn-door; Madame Barbedette, the Sisters in charge of the parish school, the venerable curé, and more than sixty other persons, but of all these, only two shared the happiness of the Barbedette children. These two were also children, boarders at the convent. Frances Richer, aged eleven years, and Jane Mary Lebossé, aged nine and a half. The other spectators were witnesses only of the joy and happiness of the four privileged ones, but all were convinced that it was truly the Blessed Virgin who had appeared.

"The Blessed Virgin's attitude was at first, that seen in the Miraculous Medal. After the parish priest arrived, a circle of blue was formed around the apparition, and a small red cross like that worn by pilgrims, appeared on the Blessed Virgin's heart. All began to pray. Suddenly the vision was enlarged, and outside the blue circle, appeared a long white strip or band, on which the children saw letters successively traced and forming those words: 'But pray, my children. God will, in a short time hear you. My Son allows himself to be touched by your supplications. ' Then, raising her hands, as if in unison with the singing of the canticle, 'Mother of hope,' there appeared in them a red crucifix at the top of which was the inscription: Jesus Christ.

"This prodigy was visible for three hours. After juridical information, Mgr. Wicart, Bishop of Laval, confirmed by a solemn judgment, the reality of the apparition.

"On the 17th of January 1872, the first anniversary of the event, a beautiful statue representing the apparition, was solemnly set up, in presence of more than eight thousand pilgrims, and a magnificent church is now in course of erection on the spot.

"The Holy See has authorized the clergy of the diocese of Laval to recite the Office and celebrate the Mass of the Immaculate Conception, every year, on the 17th of January; and by Papal brief, an archconfraternity, under the title of Our Lady of Hope, has been instituted in the parish of Pontmain." [36]

We could enumerate many other apparitions of the Blessed Virgin in France, but, not having been approved, by ecclesiastical authority, we dare not give them as authentic. We shall mention only the apparitions with which Miss Estelle Faguette was favored with at Pellevoisin, in the diocese of Bourges. The instantaneous cure of this lady, afflicted by a malady judged incurable, may be regarded as evidence of the truth of the account. Moreover, the Archbishop of Bourges appears to have considered it reliable, as he has authorized the erection of a chapel in memory of the event. On the 14th of February 1876, the Blessed Virgin appeared to Miss Faguette, and the vision was repeated fifteen times in the space of ten months. Mary's attitude was similar to that represented on the Miraculous Medal, except that the rays proceeding from her hands were replaced by drops of dew, symbols of grace. A scapular of the Sacred Heart of Jesus was on her breast.

Mary expressed her love for France but complained of her admonitions being disregarded. She recommended fervent prayer, by the fulfillment of which duty we may confidently rely upon God's mercy.

"What have I not done for France?" said she. "How many warnings have I not given! Yet, this unhappy land refuses to listen. I can no longer restrain my Son's wrath. France will suffer. Have courage and confidence. I come especially for the conversion of sinners. You must pray; I set you the example. My Son's heart has so great love for my heart that He cannot refuse my petitions. You must all pray and have confidence!" Showing the scapular, she said: "I love this devotion."

Who has not heard of the wonderful manifestations of the Blessed Virgin in Italy of late years? How many thousands of persons, moved by piety or curiosity, have visited the Madonnas of Rimini, of San Ginesio, of Vicovaro, of Prosessi, etc., and have witnessed the movement of the eyes, the change of color, and other miraculous signs certainly attributable to none but a supernatural power. It does not appear, however, that Mary has, in this country, presented herself in person, though here she receives the most sincere and abundant tributes of affection. Doubtless, she considers any stimulus to the faith of its people unnecessary. And besides, may we not say that she has fixed her abode in Italy, since her own house, the house of Nazareth, wherein the mystery of the Incarnation was accomplished, and where dwelt the Holy Family, has been transported thither by the hands of angels?

Whilst the Prussian government is persecuting the Church, the Blessed Virgin vouchsafed to appear in the two most Catholic provinces of her kingdom, and in two opposite frontiers, near the banks of the Rhine and in the Grand Duchy of Posen. Does she not seem to say to the good people of these localities, that they must have confidence and that God will conquer their enemies? We must remark that on both occasions, Mary announces herself as the Virgin conceived without sin.

We give an abridged account of these two apparitions, which we have every reason to consider supernatural. The second vision had been formally approved by the Bishop of Ermeland.

On the 3rd of July 1876, at Marpingen, an inconsiderable village of the district of Trèves (Rhenish Prussia), the Blessed Virgin appeared to three little girls, in a pine forest about the hour of the evening. The three children were each about eight years of age, and belonged to families of poor, honest farmers residing in the village. They perceived a bright light, and in the midst of it a beautiful Lady seated, holding a child in her right arm. The Lady and child were clad in white, the Lady crowned with red roses, and in her clasped hands, a little cross.

The vision was renewed several times. To the children's questions as to her name, she answered, "I am she who was conceived without sin;" and when asked what she desired, the reply was: "That you pray with fervor, and that you commit no sin." Several sick persons were cured by touching the place which the children pointed out as that occupied by the Blessed Virgin. These facts are incontestable; but they have not yet been examined by ecclesiastical authority.[37]

In the village of Grietzwald, in Varmia, one of the ancient provinces of Poland annexed to Prussia, four young girls, poor and of great innocence, were favored on various occasions for two months, beginning June 27th, 1877, with apparitions of the Blessed Virgin, who appeared sometimes alone, sometimes carrying the Child Jesus, holding in his hands a globe surmounted by a cross. Both Mother and Child were clothed in white.

To the children's question: "Who are you?" the apparition answered, on one occasion: "I am the Blessed Virgin Mary, conceived without sin;" and another time, "I am the Immaculate Conception."

In the first apparition, our Lady's countenance was sad, and she even shed tears; afterwards, it betokened joy. She asked that a chapel be erected, and a statue of the Immaculate Conception placed therein. At each apparition she blessed the crowd, which was always numerous; she also blessed a spring, which has since then furnished an abundant supply of water, effecting miraculous cures. She recommended the recitation of the Rosary, and exhorted all to fervent prayer, and confidence in the midst of the trials which were to come.[38]

These recent apparitions of the Blessed Virgin have founded new pilgrimages, the faithful flocking to the favored spots in honor of the Mother of God, and ask for the graces which she bestows with a truly royal liberality. At the same time her ancient sanctuaries, far from being neglected, have only become more endeared to piety, many having been reconstructed with magnificence, or at least most handsomely embellished; it suffices to mention Fourvières, Notre-Dame-de-la-Garde, Rocamadour, Boulogne-sur-mer, Liesse and Buglose.

The coronation of the most celebrated statues of the Blessed Virgin, in the name and by the munificence of Pius IX, was the occasion of imposing solemnities, and a means of infusing into the devotion of the people greater vigor and fervor.

The exercises of the Month of Mary have extended to the humblest villages, and there is scarcely a parish without its confraternity in honor of the Blessed Virgin.

Science, eloquence, poetry, music, sculpture, painting, and architecture have rivalled one another in celebrating the glory of the Virgin Mother.

What may we deduce from this wonderful increase of devotion to the Immaculate Mary?

The impression naturally produced is that of confidence. A society which pays such homage to Mary, cannot perish. If, as St Bernard says, it is unheard of that any one has been forsaken who had recourse to her intercession, how were it possible that the fervent prayers of an entire people should fail to touch her heart? No, the future is not without hope; the mediation of Mary will save us.

The venerable Grignion of Montfort, in his Treatise on true devotion to the Blessed Virgin has written these lines: "It is by the Blessed Virgin Mary, Jesus Christ came into the world; it is also by her, that he is to reign in the world. If then, as is certain, the reign of Jesus Christ will come, so likewise is it certain that this reign will be a necessary consequence of the knowledge and reign of the Blessed Virgin. Mary, by the operation of the Holy Ghost, produced that most stupendous of all creations, a Man-God, and she will produce by the power of this same Holy Spirit, the greatest prodigies in these latter times. It is through Mary the salvation of the world began; it is through Mary the salvation of the world is to be consummated. Mary will display still greater mercy, power, and grace in these days. Mercy, to bring back poor sinners; power, against the enemies of God; grace, to sustain and animate the valiant soldiers and faithful servants of Jesus Christ, combating for His interests. Ah! when will arrive the day that establishes Mary mistress and sovereign of hearts, to subject them to the empire of Jesus? ... Then will great and wonderful things be accomplished.... When will this joyful epoch come, this Age of Mary, in which souls absorbed in the abyss of the interior of Mary, will become living copies of the sublime, original, loving, and glorifying Jesus Christ?"

Father de Montfort adds, in addressing our Saviour: Ut adveniat regnum tuum, adveniat regnum Mariæ! May the reign of Mary come that they reign, O Jesus, may come!

Is not this the Age of Mary? Was there ever in the Church, a period in which Mary was, if we may thus express it, so lavish of favors as in these, our days? Was there ever a period in which she appeared so frequently and familiarly, in which she has given to the world, admonitions so grave and maternal; in which she has worked so many miracles; and poured out graces so abundantly? The reader of this volume will answer unhesitatingly that no period of history offers anything comparable to what we have witnessed in our own days.

It is true, that the day of triumph announced by the venerated Montfort, appears far distant; one might say that the kingdom of God on earth is more compromised than ever. The wicked make unexampled efforts to demolish the social edifice; they are numerous, powerful, and possessed of incalculable resources. But for the Church, when all seems lost, then is her triumph at hand. God sometimes permits the malice of men to exceed all bounds, that His power may be the more manifest when the moment of their defeat arrives.

All the united efforts of the Church's enemies in the course of ages, all their errors, hatred and violence directed against her, the Spouse of Christ, are now concentrated in what is termed the Revolution—that is, anti-Christianity reduced to a system and propagated throughout the world, it is Satan usurping the place of Jesus Christ.

But He who has conquered the world, and put to flight the prince of the world, will not permit Himself to be dethroned. He will reign, and even now, before our eyes, is His kingdom being prepared, by the mediation of the Immaculate Mary, of whom the promise was made that she should crush the serpent's head, and to whom alone belongs the privilege of destroying all heresies arising upon earth.

THE END.

# Footnotes

Chapter 1:

[1] St. Vincent desired that the sojourn which the young Sisters make at the Mother House, to be there imbued with, and instructed in, the spirit and duties of their vocation, should be called the Seminary term; he feared lest the word "novitiate," applicable to religious Orders, might cause the Daughters of Charity to be regarded as such.

[2] The Life of M. Aladel has been published; 1 volume in 12mo. It can be procured in Paris, rue du Bac, 140.

[3] Verbal process of the investigation made by order of Mgr. de Quélen in 1836, upon the origin of the medal, MS. p. 10.

[4] Verbal process of the investigation, p. 5.

[5] Verbal process of the investigation.

[6] Persons favored with supernatural communications are not thereby preserved from error. They may be deceived in misunderstanding what they see or hear, they may be duped by the illusions of the demon, they may involuntarily mingle their own ideas with those which come from God, and they may fail in transmitting with accuracy what has been revealed to them. We must also remark that prophecies are frequently conditional, and their accomplishment depends upon the manner in which the conditions are fulfilled; so that, when the Church approves these private revelations, she does nothing more than declare that, after grave examination, they may be published for the edification of the faithful, and that the proofs given are sufficient to ensure belief.

Chapter 2:

Chapter 3:

[7] M. Aladel was made Director of the Community in 1846.

[8] The rings were three on each finger; the largest next to the hand, then the medium size, then the smallest; and each ring was covered with precious stones of proportional size; the largest stones emitted the most brilliant rays, the smallest the least brilliant.

[9] We must remember that Sister Catherine's childhood was passed in the country, where she could admire the beauty of that luminous tint which precedes the sun, and colors the horizon at break of day with its increasing radiance.

[10] The author of this design is M. Letaille, editor of religious imagery.

Chapter 4:

[11] Quai des Orfevres, number 54. They are of different sizes, and the invocation is inscribed in several languages.

[12] "Life of Mgr. de Quélen," by the Baron Henrion.

[13] Look at the star, invoke Mary.

[14] In vain, Hyacinthe (de Quélen) is the tempest unchained; under the auspices of the Star of the Sea, thou wilt triumph over its fury.

Chapter 5:

[15] The Immaculate Conception had not then been defined. (Note by translator.)

[16] Conc. Trid. sess. V. Decret. de peccato originali.

[17] Prov. viii.

Chapter 6:

[18] Tob., xii, 7.

[19] Offic. Concept. B.V.M.R. viii.

[20] Manual of the Archconfraternity, edition of 1853. p. 84.

[21] Manual of the Archconfraternity, p. 7.

[22] Manual of the Archconfraternity, page 86.

Chapter 7:

[23] Several details of this account have been derived from "Illustrious Pilgrim Shrines."

Chapter 8:

[24] Letter of Mr. Boré, Aug. 13, 1854.

[25] Letter of a Sister, September 29.

[26] Letter of Mr. Boré, October 25.

[27] Report of Mr. Doumerq, 1855.

[28] Letter of a Sister, 1855.

[29] Letter of Mr. Boré, August 25, 1855.

[30] Letter of August 25, 1855.

[31] Letter of Sister M——, 1855.

[32] Letter of Mr. Turroque, July 16, 1856.

[33] Letter of Sister M——, July 9, 1857.

[34] Letter of Sister M——, July 9, 1857.

[35] Letter of Sister M., July 9, 1857.

Chapter 9:

[36] Extract of a relation approved by the Bishop of Laval.

[37] Extract from Catholic Annals.

[38] Letters from Poland.